Seats New York

150 Seating Plans to New York Metro Area Theatres, Concert Halls & Sports Stadiums

www.worldseats.com

Jodé Susan Millman

An Applause Original
Seats NEW YORK:
150 Seating Plans to New York Metro Area Theatres, Concert Halls and Sports Stadiums
By Jodé Susan Millman

Cover and title page photo: Nate Shepard

Library of Congress Cataloguing-In-Publication Data
Millman, Jodé Susan
Seats New York: Your Guide to the Best Seats in the House / by Jodé Susan Millman
p. cm.
Includes Index.
1.Theaters—New York (State)—New York—Charts, diagrams, etc.
2. Sports facilities—New York (State)—New York—Charts, diagrams, etc.
I. Title

PN227.N5M46 1997
792'.097471—dc21 97-28481
Printed in Canada CIP

British Library Cataloguing-in-Publication Data
A catalogue record for this book is available from the British Library.

ISBN: 1-55783-583-7

151 West 46th Street
New York, NY 10036
Toll Free: (800) 524-4425
www.applausepub.com

Sales & Distribution

North America:
HAL LEONARD CORP.
7777 West Bluemound Road
PO Box 13819
Milwaukee, WI 53213
Phone: (414) 774-3630
Fax: (414) 774-3259
Email: *halinfo@halleonard.com*
Internet: *www.halleonard.com*

UK:
COMBINED BOOK SERVICES LTD.
Units I/K, Paddock Wood Distribution C
Paddock Wood, Tonbridge, Kent TN12 6
Phone: (44) 01892 837171
Fax: (44) 07892 837272
United Kingdom

table of contents

take your seats

seating plans

introduction

As Irving Berlin says in *Annie Get Your Gun*, "There's no business like Show Business!" When the house lights dim, the orchestra tunes up and the curtain rises, your pulse races in eager anticipation of...the show. Before your eyes, dancers fly across the stage, singers sing their hearts out and actors emote to the back of the house. Life doesn't get any better than this!

My father was inspired by Mr. Berlin and developed ***Seats*** with one goal in mind: to make your theatrical or sporting event experience a memorable one, right from the start. From the moment you select your event and order tickets, ***Seats*** is the tool to help you locate the best seats in the house for the best price. ***Seats*** is also the guide to help you navigate the streets, buses and subways of New York City to get you to your seats.

I take pride in my father's legacy and have carefully built upon his sturdy foundation by updating and adding venues, expanding theatre and ticket information, including several ***Seats*** Theatre District maps and giving ***Seats*** a slick, new pocket-sized look. In making these improvements, I have strived to remain true to ***Seats'*** original goal and dedicate this edition to my father, Sandy Millman, in loving memory.

Like my father, I want you to use ***Seats*** with the confidence that at your fingertips lies the most accurate and state-of-the-art Broadway, Off Broadway, Concert Hall and Stadium seating plans and information available.

I truly hope you find ***Seats*** to be both useful and enjoyable. Now, "Let's go on with the show!"

Jodé Susan Millman

staff

Author/Editor-in-Chief	Jodé Susan Millman
Art Director	Ethan Kaplan Emuse Design, LLC
Assistant Editor	Nichole Boucher
Graphic Design	Vinh Nguyen Ethan Kaplan Dana Linnane
Photographs	Maxwell Harris Jodé Susan Millman Nate Shepard

acknowledgments

A standing ovation and bouquet of roses for my incredible staff, especially Niki Boucher, assistant extraordinaire, for her tireless efforts and amazing research skills and Ethan Kaplan, the Renaissance man, for his artistic vision and enthusiasm.

Thanks to Dan Rutz, Director of the Dexter Performing Arts Center, Dexter High School, Dexter, Michigan, for allowing us access to the spectacular facility pictured on the cover.

Thanks to my publisher, Applause Theatre & Cinema Books, especially Mark Glubke and Kristen Schilo for their assistance, guidance and enthusiasm for this project.

Thanks to Sharon Lutzi for beating the pavements of the Big Apple and to Charlotte Ratzlaff for dotting the "eyes" and crossing the "teas."

Thanks to all of the theatre administration and box office personnel who cheerfully assisted us with this project.

Special thanks to my children, Max and Ben, for their cooperation in being relocated from New York to Michigan and for their encouragement and gathering of the troops for the photo shoot.

Very special thanks to my husband, Mike Harris, for his love, patience and support of this project and for sharing the roller-coaster ride of life with me.

Very, very special thanks to my parents, especially my father, Sandy Millman, without whose love, guidance, inspiration and legacy, *Seats* would not have been possible. I dedicate this book, in loving memory, to him.

theatre seat prices

$$$$$	Most Expensive
$$$$	
$$$	
$$	
$	Least expensive

stadium seat prices

Most Expensive

Least expensive

All seats are one price

Subways/Trains

Buses

Automobile directions

Parking

Theatre location on the *Seats* Theatre District Map

Theatres that are completely wheelchair accessible.*

*Most theatres are partially wheelchair accessible, and wheelchair seating may be available by contacting the box office.

Theatres offering assisted hearing devices.*

*Devices are available by depositing a valid ID or driver's license at the Infra-Red Booth in the theatre lobby.

Devices are available at most other theatres by reservation at the Infra-Red Division of Sound Associates, (212) 582-7678.

subways and buses

MTA subways and buses connect you to all theatres, concert halls, sports stadiums and events around New York City with a base fare of $1.50 no matter how far you ride.

SUBWAY TIPS:

- As the Theatre District is located in the TIMES SQUARE area, here are some subway lines that will take you to TIMES SQUARE - 42nd Street: **N, Q, R, S, W, 1, 2, 3, 7**

- Still confused about taking the NYC subway? You can create your own subway route, including travel times and sites along the way at *www.subwaynavigator.com.*

BUS TIPS:

- As the Theatre District is located in the TIMES SQUARE area, here are some bus lines that will take you to TIMES SQUARE - 42nd Street:

M6	**Broadway/6th Ave.**
M7	**Columbus/Amsterdam Aves.**
M10	**Central Park West**
M20	**7th/8th Aves.**
M27	**49/50 Sts. Crosstown**
M42	**42nd St. Crosstown**
M104	**Broadway**

- All MTA buses are user-friendly because they lower themselves to curbside for easy entrance and are equipped with wheelchair lifts.

- Children under 44” tall are invited to ride the buses for FREE!!

- For fares, use your MetroCard or pay as you go, but remember you need exact change or tokens for the buses and don’t forget to ask for your transfers.

The subways and buses you need to get you to your destination are indicated on each *Seats* seating plan. Our *Seats* Theatre District maps highlight the important MTA transportation stops in the Midtown, Westside and Downtown Theatre Districts.

metrocard

The MetroCard is the smart and convenient way to travel around New York City. The card allows you to take the subway, hop the buses and transfer between buses and subways (good for two hours from the time you pay your fare). The basic fare is $1.50, but the more you ride, the cheaper your trips!

A super buy is the The Fun Pass, which gives you a day of unlimited subway and local bus rides for $4.00. There are many other riding options, so select the card that fits your needs. MetroCards are available from all subway stations, MetroCard merchants and vending machines and tourist information centers.

Also, seniors and people with disabilities who have proper identification are eligible for reduced fares on all MTA services. Call (212) METROCARD (within NYC) and (800) METROCARD (outside NYC) for information, or visit *www.mta.nyc.ny.us*.

taxi

One of the most convenient yet most frustrating ways around town is by taxi cab. Hailing a cab is no easy task, so here are a few rules of the road:

TAXI TIPS:

- Look for the yellow medallion cabs with the center roof light ON. These cabs are empty and are looking for fares.

- If the center light is OFF and the end lights are ON, the cab is OFF DUTY. These drivers will not stop for you.

- If the entire set of top lights is OFF, the cab is occupied.

When you can't catch a cab, look for alternate transportation or, in nice weather, just hoof it!!

The taxi directions you need to get you to your destination are indicated in brackets [ ] near the venue address on each *Seats* seating plan.

parking

The parking facilities convenient to your destination are indicated on each *Seats* seating plan.

For additional parking locations in NYC, log on to *www.ci.ny.us* or *www.newyorktransporation.com* or call (212) 225-5368.

limousines and car services

A show-stopping way to get to and from your event is to splurge and hire a car or limousine service. These services often cost more than a taxi and the fee depends upon your specific request. For a special treat, plan ahead by checking your local phone book or contacting LimoLink at (877) 798-5466 or *www.limolink.com.*

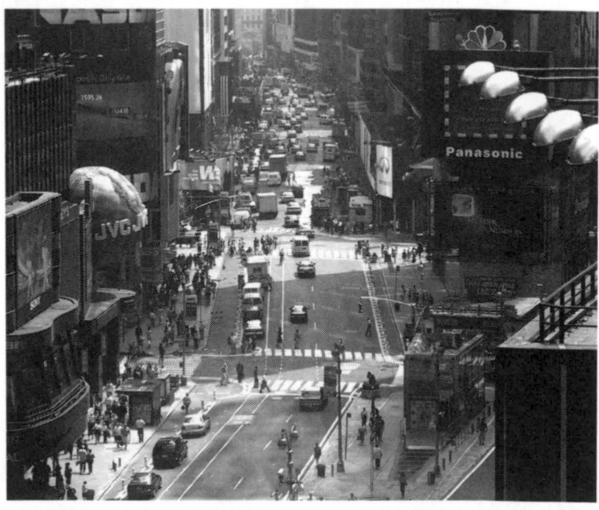

GENERAL THEATRE RULES

- Before you leave the box office, be sure to carefully examine your tickets for the correct performance date, time, seat location and price. Ticket sales are final and non-refundable.
- No smoking is allowed in the theatres; patrons may smoke outside during intermission.
- No outside food is allowed in the theatres.
- No recording devices are allowed in the theatres, including still cameras.
- Patrons are requested to turn off all pagers and cell phones prior to entering the theatre.
- Arrive before curtain time; latecomers will be seated at the discretion of management.

counterfeit tickets

Buyers beware!!! Do not purchase tickets sold on the street. Tickets that have not been purchased from theatre box offices, the internet, legitimate ticket brokers or TKTS may be counterfeit and the theatres will not honor them.

children

Check with your theatre to determine whether the production is age appropriate for your children and for policies restricting admission to children under the age of five. Also inquire as to whether children are required to purchase an adult ticket, or may attend for free.

security

Some venues may require the checking or searching of oversized purses, backpacks, briefcases and bags. If you carry such items, plan to arrive early as you may be required to proceed to baggage check.

prices and views

When ordering your tickets, it is recommended that you select rows behind or next to the highest price seats and enjoy virtually the same view. Be sure to ask the box office if your seats have an obstructed or partial view.

Our *Seats* seating plans do not note obstructed views or changes warranted by a specific production.

the broadway line

[(888) BROADWAY; (888) 276-2392]

"The Official Hotline for Show Information and Tickets" is Broadway's first toll-free, interactive telephone hotline. Using the interactive menus, search for Broadway shows by title, location or genre. Information such as show synopsis, performance schedules, student discounts and ticketing are available at your fingertips. For more information, check out *www.livebroadway.com.*

broadway ticket center at times square visitors center

1560 Broadway [between 46th & 47th Street]

Theatre-goers can enjoy one-stop shopping for Broadway and Off-Broadway tickets at the visitors center. Tickets are full price plus a service fee of $4.50 per ticket. The Broadway Ticket Center at Times Square is open Monday through Saturday 8am–7pm and Sunday 12pm–6pm for advance or same-day ticket purchases. For more information check *www.timessquarebid.org.*

new york city's official visitors information center

810 7th Avenue [between 52nd & 53rd Street]

[(212) 484-1222]

Planning a trip to the Big Apple? Visit the city's official tourism website at *www.nycvisit.com* for the most up-to-date information you need for a fun-filled visit to NYC. Winter and summer bring special theatre-related celebrations, which save you money all around the town. Discover discount theatre coupons every day at the Visitors Information Center. Hours of operation are Monday through Friday 8:30am–6pm and Saturday and Sunday 9am–5pm. To receive a free NYC visitors kit call: (800) NYC-VISIT.

the off-broadway theatre information center

251 W. 45th St. [between Broadway and 8th Avenue]

[(646) 728-0960]

OBTIC is dedicated to introducing the public to the exciting world of Off-Broadway theatre. The center offers theatre locations, neighborhood information, performance times, as well as advance and same-day tickets and discounts for the current productions. OBTIC employees are required to see all subscribing shows so there is always someone familiar with the show to assist you. Hours of operation are Sunday and Monday 12pm–6pm; Tuesday through Thursday 12pm–8pm; Friday and Saturday 12pm–11pm. Find out their current listings at *www.offbroadway.com.*

what's playing and where

To find out what's playing and where, several publications list Broadway, Off-Broadway and dance, cabaret, music and theatrical events. *New York, The New Yorker* and *Time Out New York* magazines offer excellent weekly listings of Broadway and Off-Broadway shows. The Sunday Arts & Leisure Section of *The New York Times* offers the most comprehensive picture of the current arts and entertainment scene in the New York metropolitan area. For dedicated professionals and true afficionados, *Performing Arts Insider* magazine lists every show in every nook and cranny of NYC and what will be playing during the next year.

purchasing your seats

It is always showtime in NYC. For smaller productions tickets are available at the venue box office; for larger venues, purchase tickets through one of the following telephone or internet ticket services, which charge an additional processing fee:

TICKETMASTER:	(212) 307-4100 *www.ticketmaster.com*
TELECHARGE:	(212) 239-6200 *www.telecharge.com*
TICKETCENTRAL:	(212) 279-4200 *www.ticketcentral.org*
TICKETWEB:	(800) 965-4827 *www.ticketweb.com*

box offices

The box office telephone numbers you need to purchase your seats are indicated on each *Seats* seating plan.

tdf

1501 Broadway, 21st Floor, N.Y., N.Y.,10036.

The Theatre Development Fund (TDF) is the largest not-for-profit service organization for the performing arts in the United States. While TDF is best known for its operation of the TKTS discount ticket booths and the TDF vouchers, it also sponsors many other theatre-related programs and annual events such as "Kids Night on Broadway," "Teacher's Night on Broadway" and the Annual Broadway Holiday Tree Lighting at Duffy Square, where members of Broadway and Off-Broadway strut their stuff at Christmas time.

tdf mailing list

The TDF mailing list is composed of dedicated theatre-goers to whom offers of discounted tickets are mailed on a rotating basis (approximately every 4–6 weeks). However, the list is restricted to students, teachers, union members, retired persons, performing arts professionals, the clergy and members of the Armed Services. Members are also eligible to purchase the performing arts TDF vouchers. Applications are available with a self-addressed stamped envelope mailed to TDF, Attn: Applications or online at *www.tdf.org*. There is a small application processing fee for those eligible for the list.

vouchers

TDF vouchers are your "passport to the cutting-edge world of performance." Experience the exciting world of emerging Off-Off Broadway music, theatre and dance with a set of four vouchers, which are open tickets of admission good for one year. The voucher pack can be purchased for $28.00 by individuals registered on the TDF mailing list. Applications are also available by mail with a self-addressed stamped envelope addressed to TDF, Attn: Applications. The vouchers are accepted wherever you see the TDF logo or check the TDF website, *www.tdf.org*, for events accepting the vouchers.

theater access program (tap)

TDF is proud to provide access to the NYC performing arts to individuals with physical disabilities. Through mail order, TAP offers tickets discounts for those who are hard of hearing, deaf, blind, partially sighted or who are medically unable to climb stairs, require aisle seats or use wheel chairs. TAP also provides special sign-language interpreted and open-captioned performances of Broadway and Off-Broadway productions. To receive information about the TDF/TAP offers and programs, call (212) 221-1103 or visit *www.tdf.org*.

nyc/on stage

Dial up a weekly recorded menu of theatre, dance and musical events for NYC area performances, TDF vouchers and TKTS information at NYC/ONSTAGE [(212) 768-1818]. At the NYC/ONSTAGE Online at *www.tdf.org*, you are one click away from TKTS Plus, a world of theatre that allows you to search the NYC boroughs as well as the national and international scenes for theatrical events and ticketing organizations.

tkts

If you are looking for the best **day of performance** Broadway and Off-Broadway seats at the best price, the TKTS booths at Times Square and Bowling Green are the places to go. Tickets are either 25% or 50% off the ticket price (plus a $3.00 per ticket service charge), and only cash and traveler's checks are accepted.

Changes in show availabilities can occur hourly, so watch the big board posted outside the ticket windows. Even though you may stand in a long line, the wait will be well worth it!

A listing of shows sold at the TKTS booths is available at *www.tdf.org*. You can also purchase TKTS gift certificates on the web, at the booths or at (212) 221-0085 [ext. 0].

Locations and Hours

Times Square [located at 47th Street and Broadway]

Monday–Saturday evening tickets:	3pm–8pm
Wednesday & Saturday matinees tickets:	10am–2pm
Sunday matinee & evening tickets:	11am–close*

[*closing time varies]

Bowling Green Park Plaza* [located at the foot of Broadway; outside the IRT 4/5 Bowling Green Subway Sta.]

Monday–Friday	11am–5:30pm
Saturday	11am–3:30pm
Sunday	Closed

*At this TKTS location, matinee tickets must be purchased the day before the performance.

TKTS TIPS:

- Try to get to TKTS at 2pm to be first on line for the popular shows.
- Tickets are made available throughout the day, so the shortest lines will be after 7pm, but your selections may be limited. However, some shows not on sale earlier in the day may release seats just prior to curtain time.
- The stand remains open until curtain time, so even if you wait until the very last minute, you can dash to the theatre without missing a beat of the overture.

audience extras

109 W. 26th St., Room 3B, N.Y., N.Y. 10001
[(212) 989-9550; Tuesday–Saturday 10:30am–5:30pm]

For $130.00 receive one complimentary ticket to as many shows as you can see in one year! Simply pay a $3.50 service charge for each reserved ticket and attend the best of over 1000 Broadway, Off-Broadway or fringe productions, dance showcases, concerts or sporting events. Contact AE on the internet at *www.audienceextras.com* or by phone. Since subscribers can experience the theatre for less than the cost of a movie, be adventurous and see a show! (**FYI**: Members critique each show by completing a survey that may assist the producers in evaluating their work during the early stages of production. These critiques also give AE an indication of the productions that are popular with its members.)

WARNING! When you arrive at the theatre to pick up your AE tickets, have your membership card out and available for the box office. Never say the words "Audience Extras" at the theatre or at the box office.

hit show club

630 Ninth Avenue, N.Y., N.Y 10036
[24 hr. Hotline: (212) 581-4211]

This free service distributes the original "two-fer" coupons, which can be redeemed for one or two tickets at one-third or more off the regular ticket price with no service charge. Redeem coupons at the theatre box office (at least one hour before the performance), by phone to the theatre box office, by mail to the theatre (requesting alternate dates) or at *www.hitshowclub.com*. You can obtain the advance ticket purchase coupons by mail with a self-addressed stamped envelope to the Hit Show Club or at the club's midtown office [between 44th and 45th Street] from 9am–4pm. To plan ahead, check the website and hotline for available show listings.

theatre membership subscriptions

Many theatres offer an innovative series of events for members and subscribers. Not only do these special theatre-goers receive super discounts, informative newsletters and priority seating, they may receive invitations to attend post-performance discussions with actors from the shows, pre- or post-theatre cocktail parties and gala events. Just contact your favorite theatre, support the arts and save!

broadway classroom

Presented by Theatre Direct International, this program offers discount tickets to Broadway shows, Theatre District workshops and educational events and materials for students as well as educators. For information, call (800) 334-8457 or contact *www.broadwayclassroom.com.*

high five tickets to the arts

Adolescents (ages 13–18) get a big break on culture with this special program designed to increase the attendance of middle and high school students at art events. Tickets to over 1000 events and museums in and around New York City can be purchased for $5.00 without a service fee from all local Ticketmaster outlets. Just visit *www.high5tix.org* or call the High5 Hotline at (212) HI5-TKTS [(212) 445-8587] for schedules and information.

kids night on broadway

Sponsored by TDF, this once-a-year winter event lets kids go free to the theatre when an adult purchases a ticket. Also, with each adult full-priced meal, receive a kids' meal free at participating restaurants. Some restrictions apply so log on to *www.tdf.org* for details.

school theatre ticket program

1560 Broadway, Suite 113, N.Y., N.Y. 10036
[(212) 354-4722; Monday–Friday 11am–5pm]

Schools, camps or organizations can obtain discount coupons to musicals and plays on and Off-Broadway, events at Lincoln Center and other events in New York City through this program. For more information, send a self-addressed stamped envelope to the program, call or go online at *www.timessquarebid.org.*

wednesday matinee workshops

Student groups should inquire whether their selected theatre offers interactive workshops prior to the production. Workshops have included backstage theatre tours, meet and greet the actors and topical discussions about the play's themes. The programs (limited to 50 students) are usually free and participants are selected on a first come, first served basis. So don't forget to ask.

student advantage card

For a membership fee of $20.00, high school, college, and graduate students as well as staff and faculty can have the "student advantage." This card not only entitles you to fantastic discounts for Broadway tickets, but super savings from other business partners such as Amtrak, USAir and Barnes & Noble. Enroll at *www.studentadvantage.com.*

student rush tickets

On the day of the performance, most theatres offer front row orchestra seats for $20.00 to students presenting valid student identification. Policies vary from theatre to theatre, but the limit is usually one ticket per student and cash is the preferred currency at the box office. Purchase times are restricted, so check your favorite show's website, the box office or *www.talkinbroadway.com* for rush ticket information.

tdf college student mailing list

1501 Broadway, 21st Floor, N.Y., N.Y. 10036

To join the TDF College Student Mailing List, just complete the online application, submit it to TDF, Attn: Student List along with a copy of your current Student ID and $5.00 to obtain tickets to great live performances throughout the five boroughs at savings up to 75% . Once enrolled, tickets can be purchased online at *www.tdf.org.*

caretix

Sponsored by Broadway Cares/Equity Fights AIDS, Care-Tix allows you to obtain the best seats in the house for sold-out Broadway, Off-Broadway and non-theatrical events. Tickets prices are twice the regular box office price, but you can claim one-half of the ticket price as a tax-deductible donation to this worthwhile cause. For information contact the Care-Tix hotline at (212) 840-0770 [ext. 229 or 230] or *www.bcefa.org*.

ebay.com

If luck is your lady tonight, try a ticket auction at *www.ebay.com*. Getting to the right page is as easy as 1-2-3. Start your search on the eBay home page, click on "Events," click on the "Theater" sub-category and hold your breath and see what pops up. Odds are there will be plenty of tickets to choose from. You may find a great theatre bargain, get tickets at just the right price or spend more than you wanted for that special night on the town. You'll never know until you try and try again.

For your information, eBay maintains a very strict ticket resale policy to promote lawful ticket sales, so whether you are buying or selling theatre tickets, be sure to read the fine print.

fund-tix

Sponsored by the Actors' Fund of America, Fund-Tix gives you another chance for those hot theatre seats. All seats are twice the regular box office price, with one-half being a tax-deductible contribution to the Actors' Fund. You must order the tickets at least 48 hours, but no more than two months, prior to your performance date. Ticket orders are filled on a first-come, first-served basis and are subject to availability. For tickets and information call (800) FUNDTIX or *www.actorsfund.org*.

gold card events

As an exclusive benefit of the American Express Gold Card Service for their Gold, Platinum or Centurion Card holders, members can purchase the most sought-after seats to sporting and entertainment events (in advance of public sale) when they use their cards. Look for the Gold Card American Express logo in the theatre advertisement or call (800) 448-TIKS or *www.americanexpress.com*.

sold-out show tickets

Even if a show is sold out, prime house seats are held by the theatre at every performance for the producers, the creative teams and the stars. If the house seats remain unclaimed on the day of the show, the VIP seats are sold to the general public at full price. House seats can go on sale as soon as the box office opens or as late as one hour before the curtain, so contact the individual theatres for details…and good luck.

stand-by/cancellation tickets

Some theatres recycle unclaimed tickets right before show time, and others may drastically reduce prices at the very last minute to fill the house. Those in the know line up early for these abandoned treasures.

standing room only tickets

Standing room only tickets are available at the box office on the day of the performance when the show is sold out. At prices around $15.00 or $20.00, it may be worth it to wear your sneakers and enjoy the show. Like the student rush tickets, show availability, prices and purchase times vary so check your favorite show's website, box office or *www.talkinbroadway.com*.

starving artist tickets

One of the best kept secrets in New York is the starving artist ticket. Most of the top shows reserve seats, usually in the first three rows, for people who love theatre but cannot afford the regular prices. The tickets are $20.00, so do your research by calling the theatre directly and asking about "starving artist tickets."

ticketsnow.com

Broadway Inner Circle presents top tickets for top dollars. If you are willing to pay the price for quick access to the top shows, this is the ticket broker for you. TicketsNow.com also provides you with a venue to sell those extra tickets and stash the cash back in your wallet. For information call (800) 927-2770 or visit *www.ticketsnow.com*.

Seats / top ten discount websites

Register for these free e-services on the web to receive ticket, hotel and restaurant discounts as well as the insider's buzz on and off the message boards of the Great White Way!!!

★**www.broadway.com**

This site presents Broadway Select, a theatre club offering discount tickets for the newest shows early in their run. Your first year's membership is free.

★**www.dealsonbroadway.com**

Tickets for many Broadway and Off-Broadway shows are a click away on the web. Contact The Walton Group for more information at (212) 840-3335.

★**www.disneyonbroadway.com**

Register to receive offers for Disney theatrical productions including the wildly popular *The Lion King*, *Aida* and *Beauty and the Beast*.

★**www.nytheatre.com**

This site offers terrific theatre listings and show reviews as well as "virtual coupons" good for ticket discounts and special offers.

★**www.nytimes.com**

Log on to *The New York Times* "Ticketwatch," an insider's e-mail service offering discount tickets to the hottest shows on Broadway.

★**www.offbroadwayonline.com**

"The official website of Off-Broadway" is sponsored by the Alliance of Resident Theatres/New York (ART/New York) and serves over 400 not-for-profit theatres and organizations. The site not only offers ticket discounts, but lists Off-Broadway shows accepting TDF vouchers.

★**www.playbill.com**

Home of the Playbill On-Line Club, members enjoy the opportunity to receive discount tickets as well as exclusive travel and dining discounts and offers. Members receive weekly e-mail updates announcing savings and specials.

★**www.theatredirect.com**

Group and single tickets at discount prices are available on the web or at (800) BROADWAY [(212) 541-8457 outside of the U.S.].

★**www.theatermania.com**

Join the TM insider club for access to their "plan ahead" theatre discounts or super saver "same day" discounts.

★**www.timessquarebid.org**

"Times Square Deals" offers selected theatre discounts, and hotel and restaurant specials. Just print the coupons and save money on your evening out.

the actors studio drama school repertory season

The world's finest aspiring actors, playwrights and directors showcase their talents during their annual repertory season, which runs from February through May. The productions, which are held at the Circle In The Square Downtown, are free, but reservations are required. Call (212) 479-1778, visit *www.newschool.edu* or e-mail *theatre@newschool.edu*. RSVP to catch the rising stars!

wall to wall...

Symphony Space presents an annual gift to New York City each March with a 12-hour musical marathon celebrating the works of a preeminent composer. Past Wall to Wall honorees have represented all musical genres, including classical, jazz, pop and Broadway. The free star-studded event features selections from the artist's best loved music, as well a parade of stars and family members paying musical tribute to the honoree. You never know what surprises are in store at the Peter Jay Sharp Theatre! There are no advance tickets, so for more information visit *www.symphonyspace.org* or call (212) 864-1414.

columbia university people's commissioning concert

Each May, the People's Commissioning Fund presents a unique, envelope-pushing, free concert featuring the "Bang on a Can All-Stars" at the Kathryn Bache Miller Theatre on the Columbia University campus at 2960 Broadway near 116th Street. Be there to experience the partnership between these extreme musical artists and the audience to create and support new music. For more information, call (212) 854-7799 or visit *www.millertheatre.com*.

traffic jam tap jam

Celebrate National Tap Dance Day with a free outdoor Dance Jam at the entrance to the Holland Tunnel at HUB Station [517 Broome Street]. On an eight-foot-high stage, tap dancers jam to live jazz, displaying their energy, creativity and talent for the outdoor crowds and rubberneckers stuck in rush-hour traffic. All tappers are welcome to jam. Just bring your tap shoes and join the fun. For more information on this May event or other seasonal tap jams call (212) 475-0588 or *www.nytap.org*.

nyc fleet week

Welcome home the Fleet at one of the largest celebrations of the year. For one week in late May, nearly two dozen U.S. Naval, Coast Guard and international ships from around the world dock in the Big Apple. During the celebration, the vessels lower their gang planks for free public tours, a Parade of Ships, a sunset parade and demonstrations, as well as a free Navy Band and USO shows. One of the week's highlights is the Memorial Day ceremony held on the flight deck of the Intrepid Sea-Air-Space Museum at Pier 86, honoring all five branches of the armed services. For a schedule of events and activities, visit *www.fleetweek.navy.mil* or *www.intrepidmuseum.org*.

new york philharmonic memorial day concert

Celebrate Spring with a free New York Philharmonic Concert at one of the most spectacular sites in NYC, the Cathedral Church of St. John the Divine, located at Amsterdam Avenue at 112th Street. The concert begins at 8pm and doors open at 7pm, so arrive early as seating is on a first-come, first-served basis. Weather permitting, additional seating will be available on the Pulpit Green located adjacent toe the Cathedral. For further information, call the Cathedral Box Office at (212) 662-2133 or *www.newyorkphilharmonic.org*.

the annual lower east side festival of the arts

Around Memorial Day, the Theater for the New City celebrates the rich artistic, cultural and ethnic diversity of this unique neighborhood. TNC presents over 70 performing groups from Manhattan's Lower East Side. Admission is free and there are plenty of activities for the whole family. For more information call (212) 254-1109 or *www.theaterforthenewcity.org*.

summer

downtown nyc river-to-river festival

From May to September, more than 500 cultural arts and musical events highlight such downtown sites as the Lawn at Historic Battery Park and the South Street Seaport. Most events are free, including superstar rock and jazz concerts, but tickets may be required. For directions and schedule of events, contact (212) 835-2789, or visit *www.downtownny.com* or *www.rivertorivernyc.org*.

met in the parks

Opera fans are treated to a summer season of performances by the Metropolitan Opera in parks throughout the five boroughs of NYC, as well as New Jersey and Connecticut. The free three-week series, starting in mid-June, consists of twelve performances, six of each of two operas. The Met In the Parks series features the Great Lawn of Manhattan's Central Park as one of its main venues. No tickets are required. For the season schedule, rain dates and directions, contact the Metropolitan Opera information line at (212) 362-6000 or visit *www.metopera.org*.

bam rhythm and blues festival

The summer solstice welcomes jazz, soul, pop, reggae and doo-wop All-Stars to the Brooklyn Academy of Music. Beginning in mid-June and throughout the summer, Brooklynites can enjoy a free outdoor concert series with BAM Rhythm & Blues Festival at the Metrotech Center Commons. For a schedule of events contact *www.bam.org*.

shakespeare in central park

During the months of June, July and August, the screen and stage's biggest and brightest stars light up the lawns of the Delacorte Theatre at Central Park. Each summer, the Public Theatre presents free performances at this open-air amphitheater, located at West 81st Street at Central Park West, near Turtle Pond, just south of the Great Lawn. The reserved seating tickets, two per patron, are free and are good for the day of issue only. They can be picked up for that evening's performance starting at 1pm at the Delacorte Theatre, or between 1pm and 3pm at the Public Theatre, 425 Lafayette Street. The ticket lines can be long, so get there early. The

Delacorte Theatre opens at 7:30pm. For information about performances and tickets, call (212) 539-8750 or visit *www.publictheater.org*.

central park summer stage

Central Park's Rumsey Playfield buzzes with free American and world musical, dance, spoken word, theatrical and opera performances during the months of June, July and August. Summer Stage is recognized for its consistent excellence and diversity of programming and is located right off the Fifth Avenue and 72nd Street entrance to Central Park. For the summer schedule, visit *www.summerstage.org*.

music at the piers

From June through October, the Chelsea Piers [West Side Highway at 22nd St.] embraces the sunny skyline and warm weather with free music concerts at Pier 62 on the Main Plaza. Every Saturday and Sunday from noon to 4pm catch two different live bands featuring the sounds of blues, rock, pop, folk, country and jazz. For directions and schedule information call (212) 336-6885 or *www.chelseapiers.com*.

celebrate brooklyn!

Join in the fun at one of New York's longest-running free summer outdoor performing arts festivals at the Prospect Park Bandshell in Brooklyn. Beginning at the end of June and continuing almost nightly through August, enjoy world-class jazz, classical, reggae, rock and roll and international musical artists at the bandshell or on the lawn. Seating is on a first-come, first-served basis and gates open one hour prior to the 7:30pm performances. Celebrate the cultural diversity and eclectic tastes of Brooklyn this summer. To view the performance schedule, click on to *www.brooklynx.org* or call (718) 855-7882.

macy's fourth of july fireworks spectacular

Brilliant bursts of color and waves of thunder explode over the skyline each July 4th when Macy's presents its annual fireworks extravaganza. Four barges stationed on the East River between 23rd and 42nd Street set off the largest display of fireworks in America. Best viewing for the 9pm display is from on the southbound lanes of the FDR Highway between 14th and 42nd Street from 7:30pm to 10pm. For further information about public viewing tips, call (212) 494-4495.

new york philharmonic concerts in the park

July brings spectacular music and fireworks to the Great Lawn of Central Park. The free concerts, featuring the New York Philharmonic with guest artists, begin at 8pm and reach a crescendo at 10pm with a pyrotechnic display sure to please the entire family. For good seats, plan to arrive between 6pm and 7pm. Bring a blanket and a picnic basket, and relax on the lawn. For details, call the hotline at (212) 875-5709 or visit *www.newyorkphilharmonic.org*.

new york grand opera

The Rumsey Playfield is alive with the sound of opera music during the month of July when the New York Grand Opera presents three free performances. For a schedule visit *www.newyorkgrandopera.org* or call (212) 246-8837.

mostly mozart

The Mostly Mozart Festival continues to showcase the greatest of classical music at Lincoln Center from late July through August. A special free outdoor event is held each year at Damrosh Park, so call (212) 875-5399 or log on to *www.lincolncenter.org* for details.

lincoln center outdoors

The rhythms of free music, dance, special events and family fun fill the plazas of Lincoln Center each August. To be added to the Out of Doors mailing list, please call (212) 875-5108 [select option #5] or contact *www.lincolncenter.org*.

battery dance company downtown dance festival

In late August, experience free live dance in Lower Manhattan at the Great Lawn at Historic Battery Park and Chase Plaza [located adjacent to Nassau Street between Pine Street and Maiden Lane]. Whether the choreography is ballet, jazz, tap or ethnic, the festival's rhythms and patterns of dance are as diverse as the ages and backgrounds of the audience enjoying this outdoor festival. This summer, head downtown and experience the grandeur of dance against the backdrop of the harbor and Statue of Liberty. For more information, call (212) 219-3910 or visit their website at *www.batterydanceco.com*.

fall

broadway on broadway

Kick off the theatre season in September with the annual free outdoor concert at Times Square. This extravaganza offers numbers from almost every musical on Broadway, with sneak peaks of upcoming musicals. Celebrate theatre at the new Times Square and join in the fun. For dates and details, click on *www.timessquarebid.org*.

manhattan school of music programs

During the academic year, the students, faculty and guest artists of MSM present a host of free music programs. No tickets are required. Whether you prefer jazz, classical, chamber, electronic or vocal renderings, there is a recital or concert to soothe your musical ear. For the schedule of events, visit *www.msnyc.edu*.

annual tugboat festival

Come and see who is the toughest tugboat in NYC when the mighty tugs parade, race and push each other around at the Intrepid Sea-Air-Space Museum each September. The Intrepid is located at Pier 86 [12th Ave. & 46th Street]. Events scheduled for the day are free and open to the public on the Intrepid's westside pier. For more information about the fun, call the public information line at (212) 245-0072 or visit *www.intrepidmuseum.org*.

macy's thanksgiving day parade

Everybody loves a parade. Along Broadway from 77th Street and Central Park all the way downtown to 34th Street at Herald Square, people line up to catch a glimpse of the world's most famous Thanksgiving Day Parade. Fabulous floats, marching bands and super-sized, eye-popping balloons of favorite cartoon characters glide by. Watch the celebrities ride on the floats down the parade route and perform at the Official Viewing Area in front of Macy's at Herald Square. To snag the best parade viewing spot along the main route, plan to arrive by 7am with your lawn chairs and blankets to enjoy the parade. For more information about the parade or the Thanksgiving Eve balloon inflations, log on to *www.nyctourist.com* or *www.macyparade.com*.

winter

christmas at rockefeller center

The most popular spot in NYC every December is Rockefeller Center on Fifth Avenue between 49th and 50th Street for the lighting and viewing of the Rockefeller Center Christmas Tree. The tree can be as tall as 125 feet and is decorated with more than 25,000 multi-colored lights strung on 5 miles of electrical wire. Kicking off the holiday season, the tree is lit during the first week of December as the highlight of a free two-hour extravaganza featuring today's hottest musical stars and, of course, the Radio City Rockettes. Bundle up and join the crowd to *ooh* and *aah* as Rockefeller Center welcomes in the holidays in NYC style. For a schedule of events, visit *www.rockefellercenter.com*.

new year's eve at times square

Ring in the New Year at the Crossroads of the World and watch the world-famous Waterford Crystal Ball drop at the stroke of midnight. Plan to start your reveling before 6pm when the bow tie of Times Square [42nd to 47th St. bet. Broadway & 7th Ave.] is fully closed to traffic. At that time, the ball will be lit and raised to its highest position on the flagpole over One Times Square. Every hour is marked by a special video countdown. Beginning at 10pm, Times Square rocks with live, world-wide televised transmissions.

At 11:59pm, a special guest stands on the Countdown Stage in the middle of Times Square to push the button signaling the ball's descent. At midnight, the New Year's sign and fireworks light up the sky over Times Square and confetti rains down on the party-goers. If you go, remember to dress warmly, bring your own food and non-alcoholic beverages, and get there early!! For more information contact *www.timessquarebid.org* or *www.nyctourist.com*.

broadway theatres

"We should have a secret meeting in the cellar of the St. James Theatre, raise $25 million, put on a million-dollar failure and split it up."

—Mel Brooks, on the success of his hit musical *The Producers*

Ambassador
American Airlines
Belasco
Booth
Broadhurst
Broadway
Brooks Atkinson
Circle In The Square (Uptown)
Cort
Ethel Barrymore
Eugene O'Neill
Ford Center for the Performing Arts
Gershwin
Helen Hayes
Henry Miller's
Imperial
John Golden
Longacre
Lunt-Fontanne
Lyceum
Majestic
Marquis
Martin Beck
Minskoff
Music Box
Nederlander
Neil Simon
New Amsterdam
New Victory
Palace
Plymouth
Richard Rogers
Royale
Shubert
St. James
Studio 54
Virginia
Walter Kerr
Winter Garden

Ambassador Theatre

219 West 49th Street // New York, NY [between Broadway & 8th Avenue]

Telecharge: (212) 239-6200 // Group Sales: (212) 302-7000

Balcony

Mezzanine

Mezzanine Row A overhangs Orchestra Row H

A
B
C
D

Orchestra

$$$$
$$$

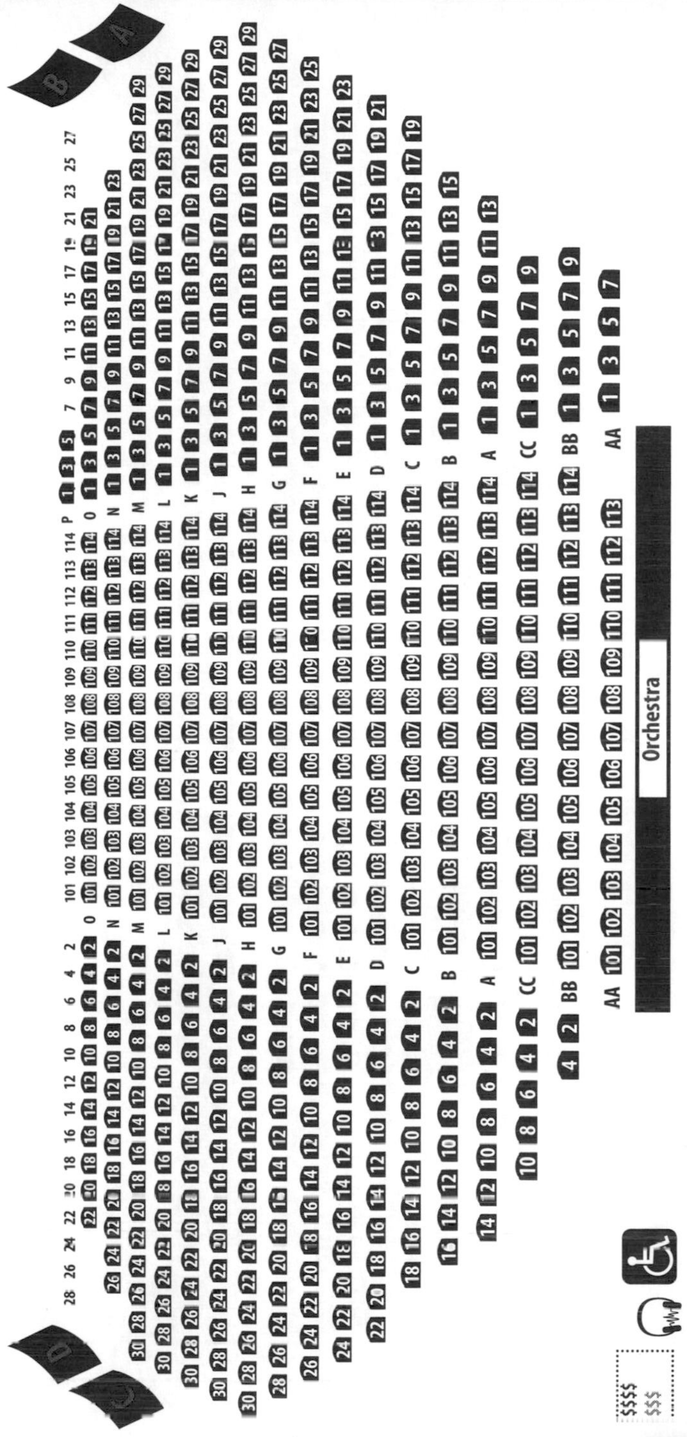

American Airlines Theatre

227 West 42nd Street // New York, NY [between 7th & 8th Avenue]

Box Office: (212) 719-1300 // Group Sales: (212) 719-9393

[www.roundabouttheatre.org]

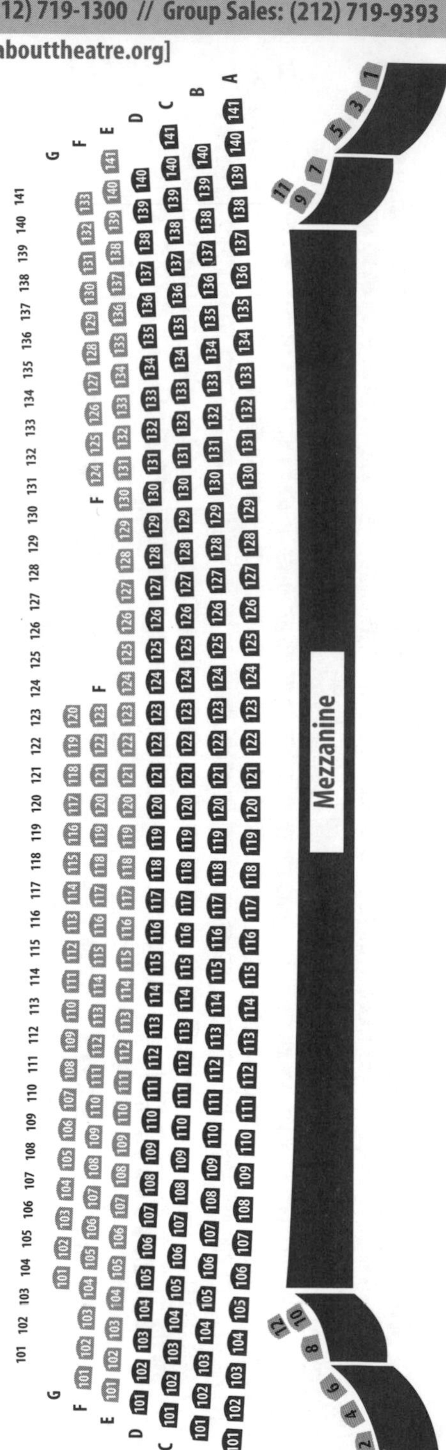

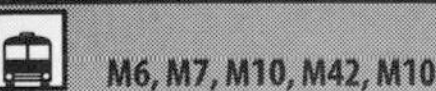

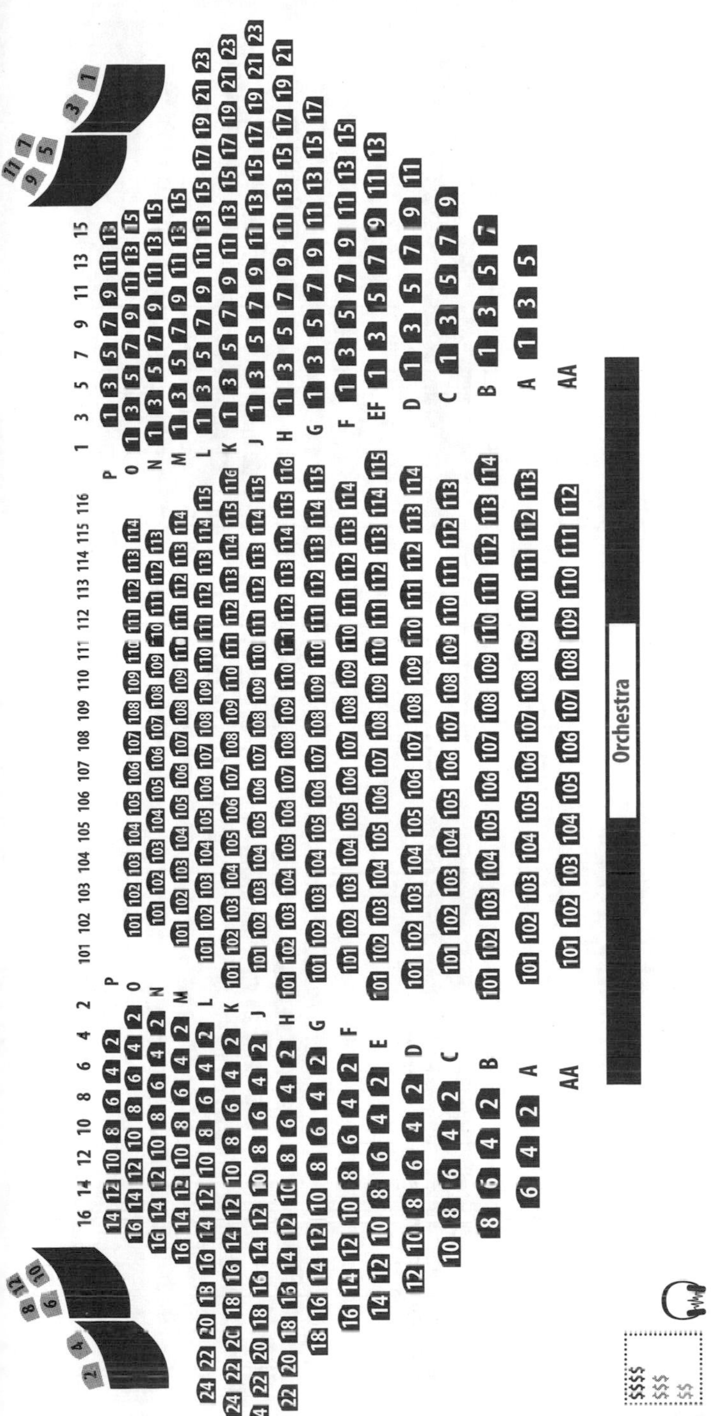

N,R,S,1,2,3,7 to 42nd St. & 7th Ave.

Kinney: 264 W. 42nd St. [bet. 7th & 8th Ave.]

M6, M7, M10, M42, M104

Midtown Map #37

Orchestra

$$$$
$$$
$$

Belasco Theatre

111 West 44th Street // New York, NY [between Broadway & 6th Avenue]

Telecharge: (212) 239-6200 // Group Sales: (877) 5-DODGER

Balcony

Balcony Row A overhangs Mezzanine Row C

Mezzanine

Mezzanine Row A overhangs Orchestra Row J

N,R to 42nd St. & 7th Ave.
B,D,F,Q to 42nd St. & 7th Ave.

Kinney: 100 W. 44th [bet. 6th & 7th Ave.]

M5, M6, M7, M10, M 42, M104

Midtown Map #30

Orchestra

$$$$
$$$

Booth Theatre

222 West 45th Street // New York, NY [between Broadway & 8th Avenue]

Telecharge: (212) 239-6200

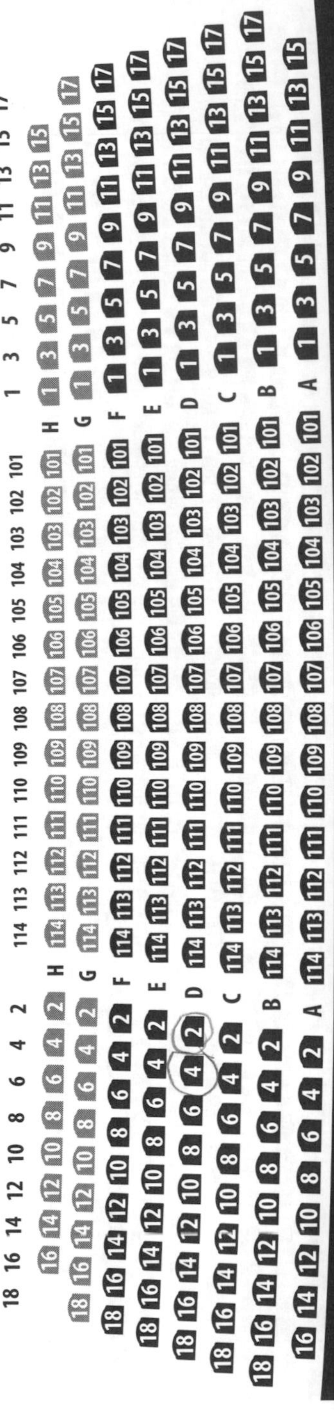

Orchestra

$$$$
$$$

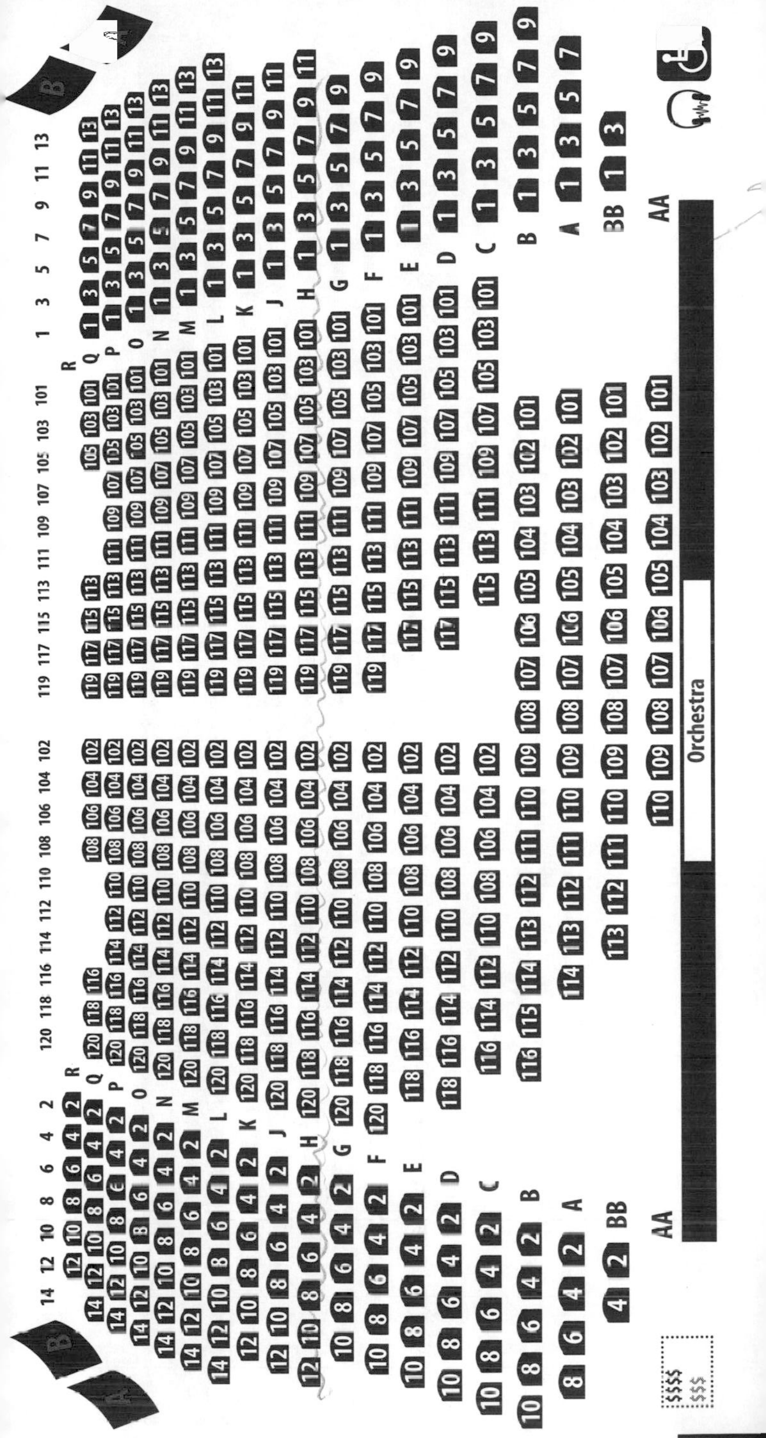

Broadhurst Theatre

235 West 44th Street // New York, NY [between Broadway & 8th Avenue]

Telecharge: (212) 239-6200 // Group Sales: (877) 5-DODGER

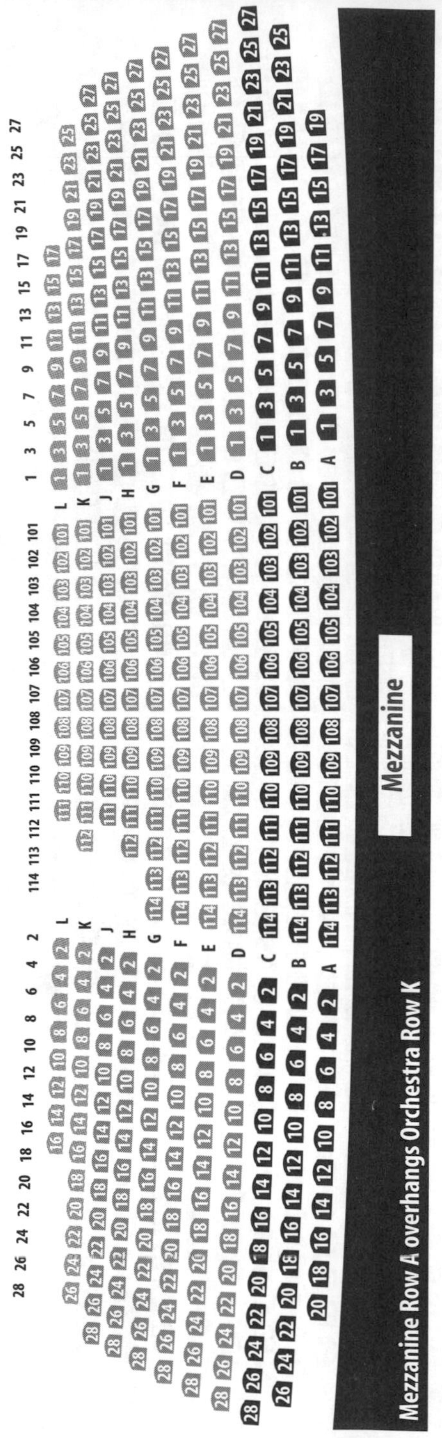

Mezzanine

Mezzanine Row A overhangs Orchestra Row K

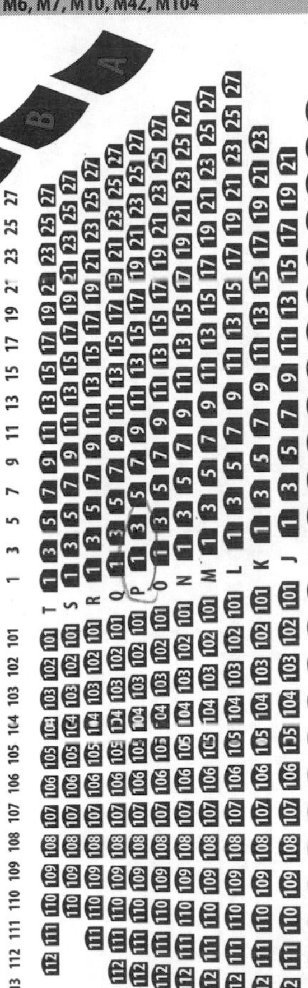
Orchestra

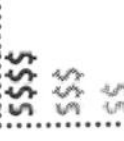

$$$$
$$$
$$

Broadway Theatre

1681 Broadway // New York, NY [between 52nd & 53rd Street]

Telecharge: (212) 239-6200

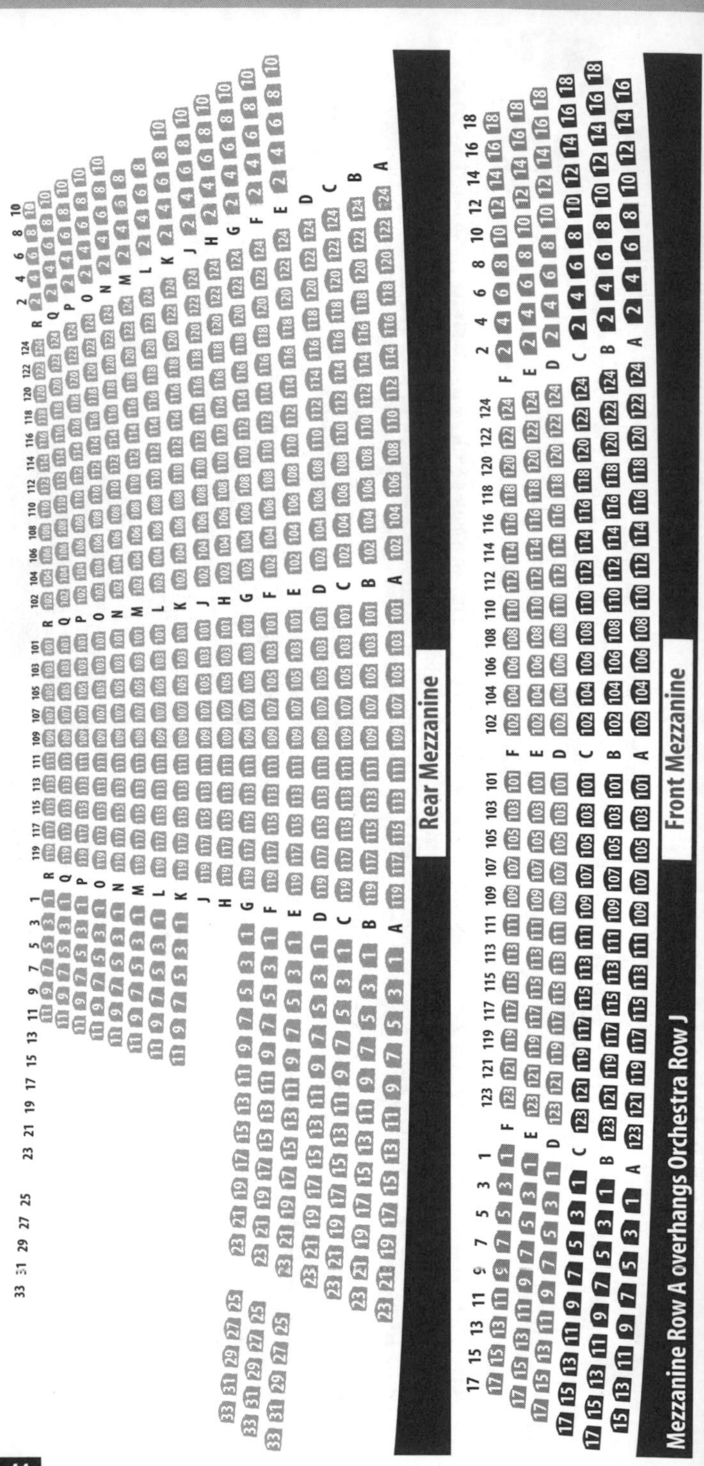

Rear Mezzanine

Front Mezzanine

Mezzanine Row A overhangs Orchestra Row J

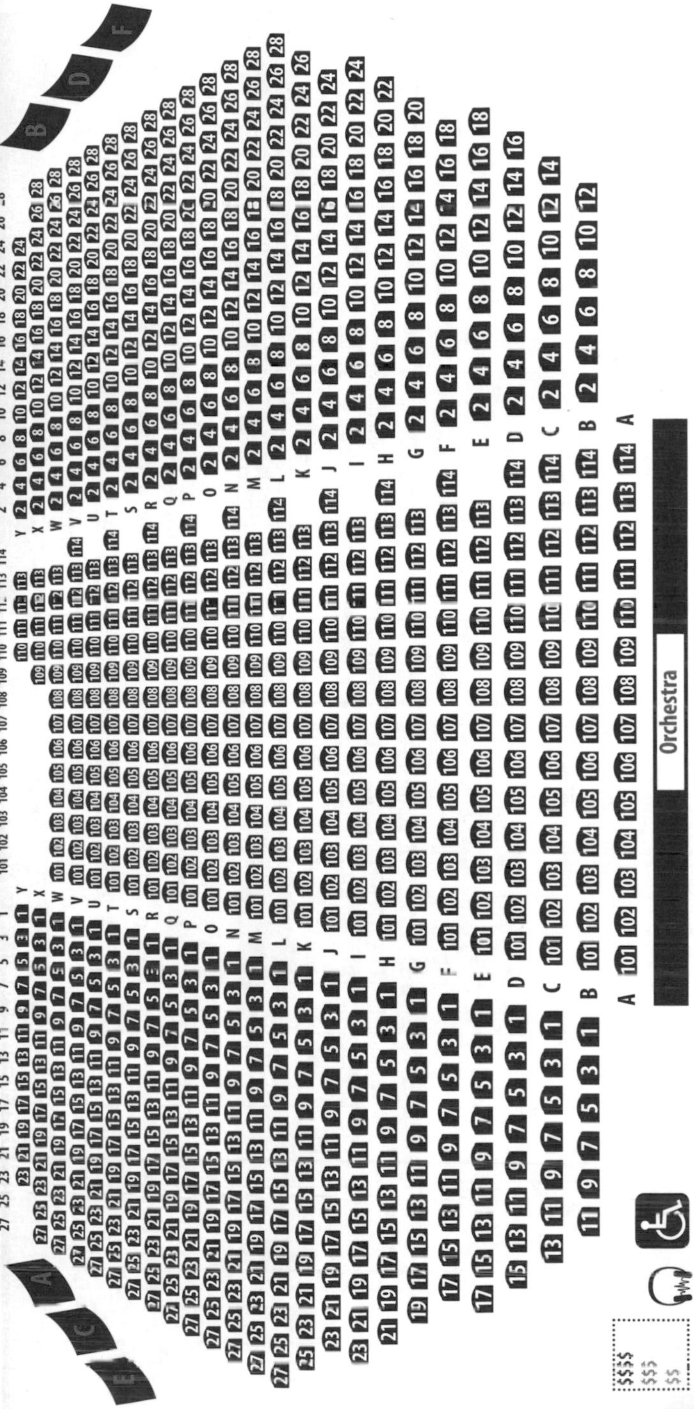

Orchestra

$$$$
$$$
$$

Brooks Atkinson Theatre

256 West 47th Street // New York, NY [between Broadway & 8th Avenue]

Ticketmaster: (212) 307-4100 // Group Sales: (212) 398-8383

[www.nederlander.org]

Balcony

Mezzanine

Mezzanine Row AA overhangs Orchestra Row K

Orchestra

A B C

$$$$
$$$

Circle In The Square Theatre (Uptown)

1633 Broadway // New York, NY [corner of 50th Street]

Telecharge: (212) 239-6200 // Group Sales: (212) 889-4300

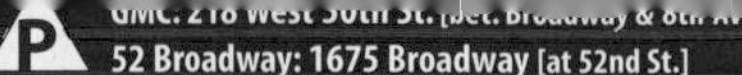

1,9,C,E to 50th Street

GMC: 218 West 50th St. [bet. Broadway & 8th Ave.]

52 Broadway: 1675 Broadway [at 52nd St.]

M6, M7, M10, M27, M50, M104

Midtown Map #5

G 201 203 205 207 209 211 219 221 223 225 227 229 231 233 235 237 239 241 243 245 247 G
F 201 203 205 207 209 211 213 215 217 219 221 223 225 227 229 231 233 235 237 239 241 243 245 247 F
E 201 203 205 207 209 211 213 215 217 219 221 223 225 227 229 231 233 235 237 239 241 243 245 247 E
D 201 203 205 207 209 211 213 215 217 219 221 223 225 227 229 231 233 235 237 239 241 243 245 D
C 201 203 205 207 209 211 213 215 217 219 221 223 225 227 229 231 233 235 237 239 241 243 C
B 201 203 205 207 209 211 213 215 217 219 221 223 225 227 229 231 233 235 237 239 241 B
A 201 203 205 207 209 211 213 215 217 219 221 223 225 227 229 231 233 235 237 239 A

A 202 204 206 208 210 212 214 216 218 220 222 224 226 228 230 232 234 236 238 240 A
B 202 204 206 208 210 212 214 216 218 220 222 224 226 228 230 232 234 236 238 240 242 B
C 202 204 206 208 210 212 214 216 218 220 222 224 226 228 230 232 234 236 238 240 242 244 C
D 202 204 206 208 210 212 214 216 218 220 222 224 226 228 230 232 234 236 238 240 242 244 246 D
E 202 204 206 208 210 212 214 216 218 220 222 224 226 228 230 232 234 236 238 240 242 244 246 248 E
F 202 204 206 208 210 212 214 216 218 220 222 224 226 228 230 232 234 236 238 240 242 244 246 248 F
G 202 204 206 208 210 212 220 222 224 226 228 230 232 234 236 238 240 242 244 246 248 G

Cort Theatre

138 West 48th Street // New York, NY [between 6th & 7th Avenue]

Telecharge: (212) 239-6200

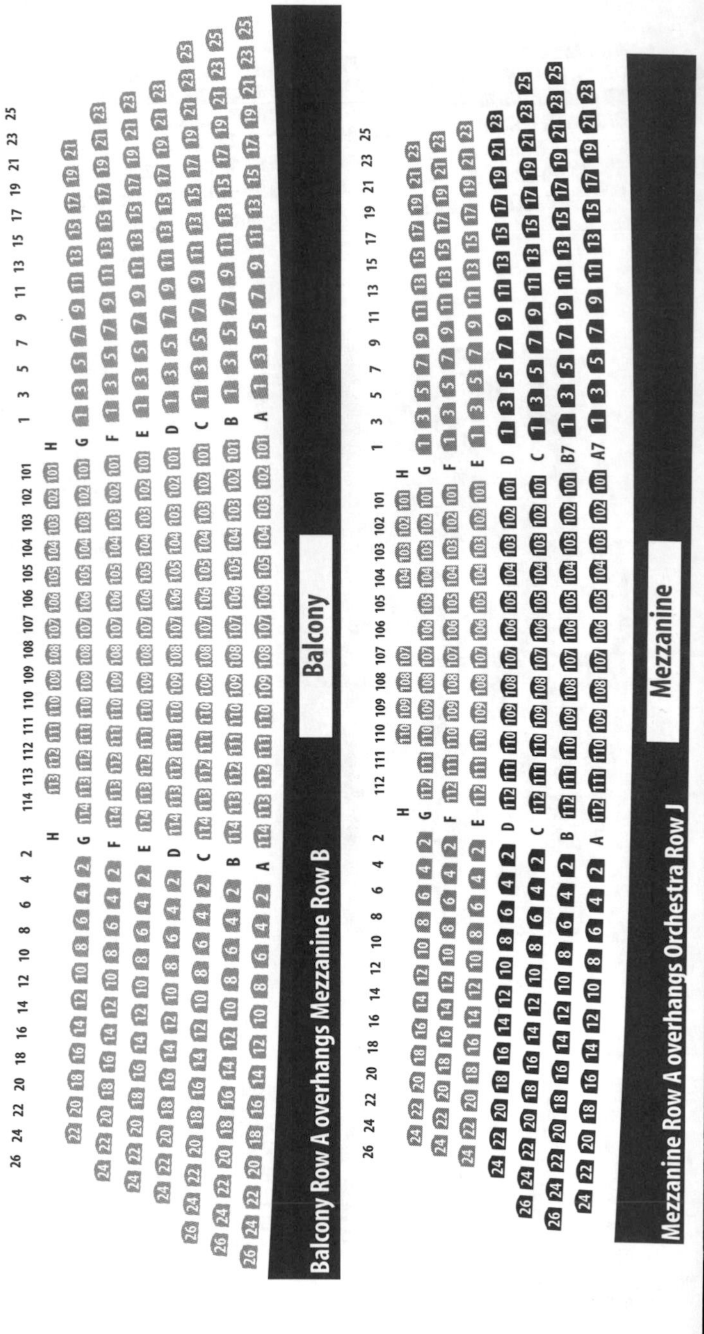

Balcony

Balcony Row A overhangs Mezzanine Row B

Mezzanine

Mezzanine Row A overhangs Orchestra Row J

B,D,F,V to Rockefeller Ctr. [47-50th St.]

GMC: 148 West 48th St. [bet. 6th & 7th Ave.]
Kinney: 155 West 48th St. [bet. 6th & 7th Ave.]

M6, M7, M10, M27, M50, M104

Midtown Map #12

Orchestra

$$$$
$$$
$$

Ethel Barrymore Theatre

243 West 47th Street // New York, NY [between Broadway & 8th Avenue]

Telecharge: (212) 239-6200 // Group Sales: (212) 239-6262

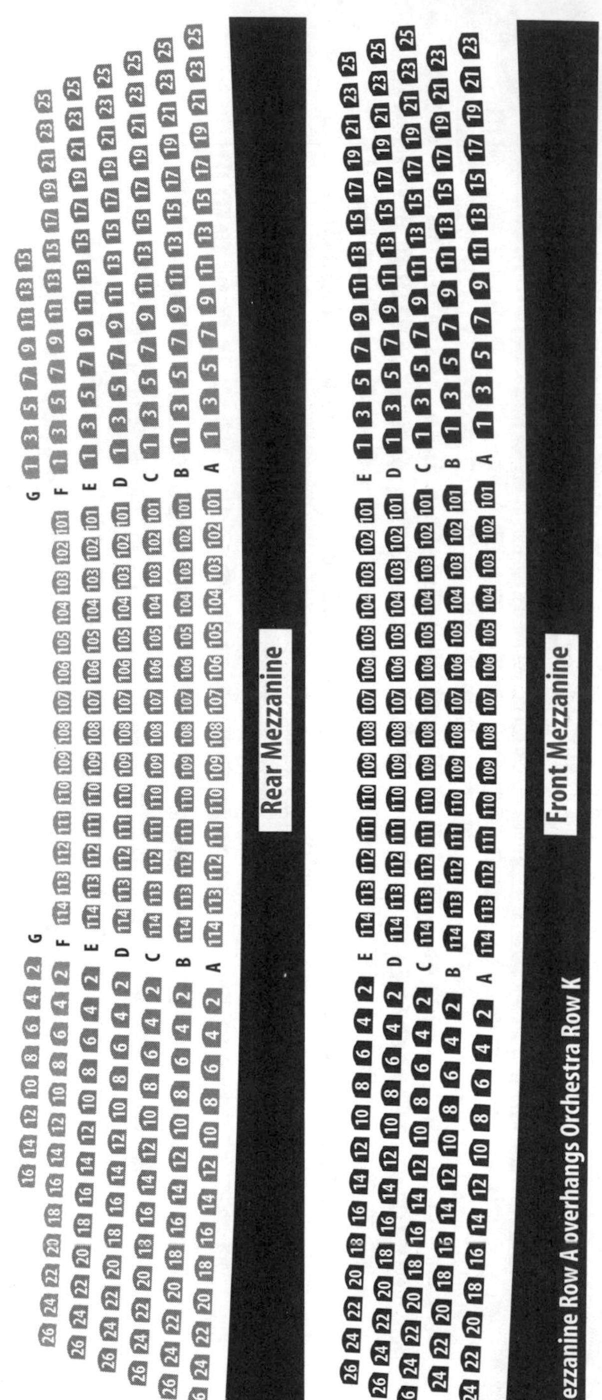

Rear Mezzanine

Front Mezzanine

Mezzanine Row A overhangs Orchestra Row K

A,C,E to 42nd St. & 8th Ave.

Kinney: 255 West 47th St. [bet. Broadway & 8th Ave.]
West 47th: 257 West 47th St. [bet. Broadway & 8th Ave.]

M6, M7, M10, M27, M50, M104

Midtown Map #11

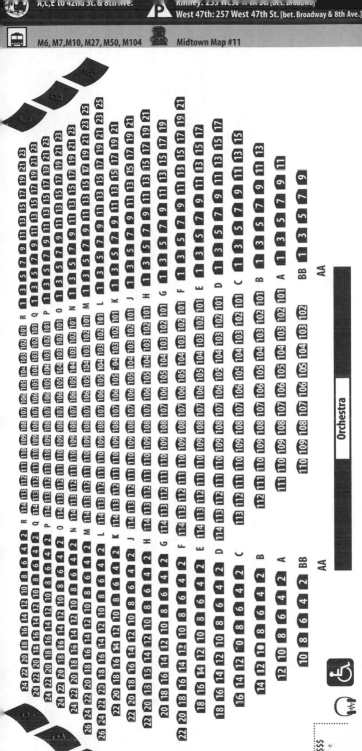

Orchestra

A B C D E F

AA BB A B C D E F G H J K L M N O P Q R

Eugene O'Neill Theatre

230 West 49th Street // New York, NY [between Broadway & 8th Avenue]

Telecharge: (212) 239-6200 // Group Sales: (212) 398-8383

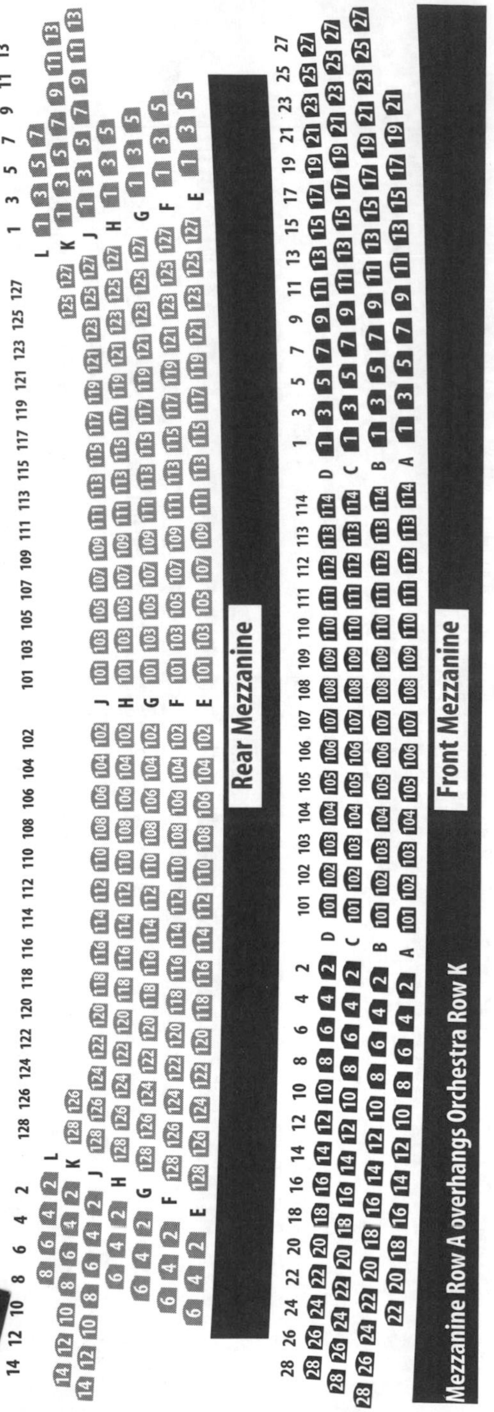

Rear Mezzanine

Front Mezzanine

Mezzanine Row A overhangs Orchestra Row K

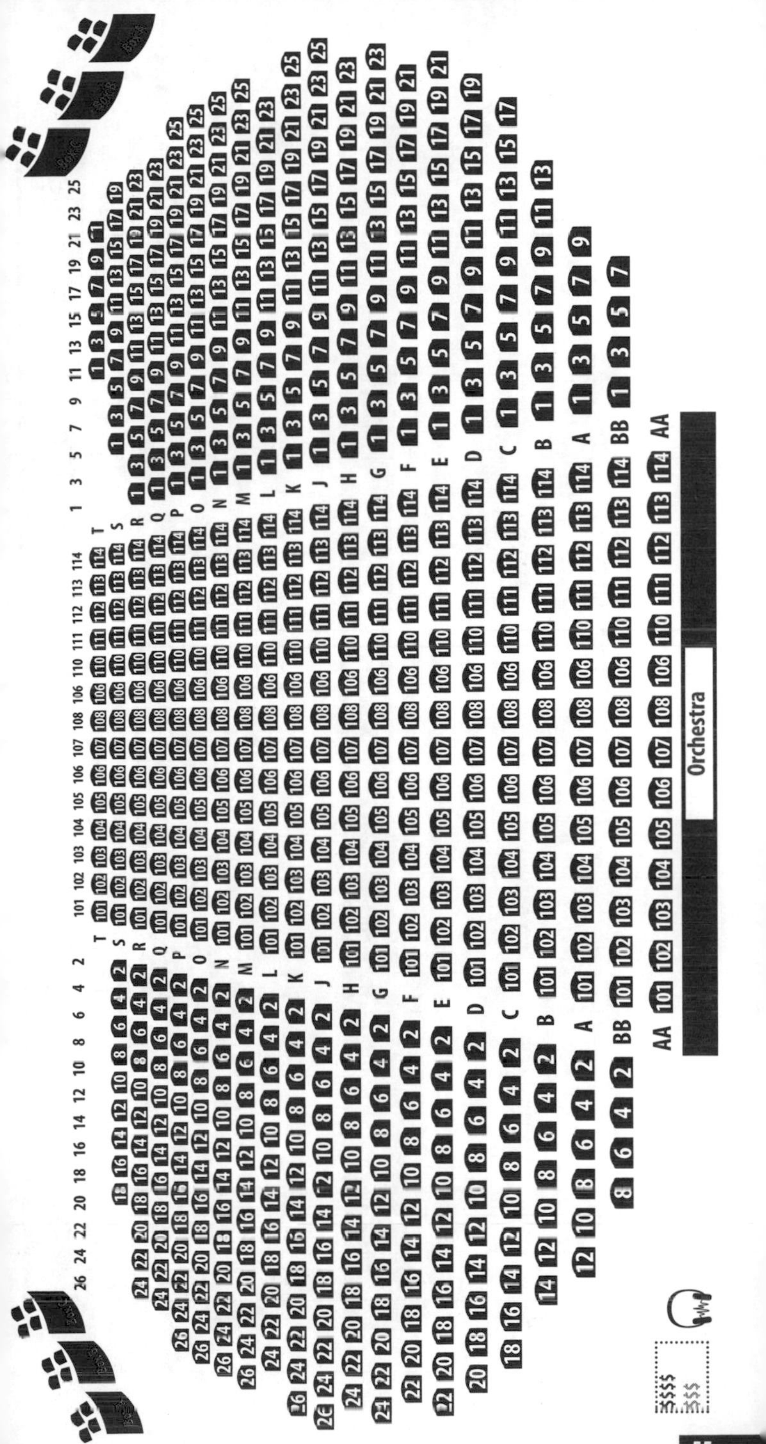

Orchestra

$$$$
$$$

Ford Center for the Performing Arts

213 West 42nd Street // New York, NY [between 7th & 8th Avenue]

Ticketmaster: (212) 307-4100 // Group Sales: (212) 398-8383

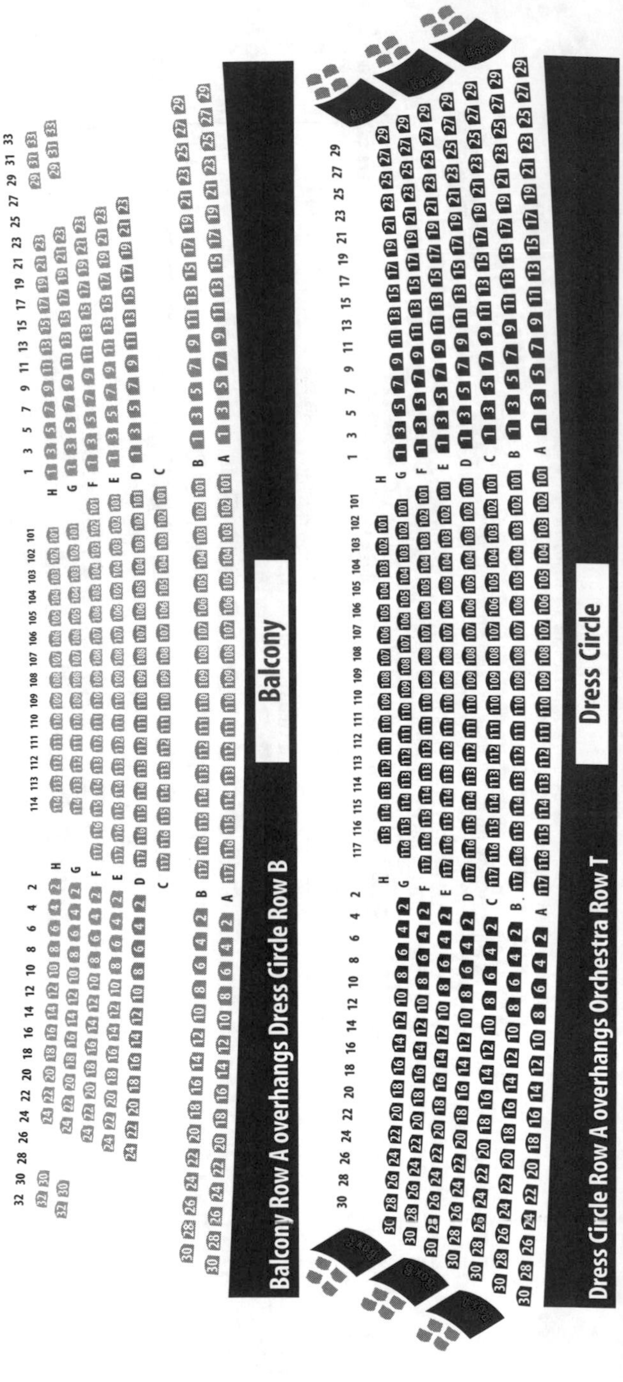

Balcony

Balcony Row A overhangs Dress Circle Row B

Dress Circle

Dress Circle Row A overhangs Orchestra Row T

1,2,3,7,S to 42nd St. & 7th Ave.
A,C,E to 42nd St. & 8th Ave.

Kinney: 250 West 41st St. [bet. 6th & 7th Ave.]

M6, M7, M10, M42, M104

Midtown Map #33

Orchestra

$$$$$
$$$$
$$$
$$

Gershwin Theatre

222 West 51st Street // New York, NY [between Broadway & 8th Avenue]

Ticketmaster: (212) 307-4100 // Group Sales: (212) 398-8383

[www.nederlander.org]

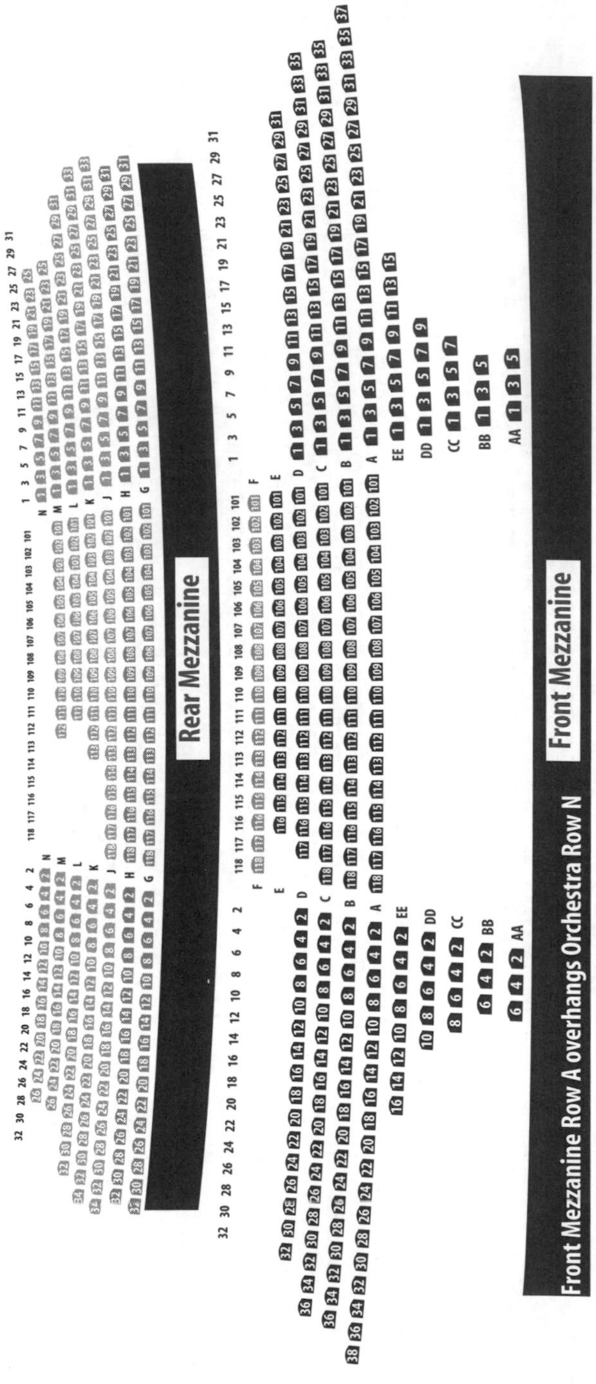

Rear Mezzanine

Front Mezzanine

Front Mezzanine Row A overhangs Orchestra Row N

1,2,9,C,E to 50th Street

Circle: 209 West 51st St. [bet. Broadway & 8th Ave.]
Zenith: 851 8th Avenue [at 51st Street]

M6, M7, M10, M27, M50, M104

Midtown Map #4

Orchestra

$$$$
$$$
$$

Helen Hayes Theatre

240 West 44th Street // New York, NY [between 7th & 8th Avenue]

Telecharge: (212) 239-6200

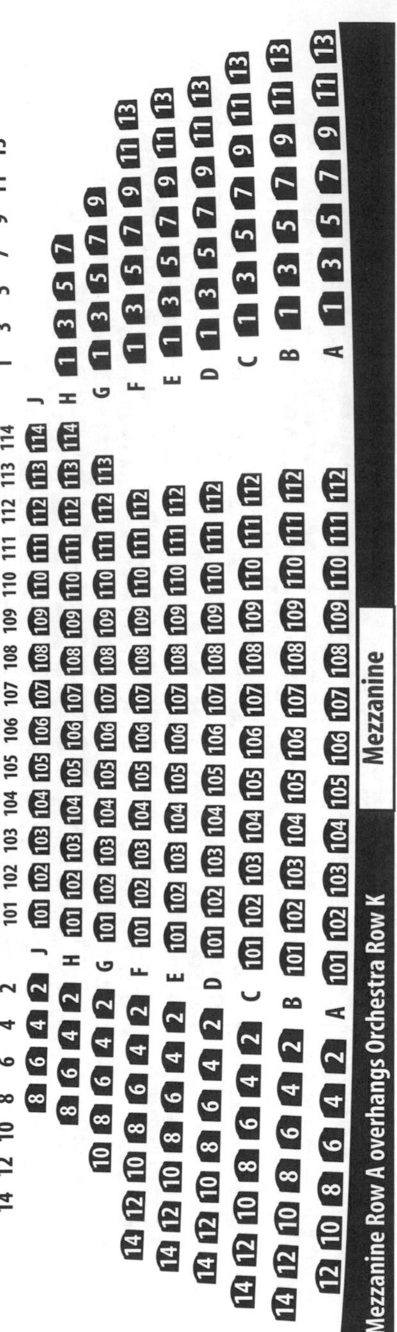

1,2,3,7 to 42nd St. & 7th Ave.
A,C,E to 42nd St. & 8th Ave.

Kinney: 100 West 44th St. [bet. 6th & 7th Ave.]

M6, M7,M10, M42, M104

Midtown Map #31

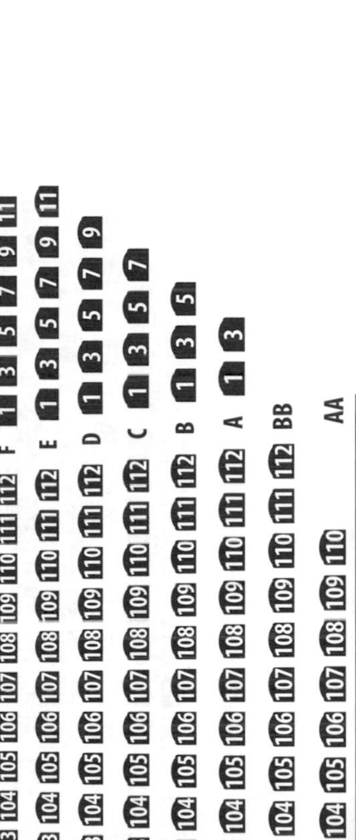

Henry Miller's Theatre

124 West 43rd Street // New York, NY [between Broadway & 6th Avenue]

Telecharge: (212) 239-6200 // Group Sales: (877) 5-DODGER

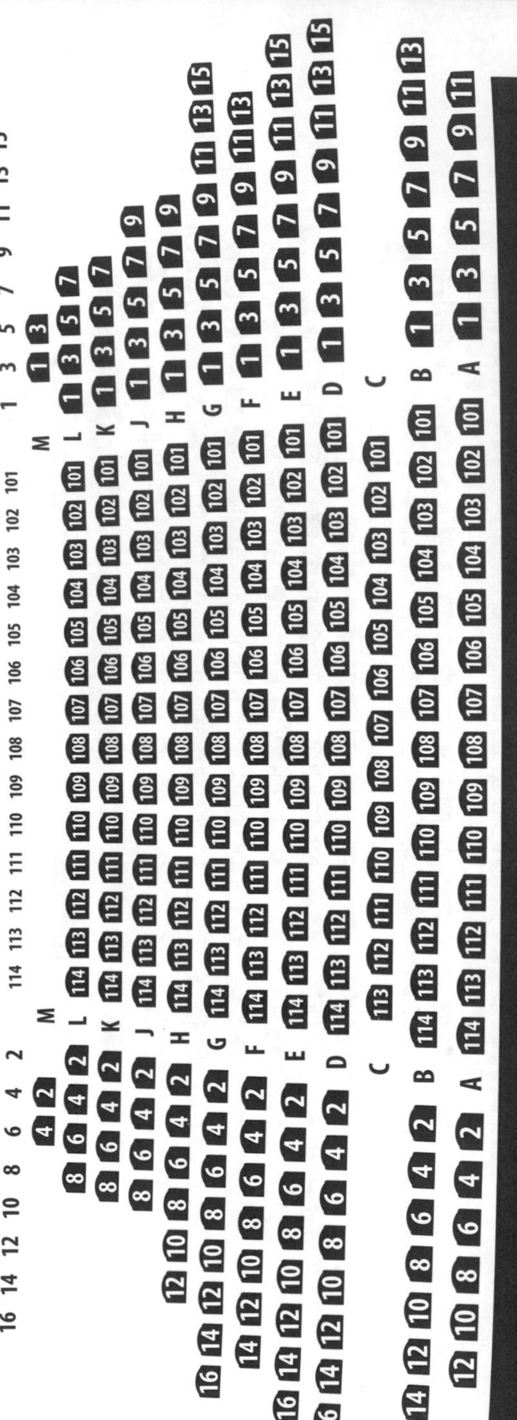

1,2,3,7 to 42nd St. & 7th Ave.
A,C,E to 42nd St. & 8th Ave.

Meyers: 141 West 43rd St. [bet. 6th & 7th Ave.]

M6, M7, M10, M27, M50

Midtown Map #40

Orchestra

Imperial Theatre

249 West 45th Street // New York, NY [between Broadway & 8th Avenue]

Telecharge: (212) 239-6200 // Group Sales: (212) 398-8383

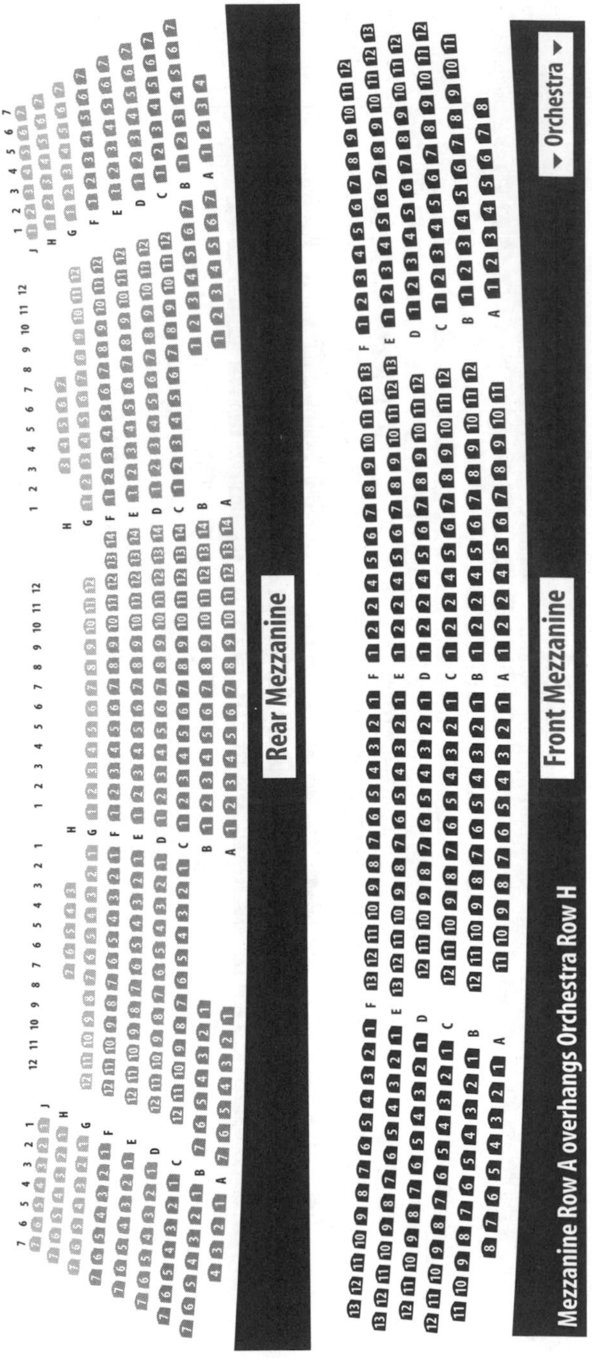

Rear Mezzanine

Front Mezzanine

Mezzanine Row A overhangs Orchestra Row H

▼ Orchestra ▼

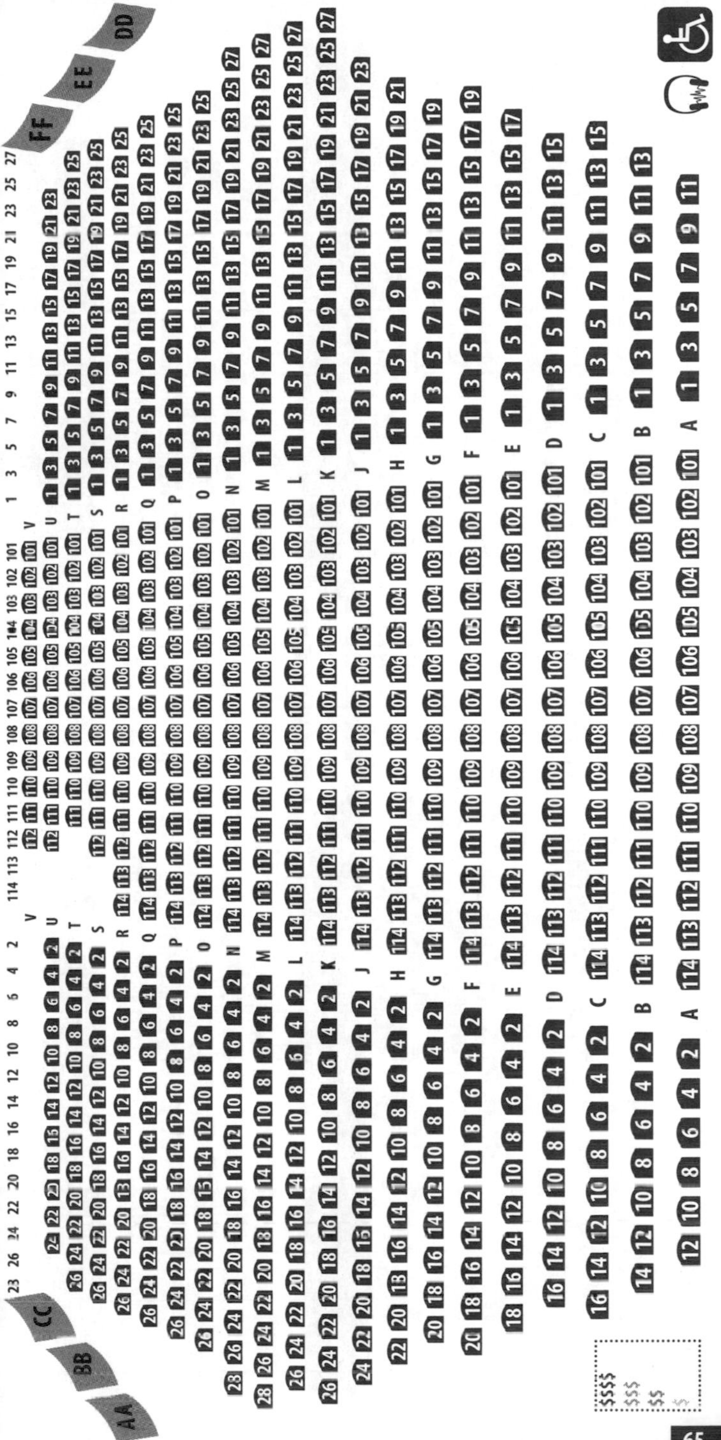

$$$$
$$$
$$
$

John Golden Theatre

252 West 45th Street // New York, NY [between Broadway & 8th Avenue]

Telecharge: (212) 239-6200 // Group Sales: (212) 239-6262

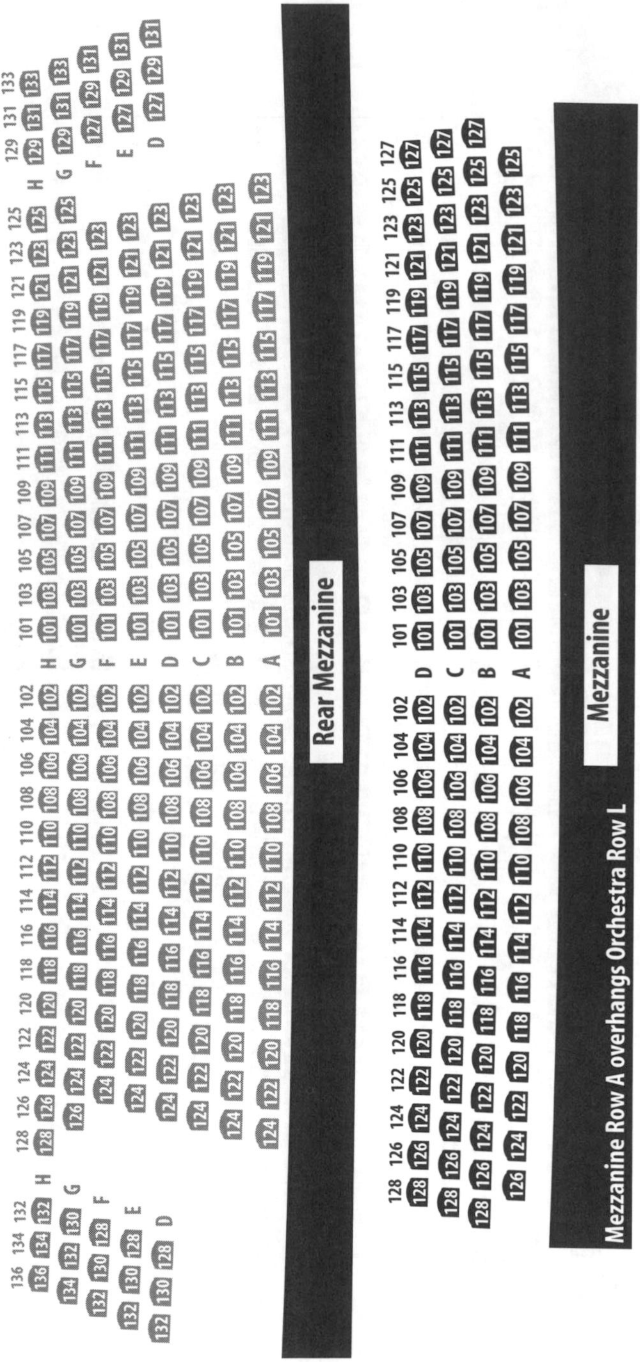

Rear Mezzanine

136 134 132 H 128 126 124 122 120 118 116 114 112 110 108 106 104 102 H 101 103 105 107 109 111 113 115 117 119 121 123 125 H 129 131 133

134 132 130 G 126 124 122 120 118 116 114 112 110 108 106 104 102 G 101 103 105 107 109 111 113 115 117 119 121 123 125 G 129 131 133

132 130 128 F 124 122 120 118 116 114 112 110 108 106 104 102 F 101 103 105 107 109 111 113 115 117 119 121 123 F 127 129 131

132 130 128 E 124 122 120 118 116 114 112 110 108 106 104 102 E 101 103 105 107 109 111 113 115 117 119 121 123 E 127 129 131

132 130 128 D 124 122 120 118 116 114 112 110 108 106 104 102 D 101 103 105 107 109 111 113 115 117 119 121 123 D 127 129 131

C 124 122 120 118 116 114 112 110 108 106 104 102 C 101 103 105 107 109 111 113 115 117 119 121 123

B 124 122 120 118 116 114 112 110 108 106 104 102 B 101 103 105 107 109 111 113 115 117 119 121 123

A 124 122 120 118 116 114 112 110 108 106 104 102 A 101 103 105 107 109 111 113 115 117 119 121 123

Mezzanine

D 128 126 124 122 120 118 116 114 112 110 108 106 104 102 D 101 103 105 107 109 111 113 115 117 119 121 123 125 127

C 128 126 124 122 120 118 116 114 112 110 108 106 104 102 C 101 103 105 107 109 111 113 115 117 119 121 123 125 127

B 128 126 124 122 120 118 116 114 112 110 108 106 104 102 B 101 103 105 107 109 111 113 115 117 119 121 123 125 127

A 126 124 122 120 118 116 114 112 110 108 106 104 102 A 101 103 105 107 109 111 113 115 117 119 121 123 125

Mezzanine Row A overhangs Orchestra Row L

1,2,3,7,N,R,S to 42nd St. & 7th Ave.
A,C,E to 42nd St. & 8th Ave.

Kinney: 100 West 44th St. [bet. 6th & 7th Ave.]
Miro: 139 West 45th St. [bet. 6th & 7th Ave.]

M6, M7, M10, M42, M104

Midtown Map #25

Row	Even seats	Odd seats
	128 126 124 122 120 118 116 114 112 110 108 106 104 102	101 103 105 107 109 111 113 115 117 119 121 123 125 127
R	124 122 120 118 116 114 112 110 108 106 104 102	101 103 105 107 109 111 113 115 117 119 121 123 125 127
Q	128 126 124 122 120 118 116 114 112 110 108 106 104 102	101 103 105 107 109 111 113 115 117 119 121 123 125 127
P	128 126 124 122 120 118 116 114 112 110 108 106 104 102	101 103 105 107 109 111 113 115 117 119 121 123 125 127
O	128 126 124 122 120 118 116 114 112 110 108 106 104 102	101 103 105 107 109 111 113 115 117 119 121 123 125 127
N	128 126 124 122 120 118 116 114 112 110 108 106 104 102	101 103 105 107 109 111 113 115 117 119 121 123 125 127
M	128 126 124 122 120 118 116 114 112 110 108 106 104 102	101 103 105 107 109 111 113 115 117 119 121 123 125 127
L	128 126 124 122 120 118 116 114 112 110 108 106 104 102	101 103 105 107 109 111 113 115 117 119 121 123 125 127
K	128 126 124 122 120 118 116 114 112 110 108 106 104 102	101 103 105 107 109 111 113 115 117 119 121 123 125 127
J	128 126 124 122 120 118 116 114 112 110 108 106 104 102	101 103 105 107 109 111 113 115 117 119 121 123 125 127
H	128 126 124 122 120 118 116 114 112 110 108 106 104 102	101 103 105 107 109 111 113 115 117 119 121 123 125 127
G	128 126 124 122 120 118 116 114 112 110 108 106 104 102	101 103 105 107 109 111 113 115 117 119 121 123 125 127
F	126 124 122 120 118 116 114 112 110 108 106 104 102	101 103 105 107 109 111 113 115 117 119 121 123 125
E	126 124 122 120 118 116 114 112 110 108 106 104 102	101 103 105 107 109 111 113 115 117 119 121 123
D	124 122 120 118 116 114 112 110 108 106 104 102	101 103 105 107 109 111 113 115 117 119 121
C	122 120 118 116 114 112 110 108 106 104 102	101 103 105 107 109 111 113 115 117 119 121
B	120 118 116 114 112 110 108 106 104 102	101 103 105 107 109 111 113 115 117 119
A	118 116 114 112 110 108 106 104 102	101 103 105 107 109 111 113 115 117
CC	116 114 112 110 108 106 104 102	101 103 105 107 109 111 113 115
BB	112 110 108 106 104 102	101 103 105 107 109 111

Orchestra

$$$$
$$$

Longacre Theatre

220 West 48th Street // New York, NY [between Broadway & 8th Avenue]

Telecharge: (212) 239-6200

Balcony

Balcony Row A overhangs Mezzanine Row B

Mezzanine

Mezzanine Row A overhangs Orchestra Row K

1,9 to 50th Street // N,R to 49th Street
B,D,F,Q to 47th-50th Street

Kinney: 155 West 48th St. [bet. 6th & 7th Ave.]
GMC: 148 West 48th St. [bet. 6th & 7th Ave.]

M6, M10, M27, M50, M42, M104

Midtown Map #10

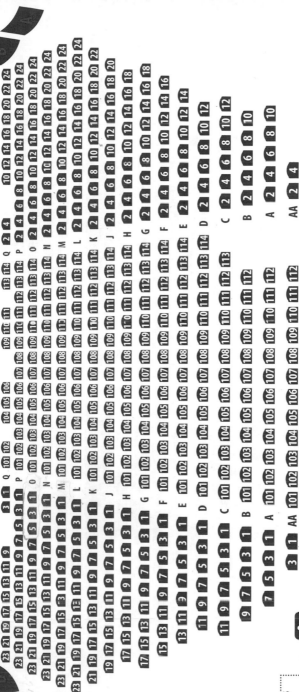

Orchestra

$$$$
$$$
$$

Lunt-Fontanne Theatre

205 West 46th Street // New York, NY [between Broadway & 8th Avenue]

Ticketmaster: (212) 307-4747 // Group Sales: (212) 703-1040

[www.nederlander.org]

Rear Mezzanine

Front Mezzanine

▼ Orchestra ▼

Mezzanine Row A overhangs Orchestra Row J

N,R to 42nd St. & 7th Ave.
1,9,C,E to 50th Street

Trans Parking: 225 W. 46th St. [bet. Broadway & 8th Ave.]
West 47th: 257 W. 47th St. [bet. Broadway & 8th Ave.]

M6, M10, M27, M42, M50, M104

Midtown Map #15

$$$$
$$$
$$
$

Lyceum Theatre

149 West 45th Street // New York, NY [between Broadway & 6th Avenue]

Telecharge: (212) 239-6200 // Group Sales: (212) 889-4300

Balcony

Balcony Row A overhangs Mezzanine Row C

Mezzanine

Mezzanine Row A overhangs Orchestra Row L

B,D,F,Q to 47th-50th Street
N,R to 49th Street

Miro: 139 West 45th St. [bet. 6th & 7th Ave.]

M5, M6, M7, M10, M42, M104

Midtown Map #18

Orchestra

$$$$
$$$
$$

Majestic Theatre

245 West 44th Street // New York, NY [between Broadway & 8th Avenue]

Telecharge: (212) 239-6200

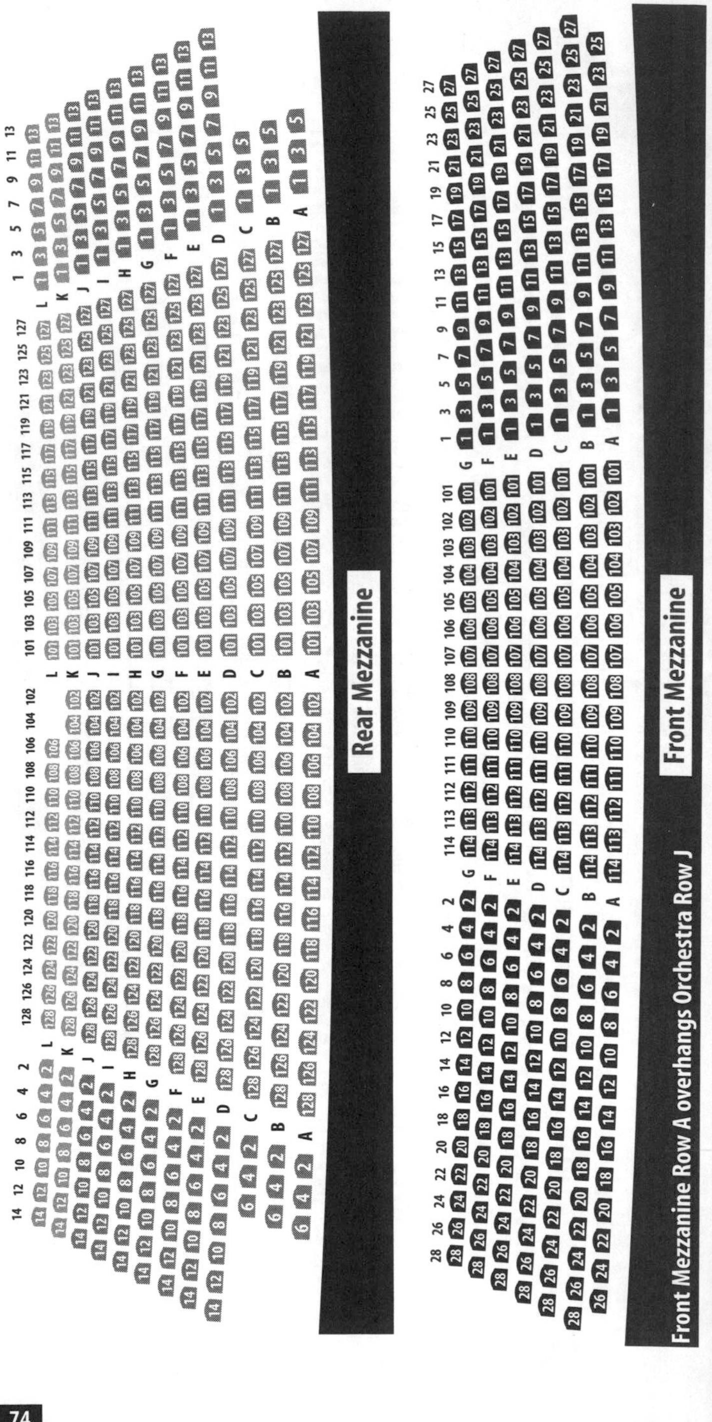

Rear Mezzanine

Front Mezzanine

Front Mezzanine Row A overhangs Orchestra Row J

1,2,3,7,N,R,S to 42nd St. & 7th Ave.
A,C,E to 42nd St. & 8th Ave.

Kinney: 100 West 44th St. [bet. 6th & 7th Ave.]

M6, M7, M10, M42, M104

Midtown Map #27

Orchestra Boxes Left

E F G

Orchestra Boxes Right

A B C

Orchestra

$$$$
$$$
$$

Marquis Theatre

1535 Broadway // New York, NY [between 45th & 46th Street]

Ticketmaster: (212) 307-4100 // Group Sales: (212) 398-8383

[www.nederlander.org]

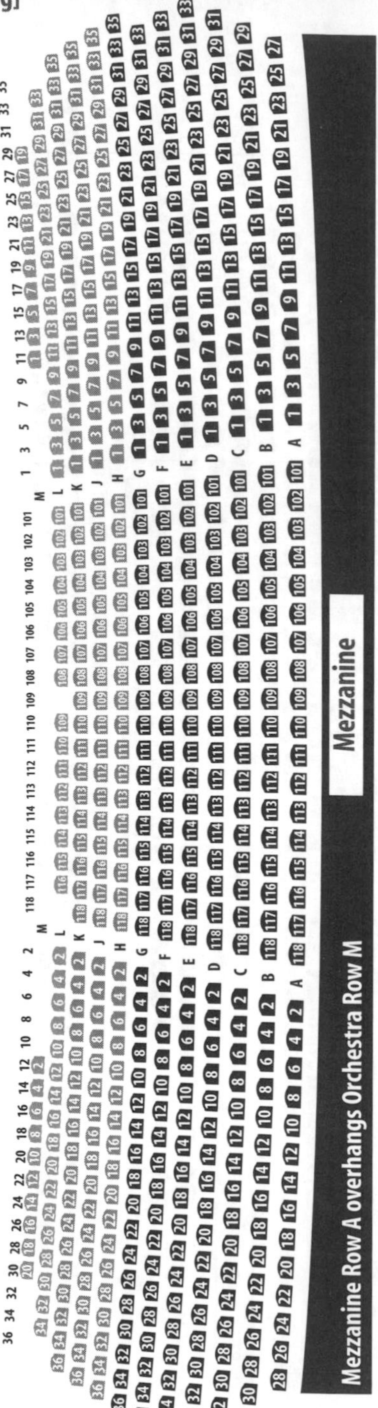

Mezzanine

Mezzanine Row A overhangs Orchestra Row M

1,2,3,7,N,R,S to 42nd St. & 7th Ave.

Astor: 1535 Broadway [at 44th Street]

M6, M7,M10, M27, M42, M50, M104

Midtown Map #17

Orchestra

$$$$
$$$
$$

Martin Beck Theatre

302 West 45th Street // New York, NY [between 8th & 9th Avenue]

Telecharge: (212) 239-6200 // Group Sales: (212) 398-8383

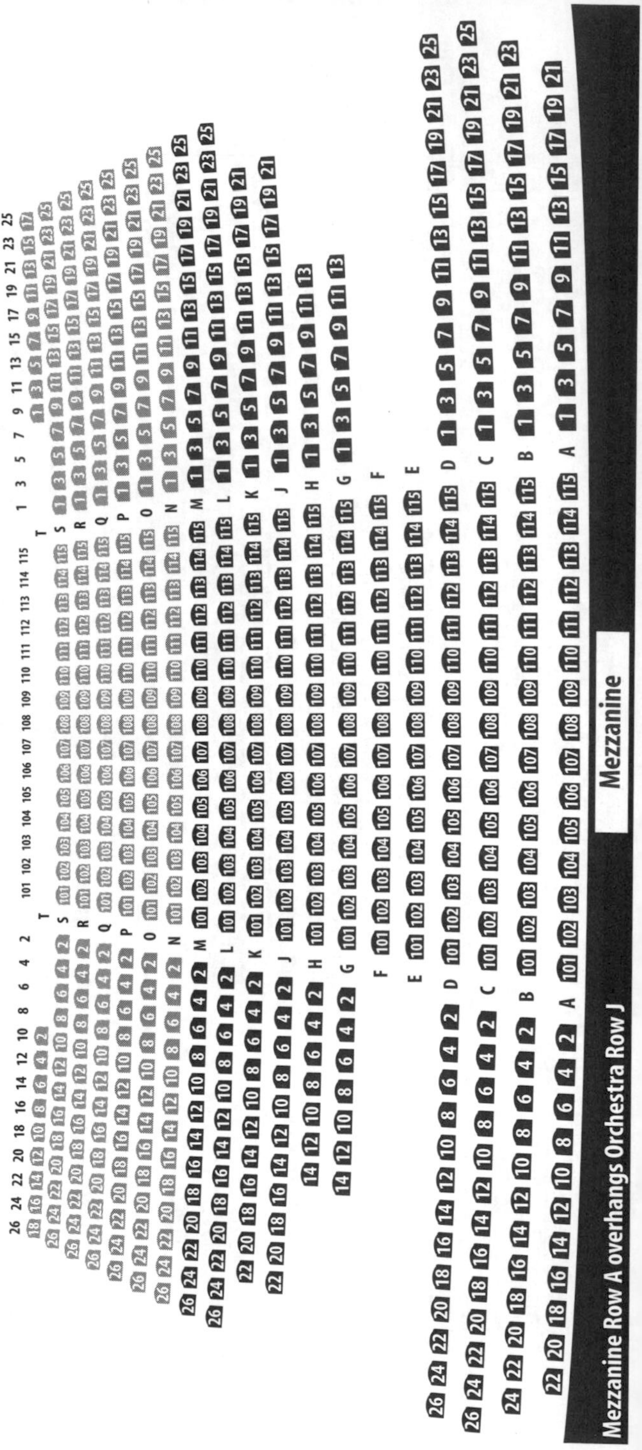

Mezzanine

Mezzanine Row A overhangs Orchestra Row J

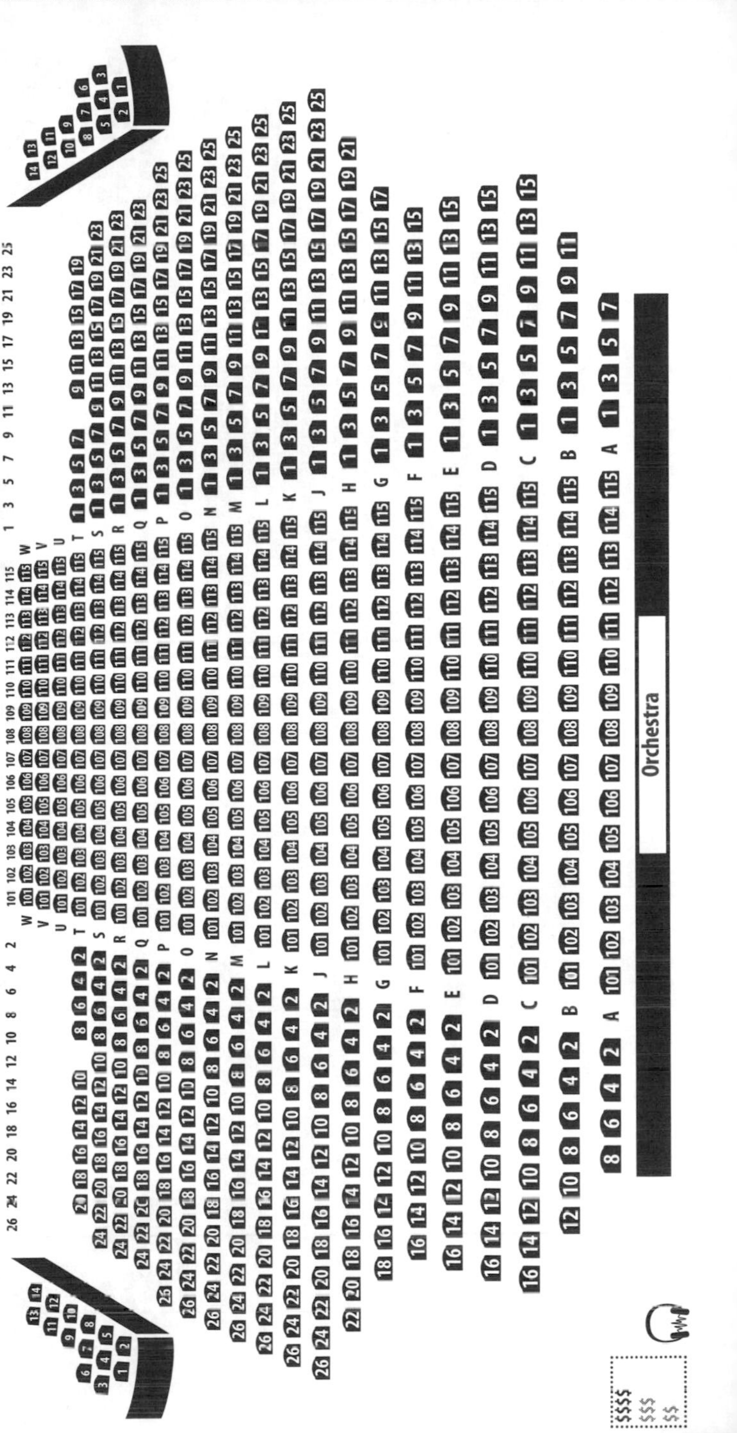

Orchestra

$$$$
$$$
$$

Minskoff Theatre

200 West 45th Street // New York, NY [between 7th & 8th Avenue]

Ticketmaster: (212) 307-4100 [www.nederlander.org]

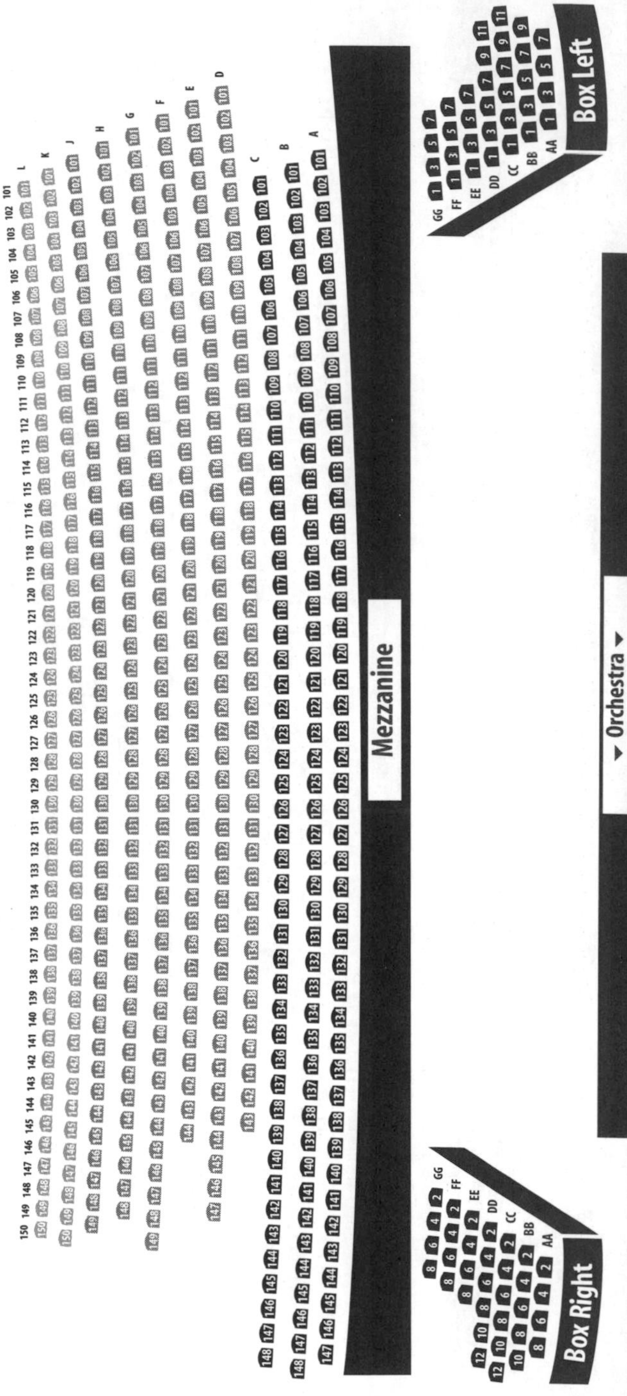

Mezzanine

▼ Orchestra ▼

Box Left

Box Right

$$$$
$$$
$$

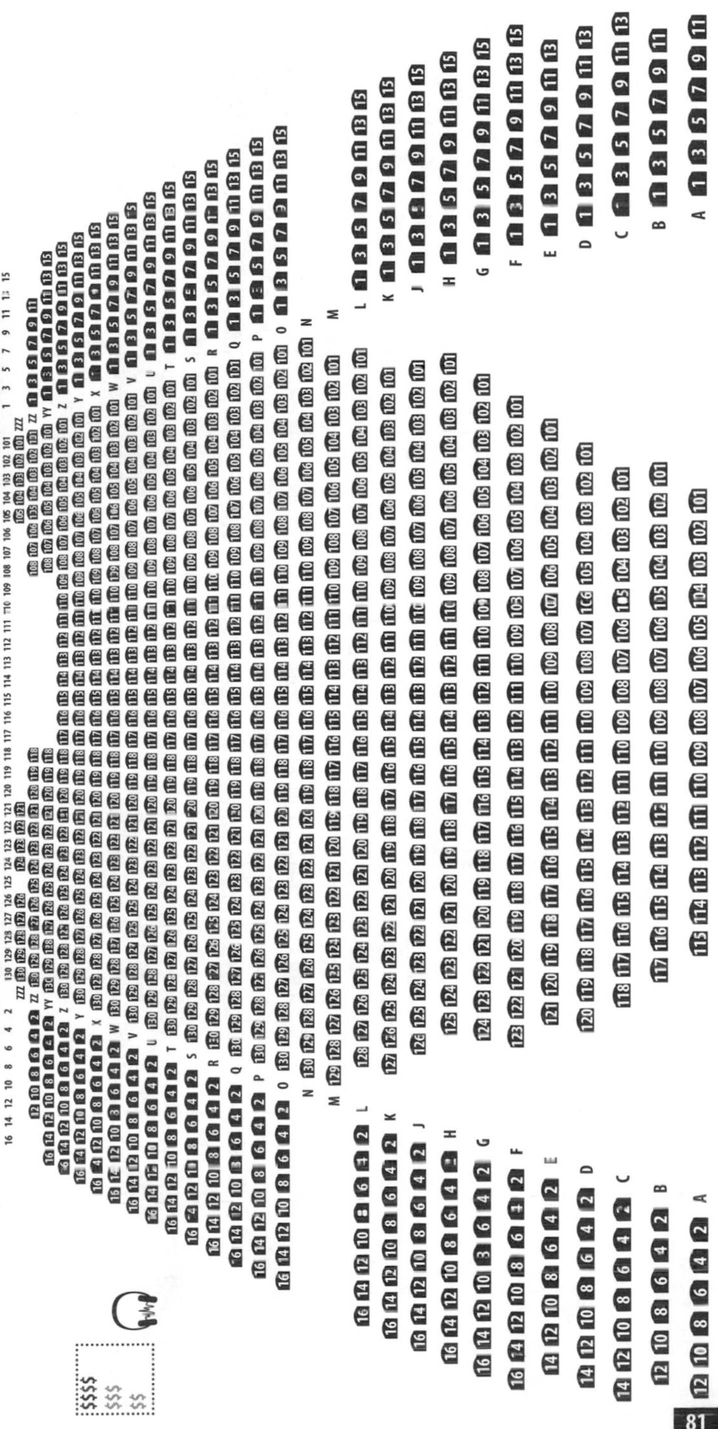

Music Box Theatre

239 West 45th Street // New York, NY [between Broadway & 8th Avenue]

Telecharge: (212) 239-6200 // Group Sales: (212) 239-6262

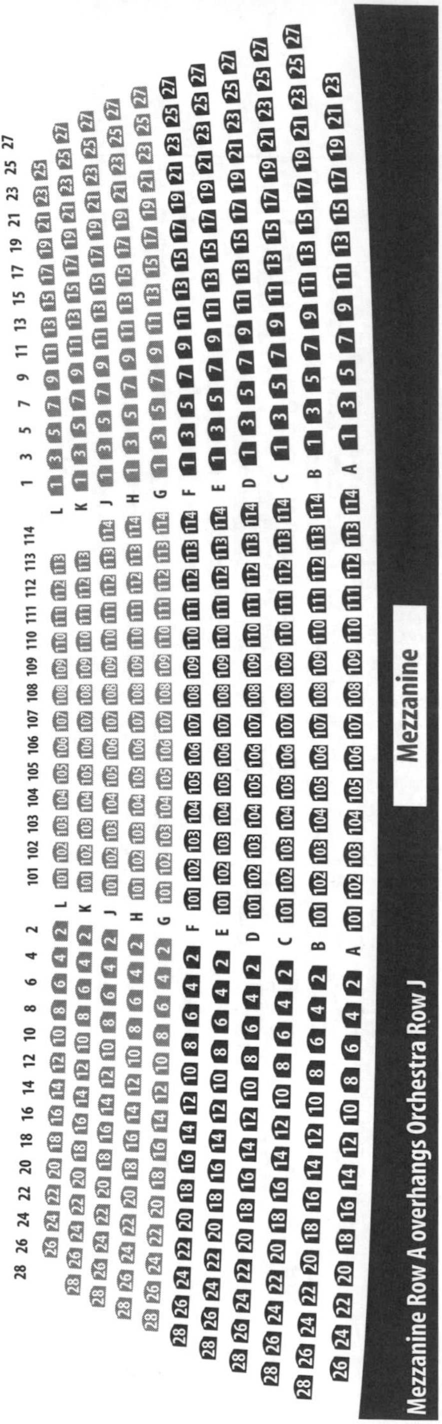

Mezzanine

Mezzanine Row A overhangs Orchestra Row J

1,2,3,7,N,R,S to 42nd St. & 7th Ave.
A,C,E to 42nd St. & 8th Ave.

Kinney: 100 West 44th St. [bet. 6th & 7th Ave.]
Miro: 139 West 45th St. [bet. 6th & 7th Ave.]

M6, M7, M10, M42, M104

Midtown Map #19

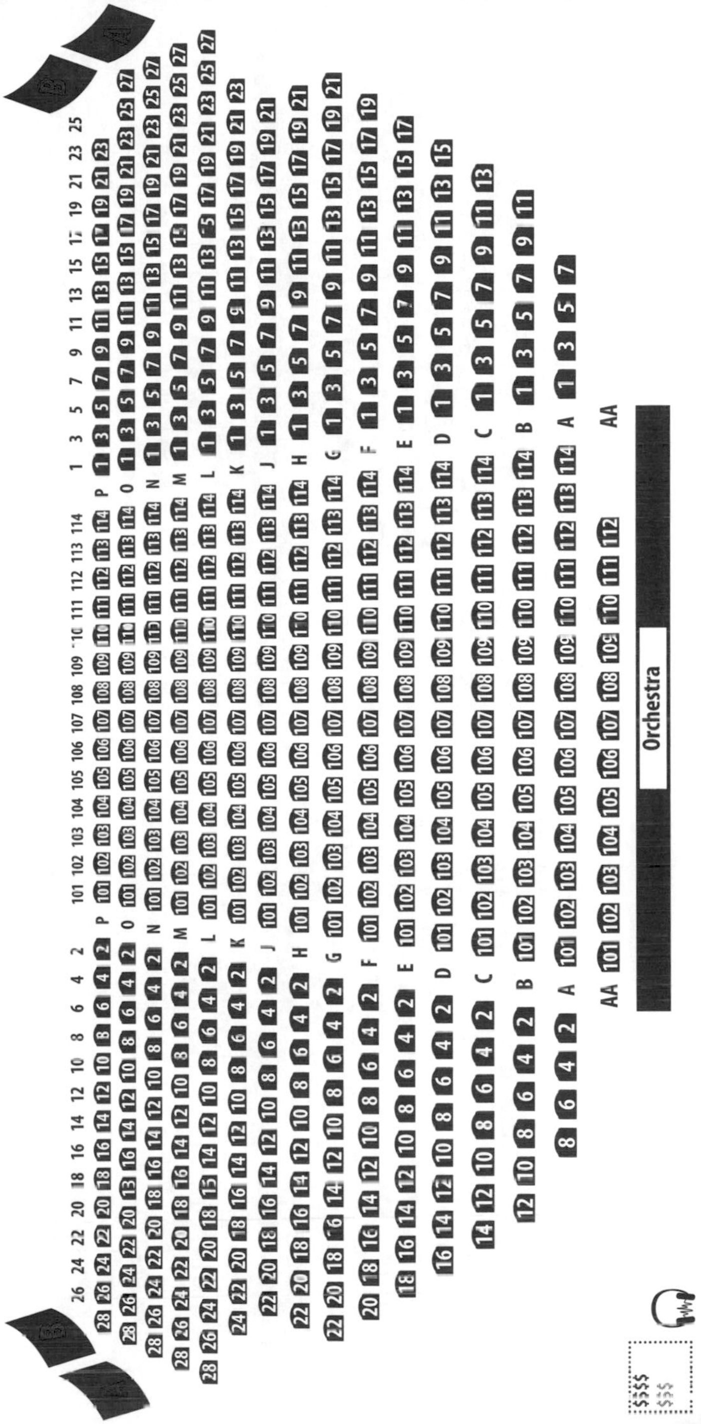

Orchestra

$$$$
$$$

Nederlander Theatre

208 West 41st Street // New York, NY [between 7th & 8th Avenue]

Ticketmaster: (212) 307-4100 // Group Sales: (212) 840-3890

[www.nederlander.org]

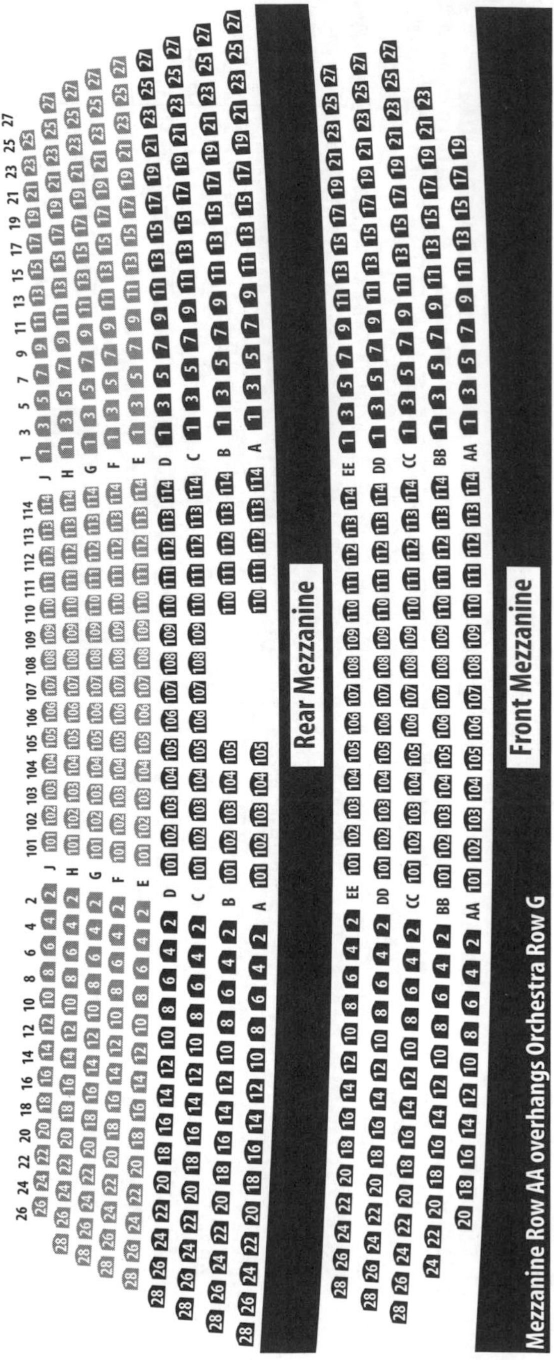

Rear Mezzanine

Front Mezzanine

Mezzanine Row AA overhangs Orchestra Row G

1,2,3,7,N,R,S to 42nd St. & 7th Ave.

Kinney: 220 West 41st St. [bet. 7th & 8th Ave.]

Kinney: 236 West 40th St. [bet. 7th & 8th Ave.]

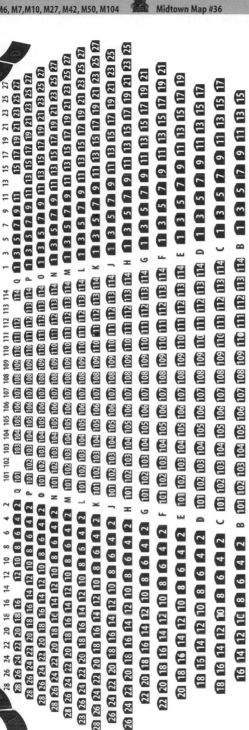

M6, M7, M10, M27, M42, M50, M104

Midtown Map #36

Orchestra Boxes Left

Orchestra Boxes Right

$$$$

$$$

Neil Simon Theatre

250 West 52nd Street // New York, NY [between Broadway & 8th Avenue]

Ticketmaster: (212) 307-4100 // Group Sales: (212) 302-7000

[www.nederlander.org]

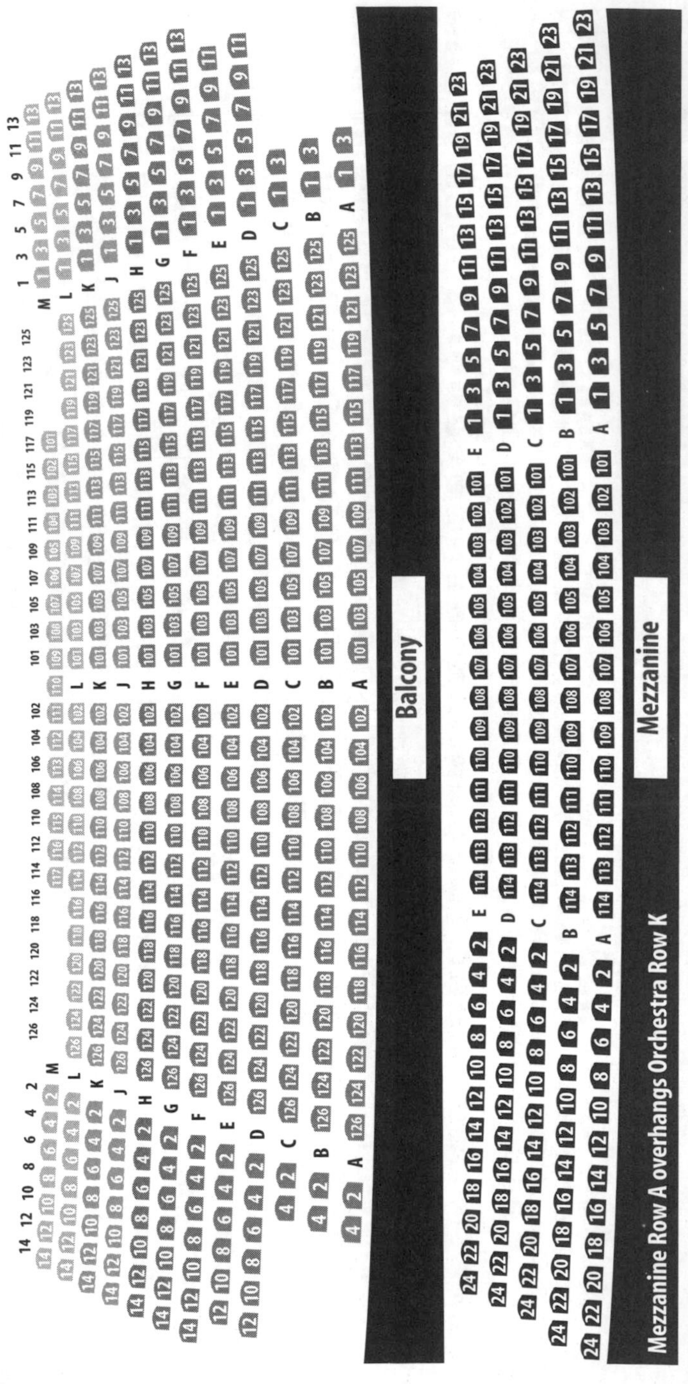

Balcony

Mezzanine

Mezzanine Row A overhangs Orchestra Row K

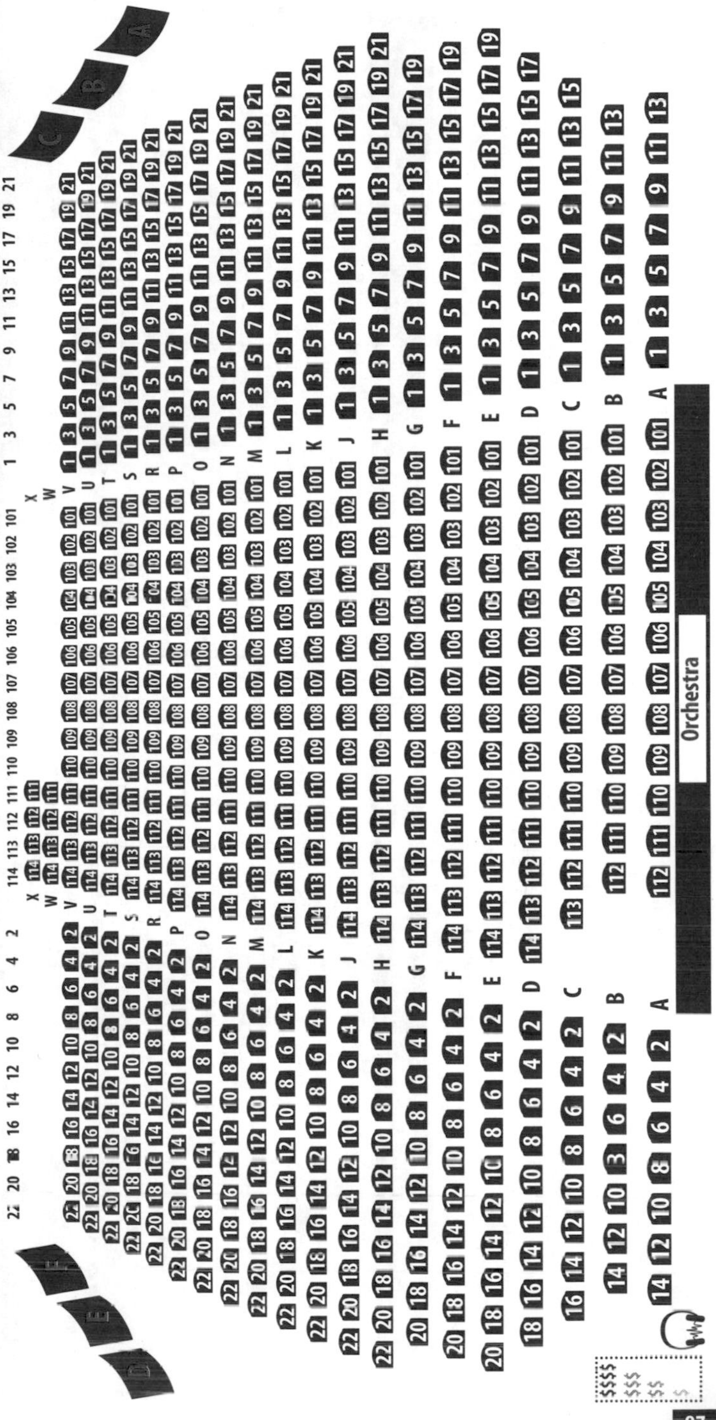
Orchestra
$$$$
$$$
$$
$

New Amsterdam Theatre

214 West 42nd Street // New York, NY [between 7th & 8th Avenue]

Ticketmaster: (212) 307-4747 // Group Sales: (212) 703-1040

[www.disneyonbroadway.com]

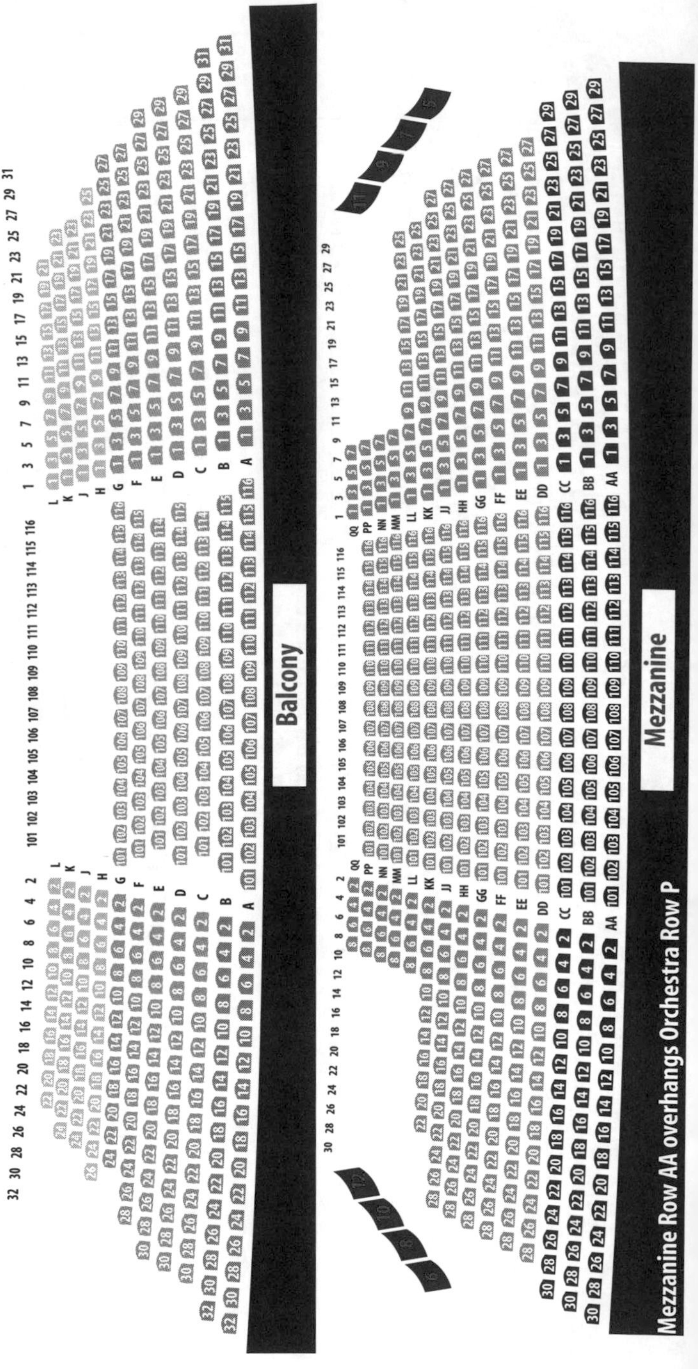

Balcony

Mezzanine

Mezzanine Row AA overhangs Orchestra Row P

1,2,3,7,N,R,S to 42nd St. & 7th Ave.

Kinney: 264 West 42nd St. [bet. 7th & 8th Ave.]

M6, M7, M10, M42, M104

Midtown Map #35

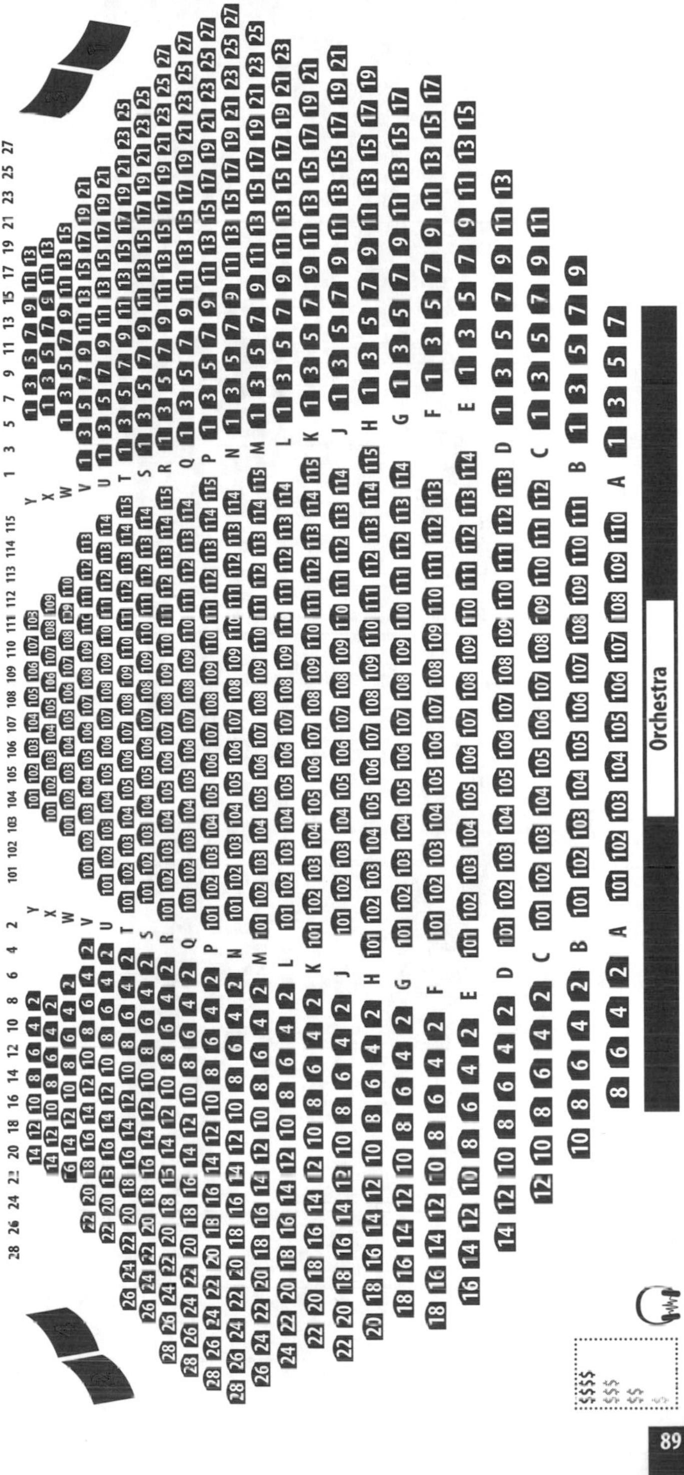

Orchestra

$$$$
$$$
$$
$

New Victory Theatre

209 West 42nd Street // New York, NY [between Broadway & 8th Avenue]

Box Office: [646] 223-3020 [www.newvictory.org]

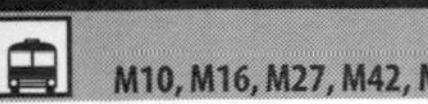
M10, M16, M27, M42, M104

Midtown Map #34

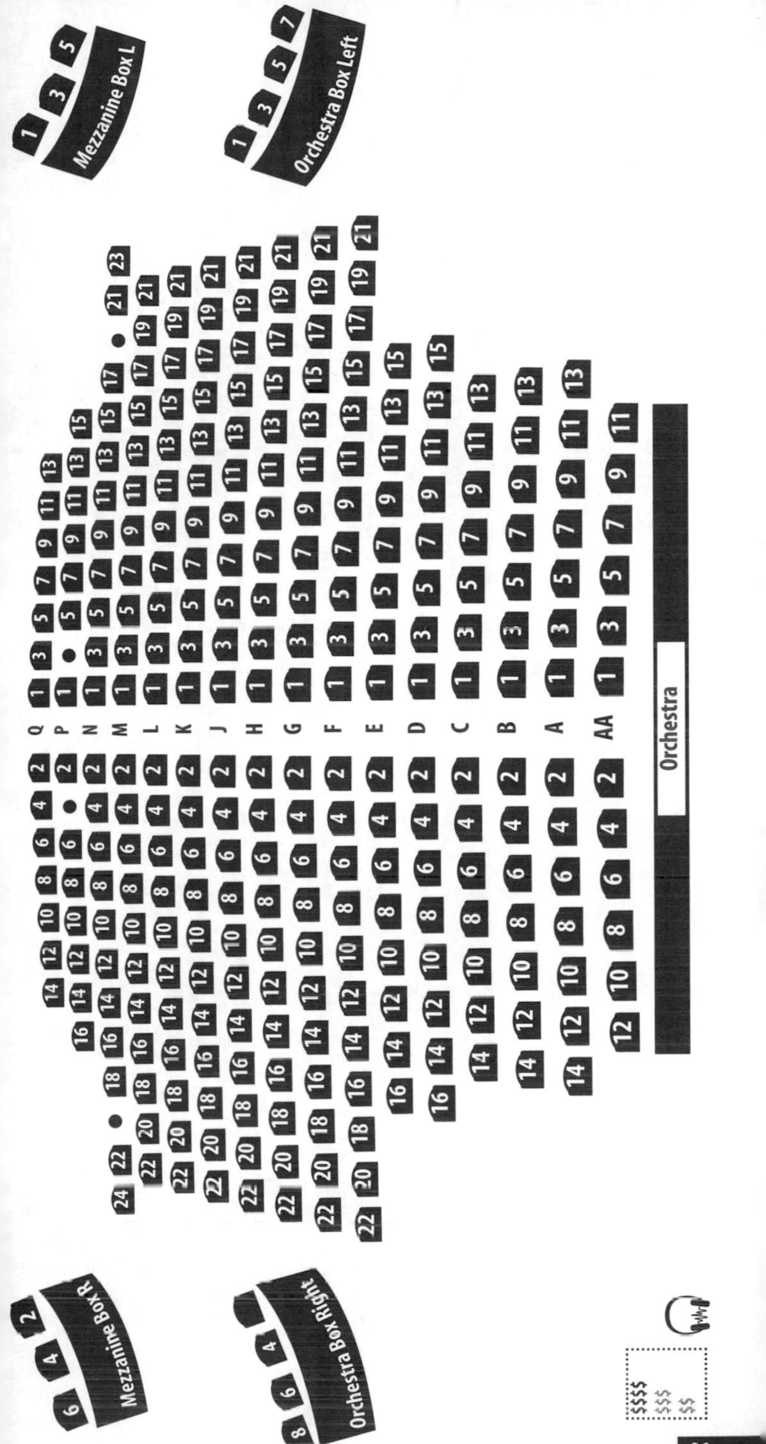

1
3
5
Mezzanine Box L

1
3
5
7
Orchestra Box Left

Orchestra

2
4
6
Mezzanine Box R

4
6
8
Orchestra Box Right

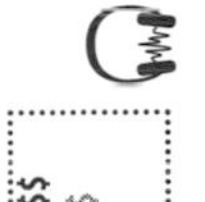
$$$$
$$$
$$

Palace Theatre

1564 Broadway // New York, NY [between 46th & 47th Street]

Ticketmaster: (212) 307-4747 // Group Sales: (212) 703-1040

[www.nederlander.org]

Balcony

Balcony Row A overhangs Mezzanine Row G

Mezzanine

Mezzanine Row A overhangs Orchestra Row K

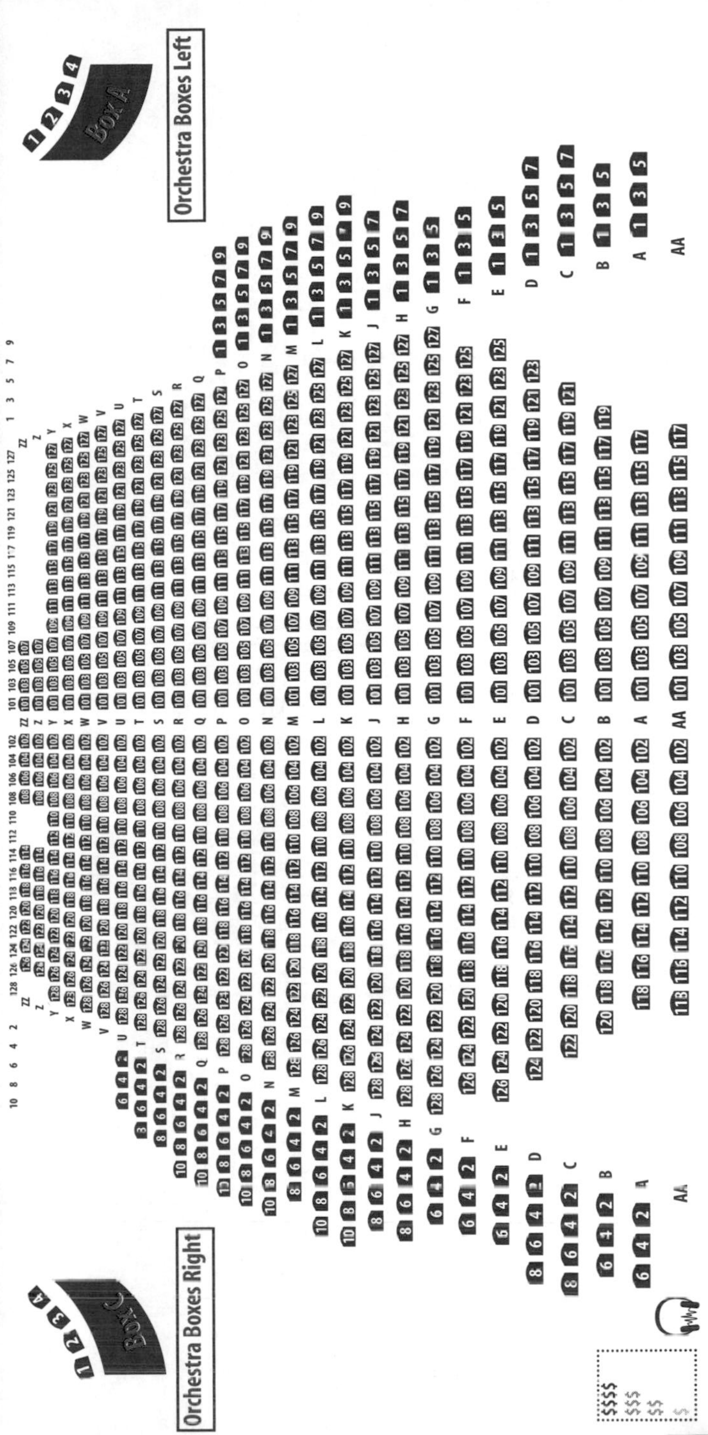

Box C 1 2 3 4

Orchestra Boxes Right

Box A 1 2 3 4

Orchestra Boxes Left

$$$$
$$$
$$
$

Plymouth Theatre

236 West 45th Street // New York, NY [between Broadway & 8th Avenue]

Telecharge: (212) 239-6200 // Group Sales: (800) BROADWAY

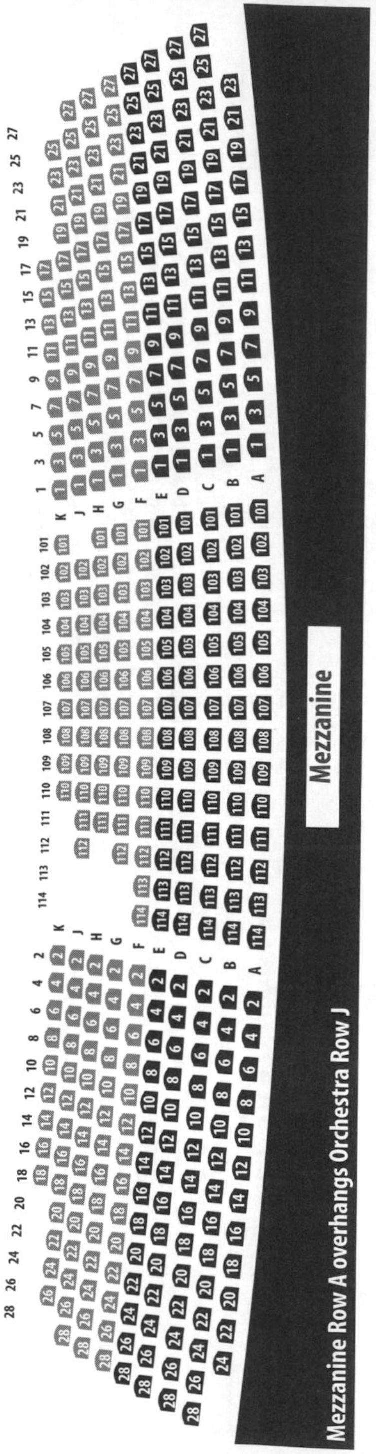

Mezzanine

Mezzanine Row A overhangs Orchestra Row J

1,9 to 50th Street

Miro: 139 West 45th St. [bet. 6th & 7th Ave.]
Astor: 1515 Broadway [at 44th Street]

M6, M7, M10, M42, M104

Midtown Map #23

Orchestra

$$$$
$$$

Richard Rogers Theatre

226 West 46th Street // New York, NY [between Broadway & 8th Avenue]

Ticketmaster: (212) 307-4100 // Group Sales: (800) 677-1164

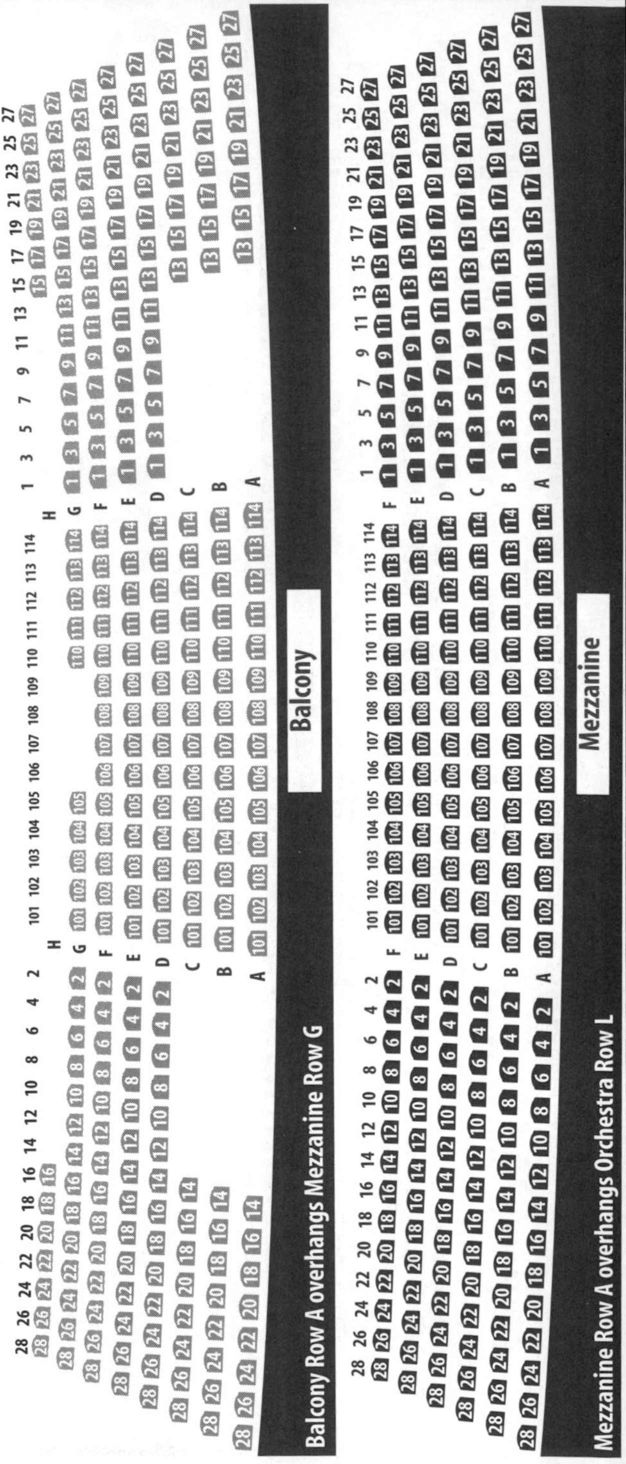

Balcony

Balcony Row A overhangs Mezzanine Row G

Mezzanine

Mezzanine Row A overhangs Orchestra Row L

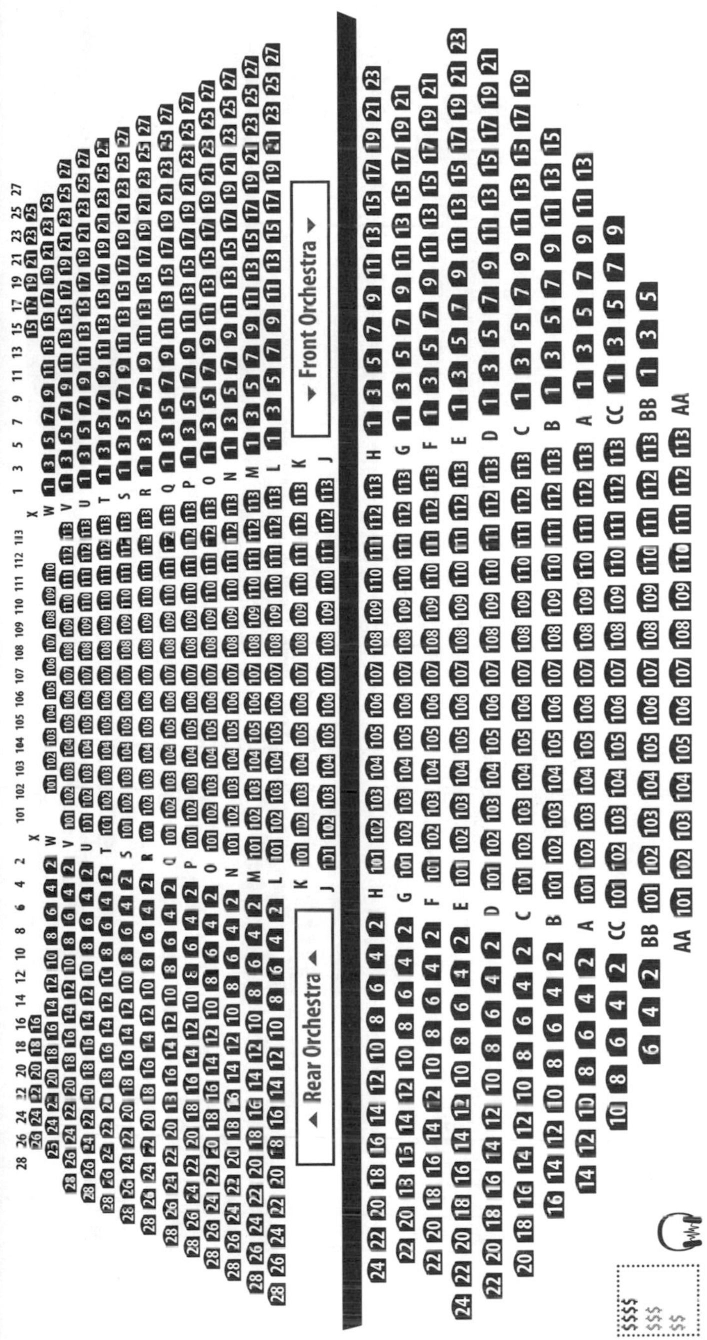

Rear Orchestra

Front Orchestra

$$$$
$$$
$$

Royale Theatre

242 West 45th Street // New York, NY [between Broadway & 8th Avenue]

Telecharge: (212) 239-6200 // Group Sales: (212) 302-7000

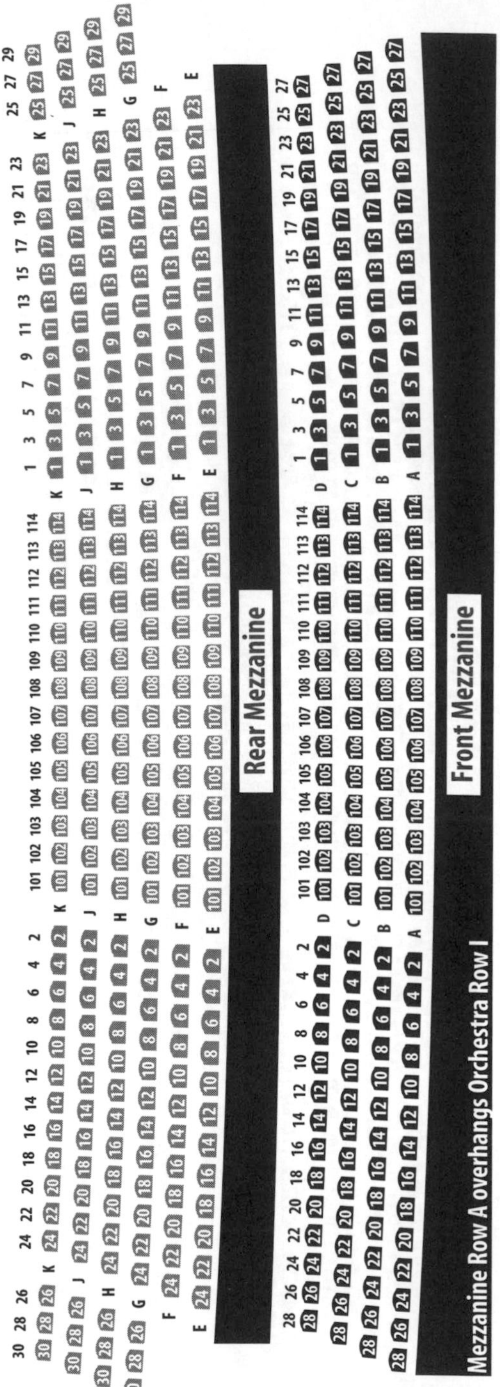

Rear Mezzanine

Front Mezzanine

Mezzanine Row A overhangs Orchestra Row I

Orchestra

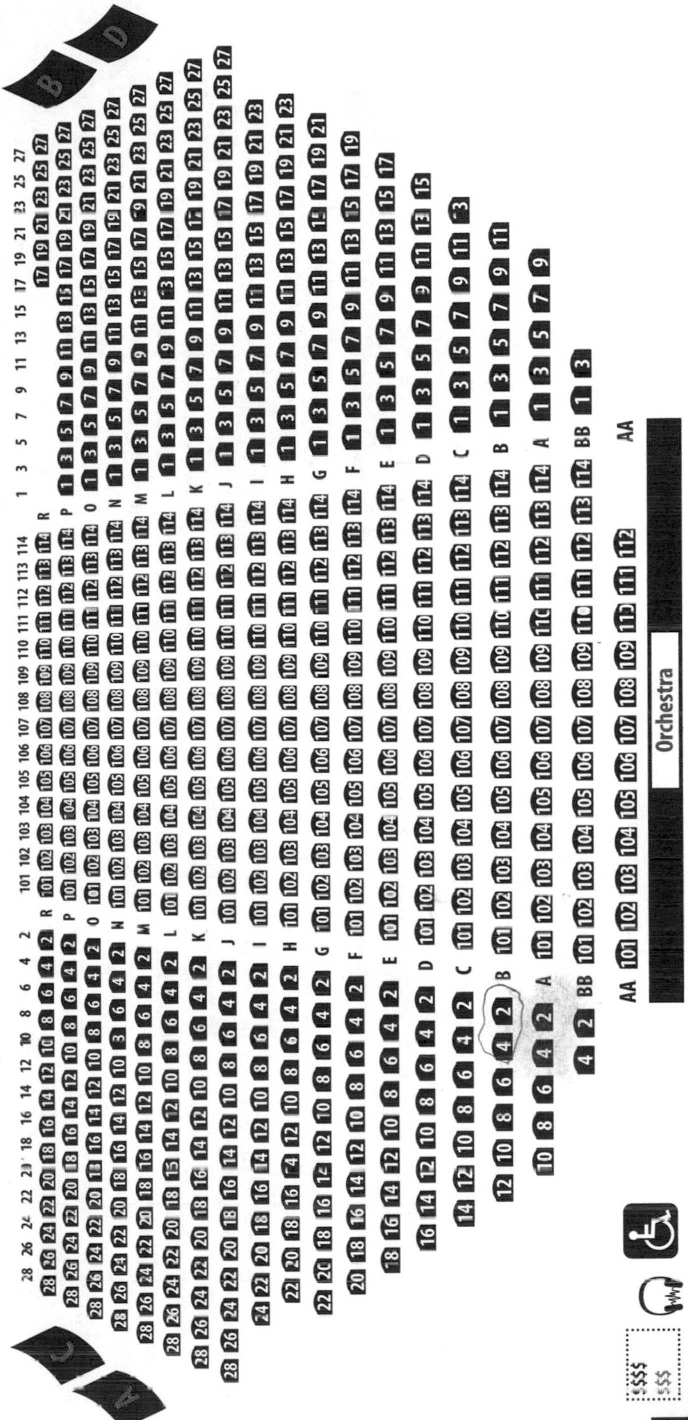

Shubert Theatre

225 West 44th Street // New York, NY [between 7th & 8th Avenue]

Telecharge: (212) 239-6200 // Group Sales: (212) 398-8383

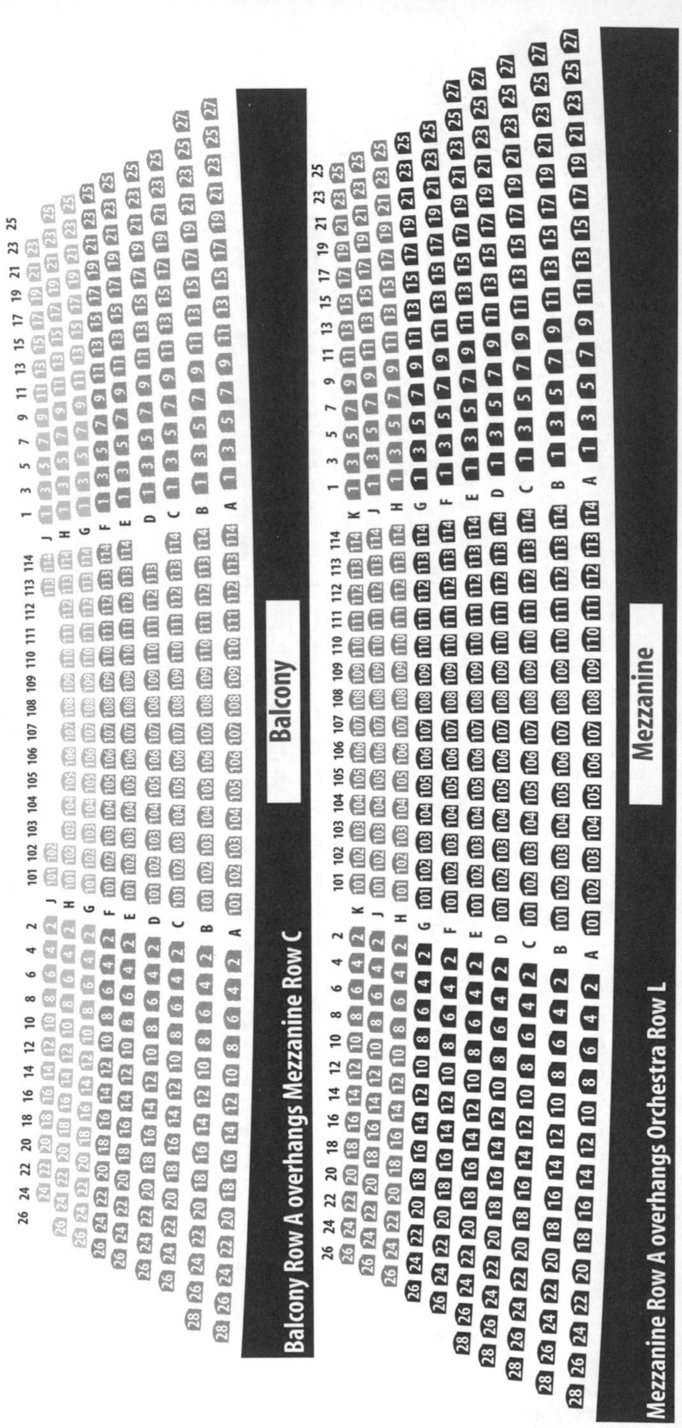

Balcony

Balcony Row A overhangs Mezzanine Row C

Mezzanine

Mezzanine Row A overhangs Orchestra Row L

1,2,3,7,N,R,S to 42nd St. & 7th Ave.
A,C,E to 42nd St. & 8th Ave.

Kinney: 100 West 44th St. [bet. 6th & 7th Ave.
43rd St: 250 West 43rd St. [bet. 7th & 8th Ave.]

M6, M7, M10, M42, M104

Midtown Map #29

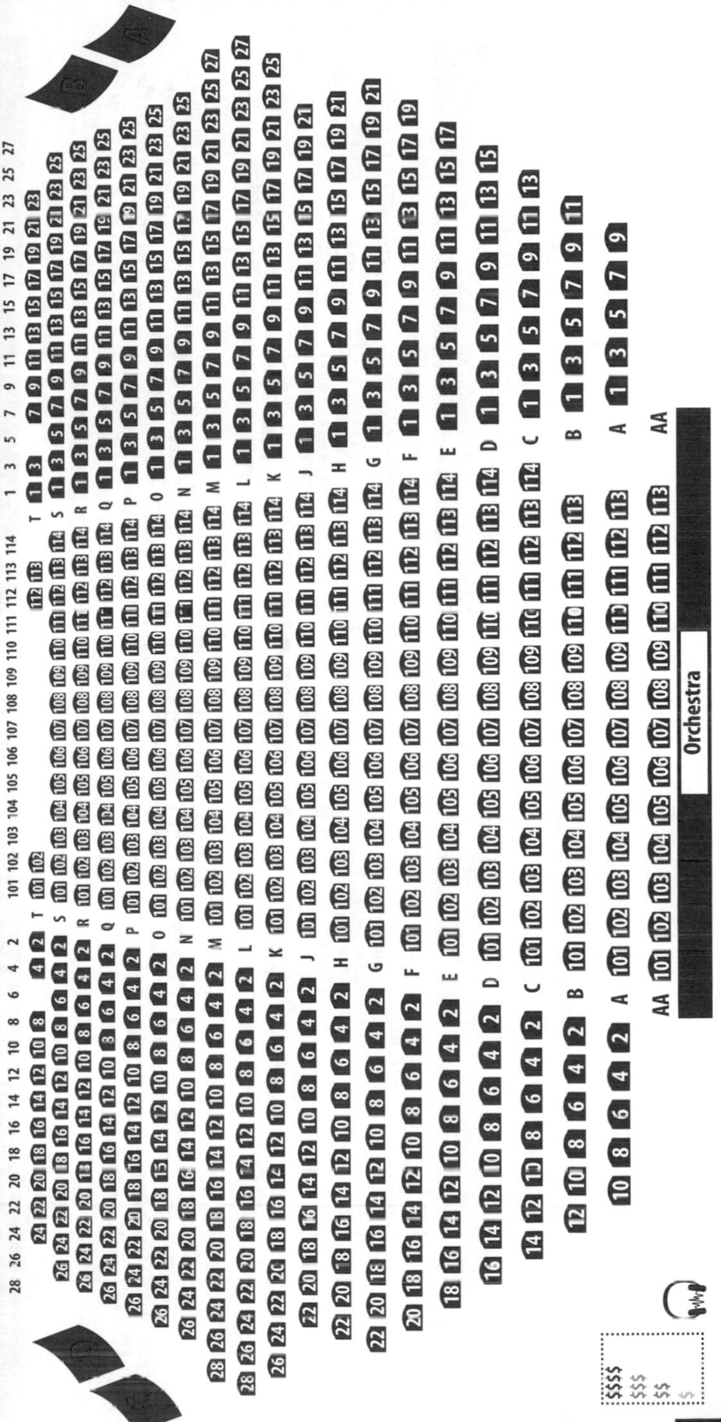

Orchestra

$$$$
$$$
$$
$

St. James Theatre

246 West 44th Street // New York, NY [between 7th & 8th Avenue]

Box Office: (212) 239-5800 // Group Sales: (212) 302-7000

[Premium Broadway Inner Circle Tickets: (212) 563-2929]

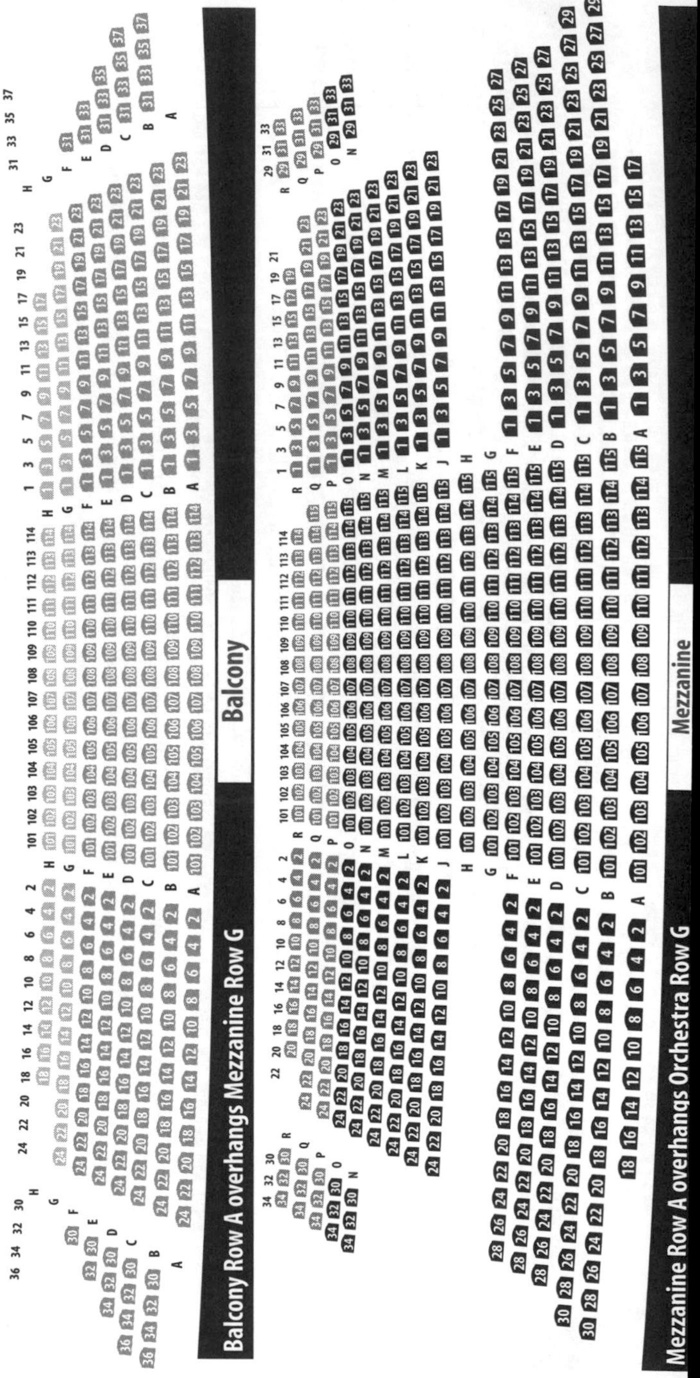

Balcony

Balcony Row A overhangs Mezzanine Row G

Mezzanine

Mezzanine Row A overhangs Orchestra Row G

1,2,3,7,N,R,S to 42nd St. & 7th Ave.
A,C,E to 42nd St. & 8th Ave.

Kinney: 100 West 44th St. [bet. 6th & 7th Ave.]
Advance: 249 West 43rd St. [bet. 7th & 8th Ave.]

M6, M7, M10, M42, M104

Midtown Map #32

Studio 54

254 West 54th Street // New York, NY [between Broadway & 8th Avenue]

Telecharge: (212) 239-6200

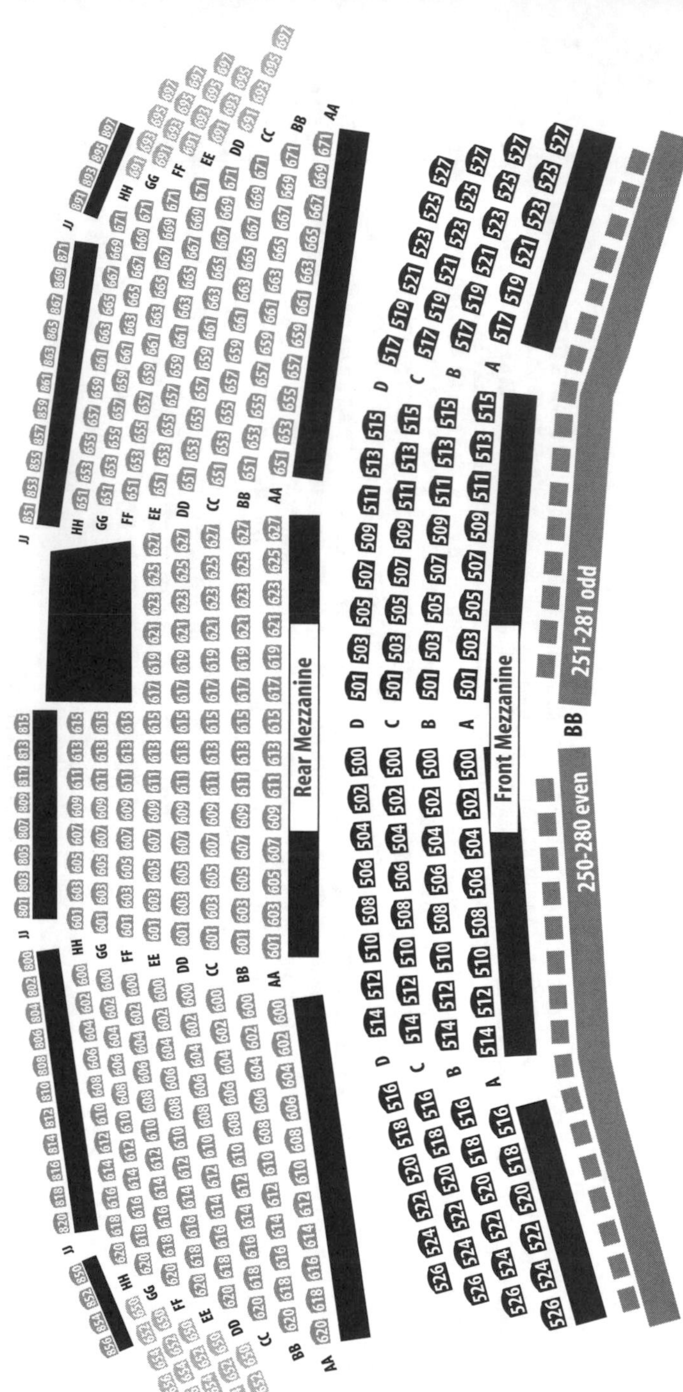

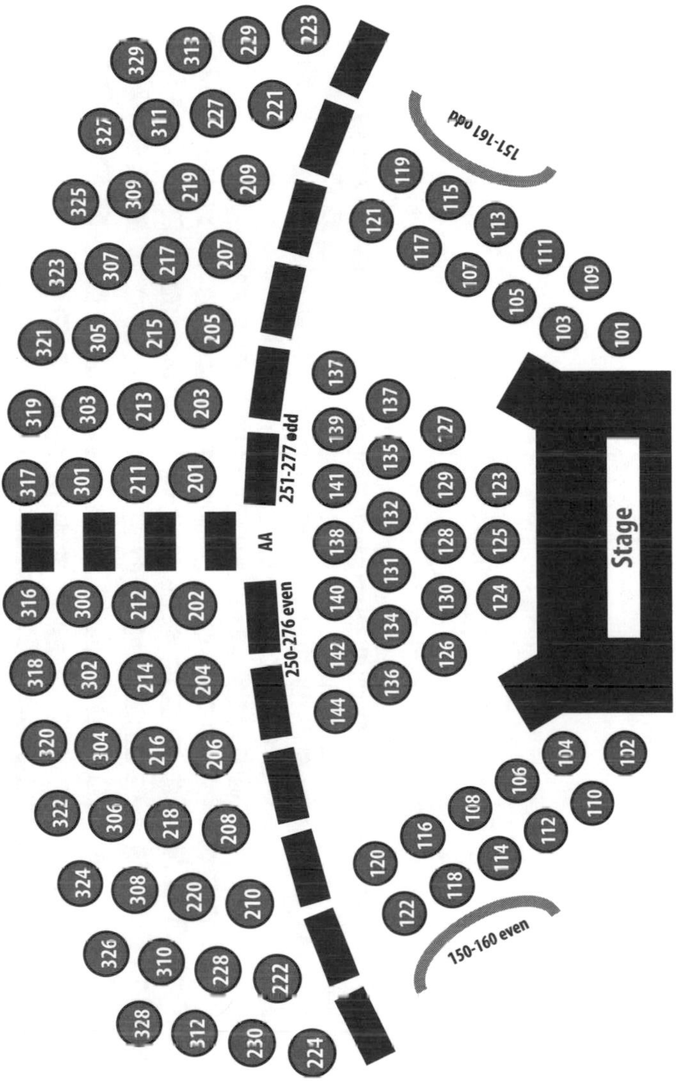

Stage

AA

251-277 odd

250-276 even

151-161 odd

150-160 even

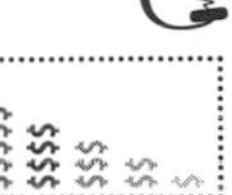

Virginia Theatre

245 West 52nd Street // New York, NY [between Broadway & 8th Avenue]

Telecharge: (212) 239-6200 // Group Sales: (212) 302-7000

Premium Broadway Inner Circle Tickets: (212) 563-2929

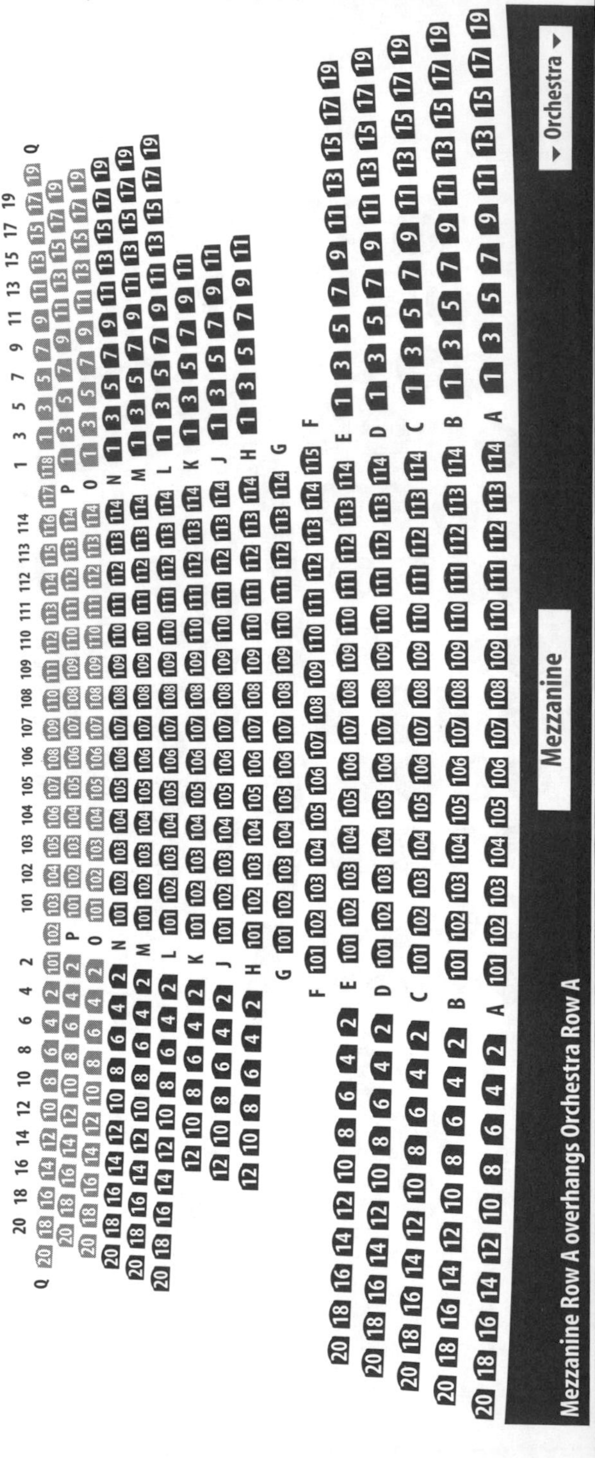

▸ Orchestra ▸

Mezzanine

Mezzanine Row A overhangs Orchestra Row A

1,9 to 50th Street

Parking 888: 888 8th Ave. [at 52nd Street]
Park: 166 West 53rd St. [bet. 6th & 7th Ave.]

M6, M7, M10, M27, M50, M104

Midtown Map #2

$$$$
$$$

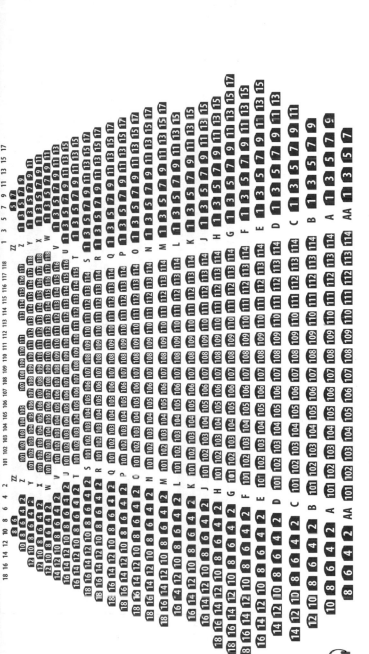

Walter Kerr Theatre

219 West 48th Street // New York, NY [between Broadway & 8th Avenue]

Telecharge: (212) 239-6200 // Group Sales: (212) 239-6262

Balcony

Mezzanine

Mezzanine Row A overhangs Orchestra Row J

1,9 to 50th Street

Quik Park: 201 West 48th St. [bet. Broadway & 8th Ave.]
Port: 235 West 48th St. [bet. Broadway & 8th Ave.]

M6, M7, M10, M27, M50, M104 — Midtown Map #9

Row	Left (even)	Center	Right (odd)
S	22 20 18 16 14 12 10 8 6 4 2	101 102 103 104 105 106 107 108 109 110 111 112	1 3 5 7 9 11 13 15 17 19 21
R	22 20 18 16 14 12 10 8 6 4 2	101 102 103 104 105 106 107 108 109 110 111 112	1 3 5 7 9 11 13 15 17 19 21
Q	22 20 18 16 14 12 10 8 6 4 2	101 102 103 104 105 106 107 108 109 110 111 112	1 3 5 7 9 11 13 15 17 19 21
P	22 20 18 16 14 12 10 8 6 4 2	101 102 103 104 105 106 107 108 109 110 111 112 113 114 115	1 3 5 7 9 11 13 15 17 19 21
N	22 20 18 16 14 12 10 8 6 4 2	101 102 103 104 105 106 107 108 109 110 111 112 113 114 115 116	1 3 5 7 9 11 13 15 17 19 21
M	22 20 18 16 14 12 10 8 6 4 2	101 102 103 104 105 106 107 108 109 110 111 112 113 114 115 116 117	1 3 5 7 9 11 13 15 17 19 21
L	22 20 18 16 14 12 10 8 6 4 2	101 102 103 104 105 106 107 108 109 110 111 112 113 114 115 116 117 118	1 3 5 7 9 11 13 15 17 19 21
K	18 16 14 12 10 8 6 4 2	101 102 103 104 105 106 107 108 109 110 111 112 113 114 115 116 117 118	1 3 5 7 9 11 13 15 17
J	16 14 12 10 8 6 4 2	101 102 103 104 105 106 107 108 109 110 111 112 113 114 115 116 117 118	1 3 5 7 9 11 13 15
H	16 14 12 10 8 6 4 2	101 102 103 104 105 106 107 108 109 110 111 112 113 114 115 116 117 118	1 3 5 7 9 11 13 15
G	16 14 12 10 8 6 4 2	101 102 103 104 105 106 107 108 109 110 111 112 113 114 115 116 117	1 3 5 7 9 11 13 15
F	16 14 12 10 8 6 4 2	101 102 103 104 105 106 107 108 109 110 111 112 113 114 115 116 117	1 3 5 7 9 11 13 15
E	14 12 10 8 6 4 2	101 102 103 104 105 106 107 108 109 110 111 112 113 114 115 116	1 3 5 7 9 11 13
D	14 12 10 8 6 4 2	101 102 103 104 105 106 107 108 109 110 111 112 113 114 115	1 3 5 7 9 11 13
C	14 12 10 8 6 4 2	101 102 103 104 105 106 107 108 109 110 111 112 113	1 3 5 7 9 11 13
B	8 6 4 2	101 102 103 104 105 106 107 108 109 110 111 112	1 3 5 7
A		101 102 103 104 105 106 107 108 109 110 111	

Orchestra

$$$$
$$$
$$

Winter Garden Theatre

1634 Broadway // New York, NY [between 50th & 51st Street]

Telecharge: (212) 563-5544

Mezzanine

Mezzanine Row A overhangs Orchestra Row O

52 Broadway: 1675 Broadway [at 52nd Street]
GMC: 218 West 50th St. [bet. Broadway & 8th Ave.]

M6, M7, M10, M27, M50, M104

Midtown Map #6

Orchestra

$$$$
$$$
$$

off-broadway theatres

"You start with the philosophy that theatre is important to people's lives. If you don't believe this, then you might as well give up."
—Joe Papp

45 Bleecker
Actor's Playhouse
Amato Opera Theatre
American Place
Astor Place
Atlantic
Bouwerie Lane
Century Center for the Performing Arts
Chelsea Playhouse
Cherry Lane
Circle In The Square (Downtown)
Classic Stage
Daryl Roth
Dicapo Opera Theatre
Douglas Fairbanks
Duffy
Ensemble Studio
Gramercy Arts Theatre & Repertorio Español
Irish Repertory
John Houseman
José Quintero
Intar
Joseph Papp Public Theatre (Anspacher)
Joseph Papp Public Theatre (Newman)
Joyce
The Kaye Playhouse
Laura Pels (Gramercy Theater)
Lucille Lortel
Manhattan Ensemble
Manhattan Theatre Club
Minetta Lane
New York Theatre Workshop
Orpheum
Pearl
Player's
Playhouse 91
Playwrights Horizons (Peter Jay Sharp)
Playwrights Horizons (Main Stage)
Primary Stages
Promenade
Samuel Beckett
Signature
Second Stage
Soho Playhouse
St. Luke's
The Duke on 42nd Street
The Theatre at St. Clements
Theater Four
Union Square
Variety Arts
Vineyard's Dimson
Westside (Downstairs)
Westside (Upstairs)
World Underground
York Theatre (St. Peter's Church)
47th Street

45 Bleecker

45 Bleecker Street // New York, NY [between Broadway & 8th Avenue]

Box Office: (212) 353.9983 **[www.45bleecker.com]**

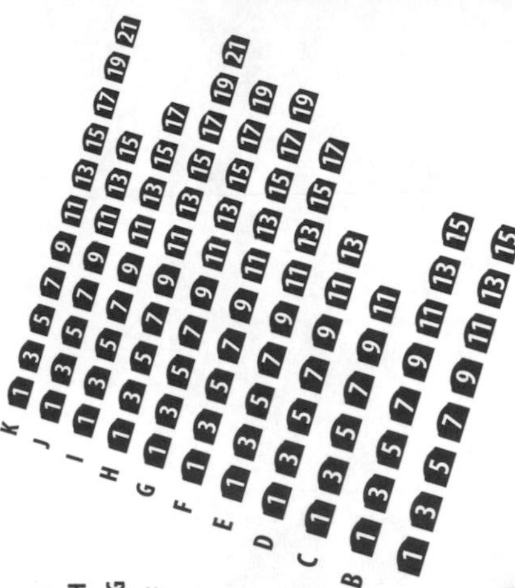

J 101 102 103 104 105 106 107 J

I 101 102 103 104 105 106 107 108 I

H 101 102 103 104 105 106 107 108 109 110 111 112 113 H

G 101 102 103 104 105 106 107 108 109 110 111 112 113 114 115 116 G

F 101 102 103 104 105 106 107 108 109 110 111 112 113 114 115 F

E 101 102 103 104 105 106 107 108 109 110 111 112 113 114 E

D 101 102 103 104 105 106 107 108 109 110 111 112 113 114 D

C 101 102 103 104 105 106 107 108 109 110 111 112 C

B 101 102 103 104 105 106 107 108 109 110 111 112 B

A 101 102 103 104 105 106 107 108 109 A

Stage

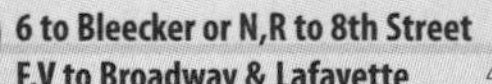

6 to Bleecker or N,R to 8th Street
F,V to Broadway & Lafayette

Bond Street Garage: 2nd St. [bet. Bowery & Lafayette]

M103

East/West Village Map #75

Actor's Playhouse

100 7th Avenue South // New York, NY [between Bleecker & Christopher St.]

Telecharge: (212) 239-6200 // Group Sales: (212) 580-9272

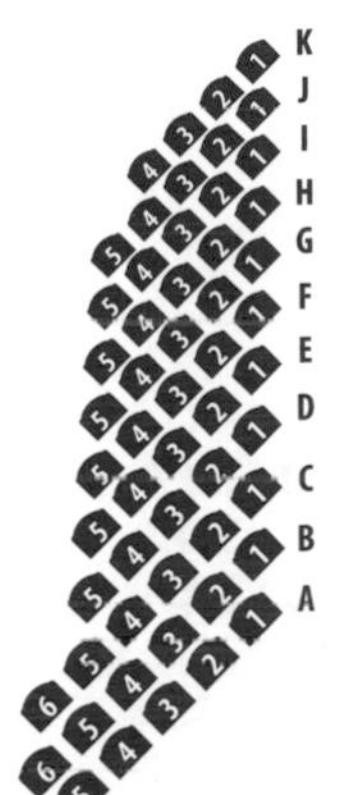

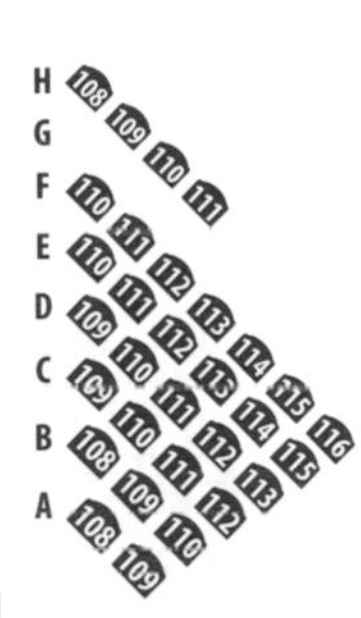

Stage

1,9 to Christopher Street

Kinney: 20 South Morton [bet. 7th Ave. & Bleecker St.]

M8, M10

East/West Village Map #72

Amato Opera Theatre

319 Bowery // New York, NY [corner of 2nd Street]

Box Office: (212) 228-8200 [www.amato.org]

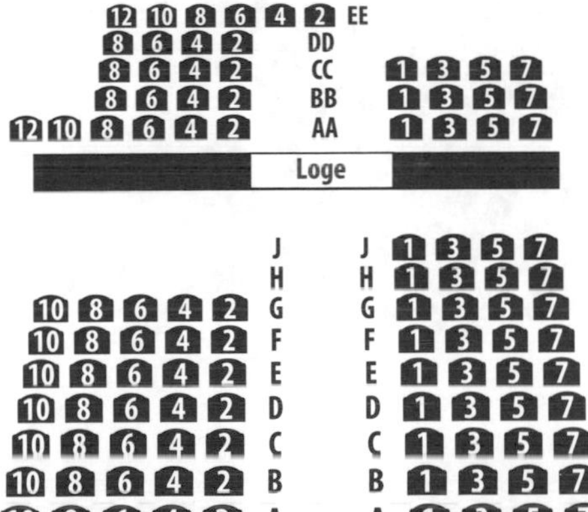

6 to Bleecker Street
B,D,F,to Broadway & Lafayette

Edison: 204 Lafayette Street
Kinney: 224 Mulberry Street

M103 to Bleecker Street

East/West Village Map #73

The American Place Theatre

111 West 46th Street // New York, NY [between 6th & 7th Avenue]

Telecharge: (212) 239-6200 // Group Sales: (212) 869-7303

[www.americanplacetheatre.org]

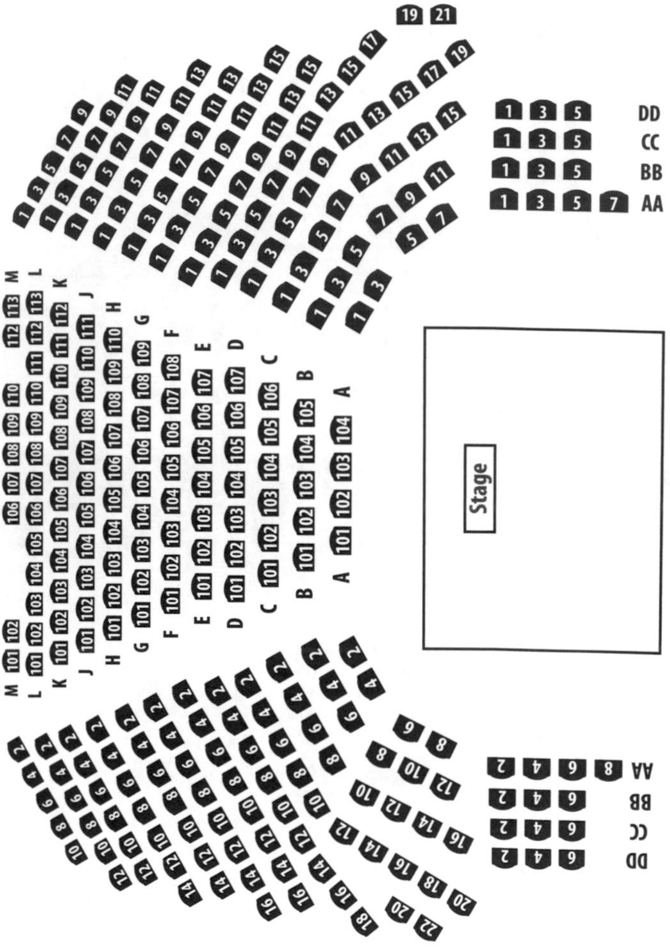

Stage

 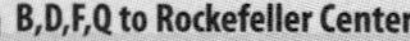
B,D,F,Q to Rockefeller Center

Resource: 164 West 46th St. [bet. 6th & 7th Ave.]

 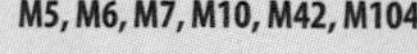
M5, M6, M7, M10, M42, M104

Midtown Map #45

Astor Place Theatre

434 Lafayette Street // New York, NY [between Astor Place & West 4th St.]

Ticketmaster: (212) 307-4100 // Group Sales: (212) 260-8993

	G	1 3 5 7 9 11 13
12 10 8 6 4 2	F	1 3 5 7 9 11 13
12 10 8 6 4 2	E	1 3 5 7 9 11
12 10 8 6 4 2	D	1 3 5 7 9 11 13
12 10 8 6 4 2	C	1 3 5 7 9 11 13
12 10 8 6 4 2	B	1 3 5 7 9 11
12 10 8 6 4 2	A	1 3 5 7 9 11

Mezzanine

Mezzanine overhangs Row HH

106 104 102	SS	101 103 105
108 106 104 102	RR	101 103 105 107
114 112 110 108 106 104 102	QQ	101 103 105 107 109 111
114 112 110 108 106 104 102	PP	101 103 105 107 109 111
114 112 110 108 106 104 102	OO	101 103 105 107 109 111
114 112 110 108 106 104 102	NN	101 103 105 107 109 111
114 112 110 108 106 104 102	MM	101 103 105 107 109 111
114 112 110 108 106 104 102	LL	101 103 105 107 109 111
114 112 110 108 106 104 102	KK	101 103 105 107 109 111
114 112 110 108 106 104 102	JJ	101 103 105 107 109 111
114 112 110 108 106 104 102	HH	101 103 105 107 109 111
114 112 110 108 106 104 102	GG	101 103 105 107 109 111
114 112 110 108 106 104 102	FF	101 103 105 107 109 111
114 112 110 108 106 104 102	EE	
114 112 110 108 106 104 102	DD	101 103 105 107 109 111
114 112 110 108 106 104 102	CC	101 103 105 107 109 111
114 112 110 108 106 104 102	BB	101 103 105 107 109 111
114 112 110 108 106 104 102	AA	101 103 105 107 109 111

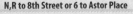

East/West Village Map #74

Atlantic Theater

336 West 20th Street // New York, NY [between 8th & 9th Avenue]

Telecharge: (212) 239-6200 [www.atlantictheater.org]

H	101 102 103 104 105 106 107 108 109 110 111 112 113 114 115
G	101 102 103 104 105 106 107 108 109 110 111 112 113 114 115 116 117
F	101 102 103 104 105 106 107 108 109 110 111 112 113 114 115 116 117
E	101 102 103 104 105 106 107 108 109 110 111 112 113 114 115 116 117
D	101 102 103 104 105 106 107 108 109 110 111 112 113 114 115 116 117
C	101 102 103 104 105 106 107 108 109 110 111 112 113 114 115 116 117
B	101 102 103 104 105 106 107 108 109 110 111 112 113 114 115 116 117
A	101 102 103 104 105 106 107 108 109 110 111 112 113 114 115 116 117
AA	101 102 103 104 105 106 107 108 109 110 111 112 113 114 115 116

Stage

C,E, to 23rd St.
1,9 to 18th St.

19th St. Garage: 250 West 19th St. [bet. 7th & 8th Ave.]
Kinney: 435 West 23rd St. [bet. 9th & 10th Ave.]

M11, M20, M23

Chelsea Map #68

Bouwerie Lane Theatre

330 Bowery // New York, NY [between Bleecker & Bond Street]

Box Office: (212) 677-0060 ext. 16 [www.jeancocteaurep.org]

12 10 8 6 4	M	3 5 7 9 11
8 6 4 2	L	1 3 5 7
8 6 4 2	K	1 3 5 7
12 10 8 6 4 2	J	1 3 5 7 9 11
12 10 8 6 4 2	I	1 3 5 7 9 11
12 10 8 6 4 2	H	1 3 5 7 9 11
12 10 8 6 4 2	G	1 3 5 7 9 11
12 10 8 6 4 2	F	1 3 5 7 9 11
12 10 8 6 4 2	E	1 3 5 7 9 11
12 10 8 6 4 2	D	
12 10 8 6 4 2	C	1 3 5 7 9 11
12 10 8 6 4 2	B	1 3 5 7 9 11
12 10 8 6 4 2	A	1 3 5 7 9 11

Stage

6 to Bleecker St. or N,R to 8th & Prince St.
B,D,F,Q to Broadway & Lafayette

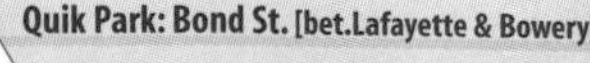
Quik Park: Bond St. [bet.Lafayette & Bowery]

M5, M101, M102

East/West Village Map #76

Century Center for the Performing Arts

111 East 15th Street // New York, NY [between Union Square & 15th St.]

Telecharge: (212) 239-6200 // Group Sales: (212) 889-4300

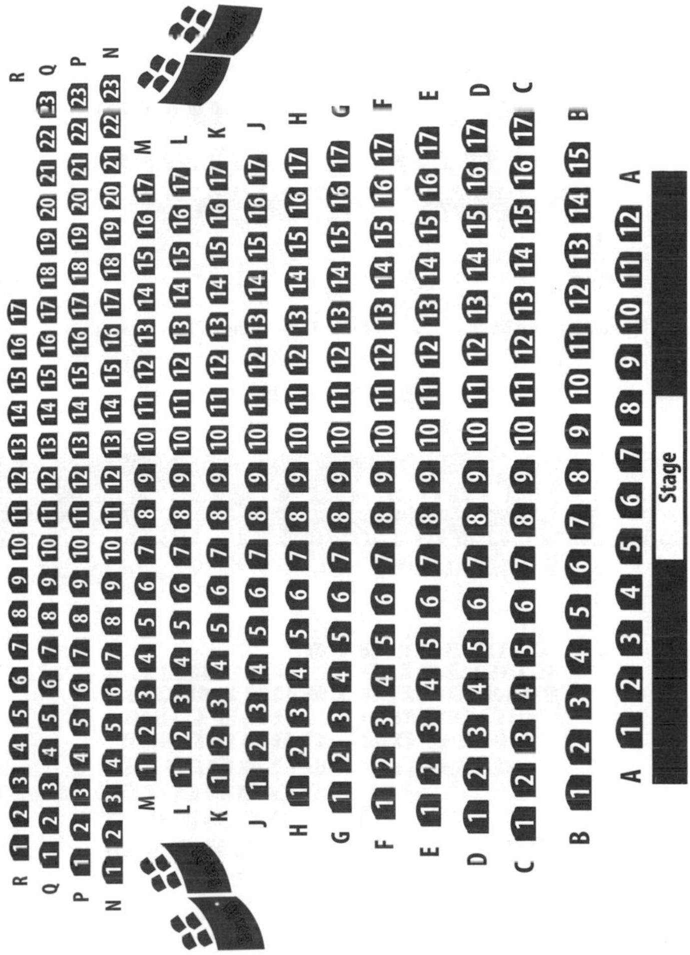

R 1 2 3 4 5 6 7 8 9 10 11 12 13 14 15 16 17 R

Q 1 2 3 4 5 6 7 8 9 10 11 12 13 14 15 16 17 18 19 20 21 22 23 Q

P 1 2 3 4 5 6 7 8 9 10 11 12 13 14 15 16 17 18 19 20 21 22 23 P

N 1 2 3 4 5 6 7 8 9 10 11 12 13 14 15 16 17 18 19 20 21 22 23 N

M 1 2 3 4 5 6 7 8 9 10 11 12 13 14 15 16 17 M

L 1 2 3 4 5 6 7 8 9 10 11 12 13 14 15 16 17 L

K 1 2 3 4 5 6 7 8 9 10 11 12 13 14 15 16 17 K

J 1 2 3 4 5 6 7 8 9 10 11 12 13 14 15 16 17 J

H 1 2 3 4 5 6 7 8 9 10 11 12 13 14 15 16 17 H

G 1 2 3 4 5 6 7 8 9 10 11 12 13 14 15 16 17 G

F 1 2 3 4 5 6 7 8 9 10 11 12 13 14 15 16 17 F

E 1 2 3 4 5 6 7 8 9 10 11 12 13 14 15 16 17 E

D 1 2 3 4 5 6 7 8 9 10 11 12 13 14 15 16 17 D

C 1 2 3 4 5 6 7 8 9 10 11 12 13 14 15 16 17 C

B 1 2 3 4 5 6 7 8 9 10 11 12 13 14 15 B

A 1 2 3 4 5 6 7 8 9 10 11 12 A

Stage

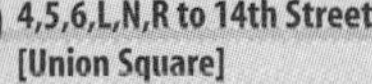
4,5,6,L,N,R to 14th Street [Union Square]

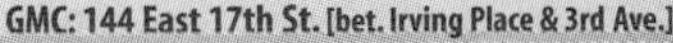
GMC: 144 East 17th St. [bet. Irving Place & 3rd Ave.]

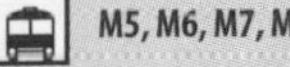
M5, M6, M7, M14

Union Square Map #62

Chelsea Playhouse

125 West 22nd Street // New York, NY [between 6th & 7th Avenue]

Box Office: (212) 924-7415

8 6 4 2	H	1 3 5 7 9
10 8 6 4 2	G	1 3 5 7
8 6 4 2	F	1 3 5 7 9
10 8 6 4 2	E	1 3 5 7
8 6 4 2	D	1 3 5 7 9
10 8 6 4 2	C	1 3 5 7
8 6 4 2	B	1 3 5 7 9
10 8 6 4 2	A	1 3 5 7

Stage

 1,9 to 23rd & 7th Street

 Kinney: 235 West 22nd St. [bet. 7th & 8th Ave.]

 M23

 Chelsea Map #69

Cherry Lane Theatre

38 Commerce Street // New York, NY [between 7th Avenue & Hudson St.]

Telecharge: (212) 239-6200 [www.cherrylanetheatre.com]

14	P	
14 12 10 8 6 4 2	O	1
14 12 10 8 6 4 2	N	3 5 7 9 11 13
14 12 10 8 6 4 2	M	1 3 5 7 9 11 13
12 10 8 6 4 2	L	1 3 5 7 9 11 13
12 10 8 6 4 2	K	1 3 5 7 9 11 13
10 8 6 4	J	1 3 5 7 9 11 13
	I	1 3 5 7 9 11 13
	H	1 3 5 7 9 11 13
12 10 8 6 4 2	G	1 3 5 7 9 11 13
12 10 8 6 4 2	F	1 3 5 7 9 11 13
12 10 8 6 4 2	E	1 3 5 7 9 11 13
12 10 8 6 4 2	D	1 3 5 7 9 11 13
12 10 8 6 4 2	C	1 3 5 7 9 11 13
12 10 8 6 4 2	B	1 3 5 7 9 11 13
12 10 8 6 4 2	A	1 3 5 7 9 11 13

Stage

 1,9 to Christopher Street

 396 Hudson Street [bet. Clarkson & Houston St.]
Kinney: 20 Morton Street [bet. Bleecker & 7th Ave.]

 M8, M10

 East/West Village Map #77

Classic Stage Theatre

136 East 13th Street // New York, NY [between 3rd & 4th Avenue]

Box Office: (212) 677-4210 ext. 2 [www.classicstage.org]

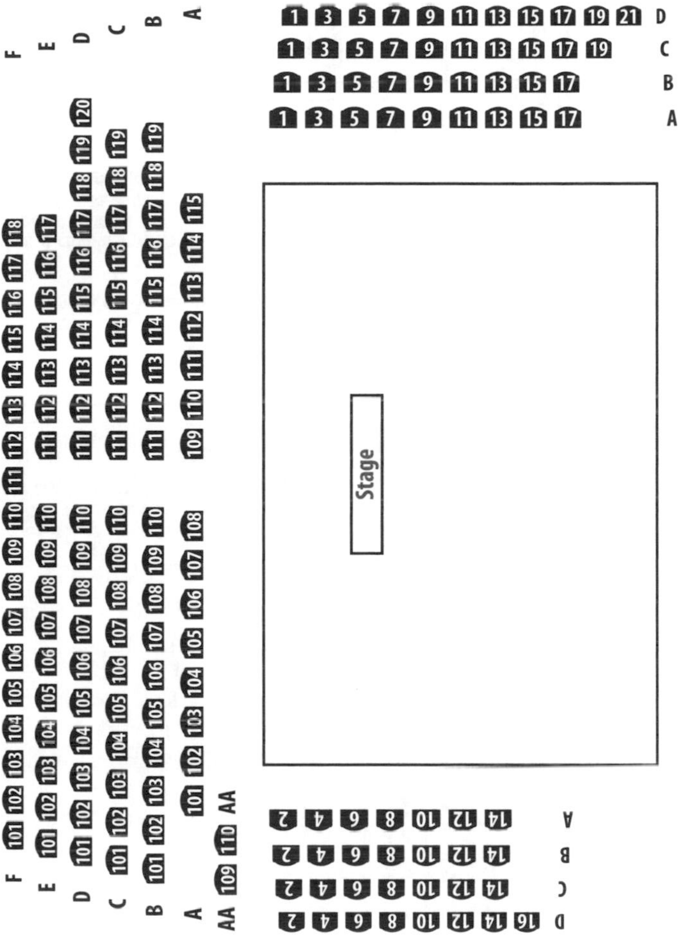

Stage

4,5,6,L,N,R to 14th Street
[Union Square]

GMC: 21 East 12th Street
Kinney: 310 East 11th Street

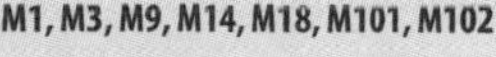

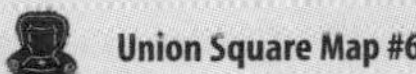

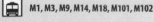

Circle In The Square (Downtown)

159 Bleecker Street // New York, NY [between Sullivan & Thompson Street]

Box Office: (212) 288-3588

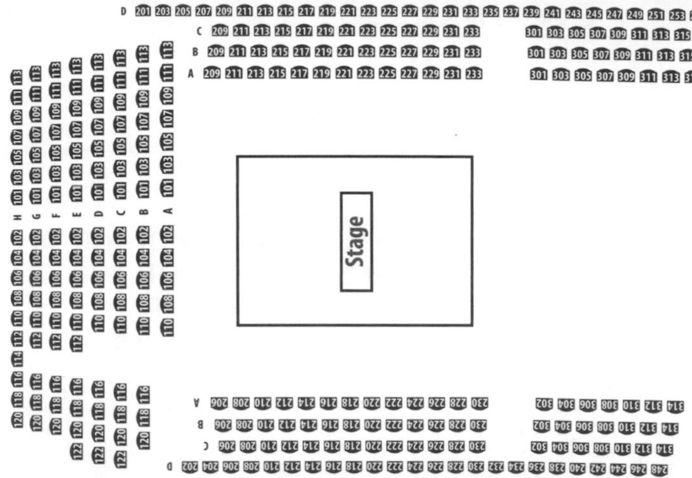

 1,9 to Christopher Street

Kinney: 20 South Morton [bet. Bleecker & 7th St.]

 M5, M6, M21

 East/West Village Map #94

Daryl Roth Theatre (DR2)

101 East 15th Street // New York, NY [between 14th & 15th St.]

Telecharge: (212) 239-6200 // Group Sales: (800) 334-8457

Row									Row
N		2	3	4	5	6	7		N
M	1	2	3	4	5	6	7		M
L	1	2	3	4	5	6	7		L
K	1	2	3	4	5	6	7		K
J	1	2	3	4	5	6	7	8	J
H	1	2	3	4	5	6	7	8	H
G	1	2	3	4	5	6	7	8	G
F	1	2	3	4	5	6	7	8	F
E	1	2	3	4	5	6	7	8	E
D	1	2	3	4	5	6	7	8	D
C	1	2	3	4	5	6	7	8	C
B	1	2	3	4	5	6	7	8	B
A	1	2	3	4	5	6	7	8	A

Stage

 4,5,6,L,N,R to 14th Street [Union Square]

GMC: 144 East 17th St. [bet. Irving Pl. & 3rd Ave.]
GMC: 104 East 15th St. [bet. 14th & 15th St.]

 M1, M2, M3,M6, M7, M9, M14

 Union Square Map #64

DiCapo Opera Theatre

184 East 76th Street // New York, NY [between Lexington & 3rd Avenue]

Box Office: (212) 288-9438 ext. 10 [www.dicapo.com]

L	17 16 15 14 13 12 11 10 9 8 7 6 5 4 3 2 1	L
K	17 16 15 14 13 12 11 10 9 8 7 6 5 4 3 2 1	K
J	17 16 15 14 13 12 11 10 9 8 7 6 5 4 3 2 1	J
I	17 16 15 14 13 12 11 10 9 8 7 6 5 4 3 2 1	I
H	17 16 15 14 13 12 11 10 9 8 7 6 5 4 3 2 1	H
G	17 16 15 14 13 12 11 10 9 8 7 6 5 4 3 2 1	G
F	17 16 15 14 13 12 11 10 9 8 7 6 5 4 3 2 1	F
E	17 16 15 14 13 12 11 10 9 8 7 6 5 4 3 2 1	E
D	17 16 15 14 13 12 11 10 9 8 7 6 5 4 3 2 1	D
C	17 16 15 14 13 12 11 10 9 8 7 6 5 4 3 2 1	C
B	17 16 15 14 13 12 11 10 9 8 7 6 5 4 3 2 1	B
A	17 16 15 14 13 12 11 10 9 8 7 6 5 4 3 2 1	A

Stage

4,5,6 to 77th Street

GMC: 332 East 76th Street [bet. 2nd & 1st]
Kinney: 155 East 76th Street [bet. 3rd & Lexington]

M101, M102, M103

Douglas Fairbanks Theatre

432 West 42nd Street // New York, NY [between 9th & 10th Avenue]

Telecharge: (212) 239-6200 // Group Sales: (212) 840-5564

N	12 11 10 9 8 7 6 5 4 3 2 1	N
M	14 13 12 11 10 9 8 7 6 5 4 3 2 1	M
L	16 15 14 13 12 11 10 9 8 7 6 5 4 3 2 1	L
K	16 15 14 13 12 11 10 9 8 7 6 5 4 3 2 1	K
J	16 15 14 13 12 11 10 9 8 7 6 5 4 3 2 1	J
H	16 15 14 13 12 11 10 9 8 7 6 5 4 3 2 1	H
G	16 15 14 13 12 11 10 9 8 7 6 5 4 3 2 1	G
F	15 14 13 12 11 10 9 8 7 6 5 4 3 2 1	F
E	15 14 13 12 11 10 9 8 7 6 5 4 3 2 1	E
D	15 14 13 12 11 10 9 8 7 6 5 4 3 2 1	D
C	16 15 14 13 12 11 10 9 8 7 6 5 4 3 2 1	C
B	16 15 14 13 12 11 10 9 8 7 6 5 4 3 2 1	B
A	16 15 14 13 12 11 10 9 8 7 6 5 4 3 2 1	A

Stage

1,2,3,7,N,R to 42nd St. & 7th
A,C,E to 42nd St. & 8th

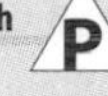
Edison: 401-471 West 42nd St. [bet. 9th & 10th Ave.]
Kinney: 352 West 43rd St. [bet. 8th & 9th Ave.]

M10, M11, M16, M42

Westside Map #49

Duffy Theater

1553 Broadway // New York, NY [corner of 46th Street]

Box Office: (212) 695-3401

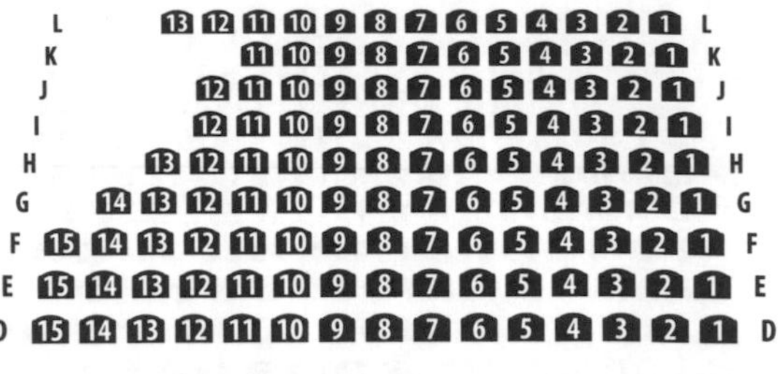

A,C,E to 42nd St. & 8th Ave.
1,2,3,7,N,R, to 42nd St. & 7th Ave.

Kinney: 253 west 47th St.
[bet. Broadway & 8th Ave.]

M6, M10, M27, M42, M104

Midtown Map #48

Ensemble Studio Theatre

549 West 52nd Street // New York, NY [between 10th & 11th Avenue]

Box Office: (212) 247-4982 [www.ensemblestudiotheatre.org]

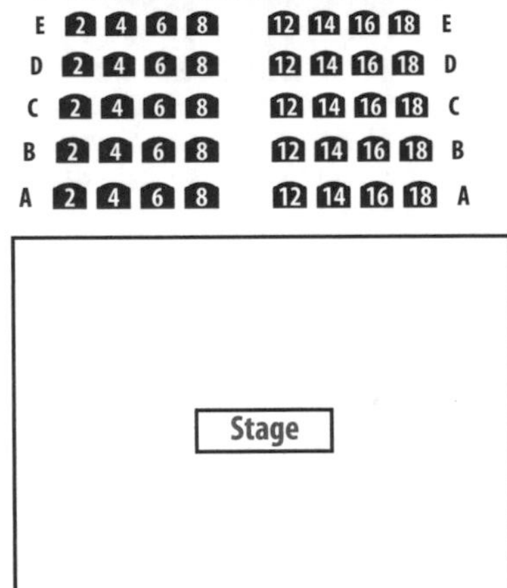

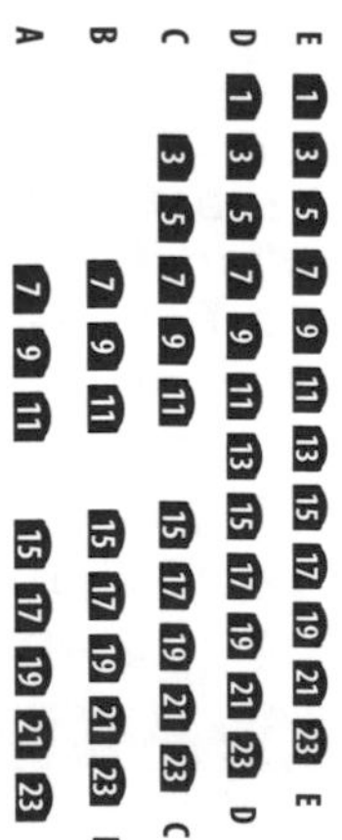

C,E to 50th Street

GMC: 622 West 57th Street [bet. 11th & 12th Ave.]

M11, M50

Gramercy Arts Theatre & Repertorio Español

138 East 27th Street // New York, NY [between Lexington & 3rd Avenue]

Box Office: (212) 889-2850 [www.repertorio.org]

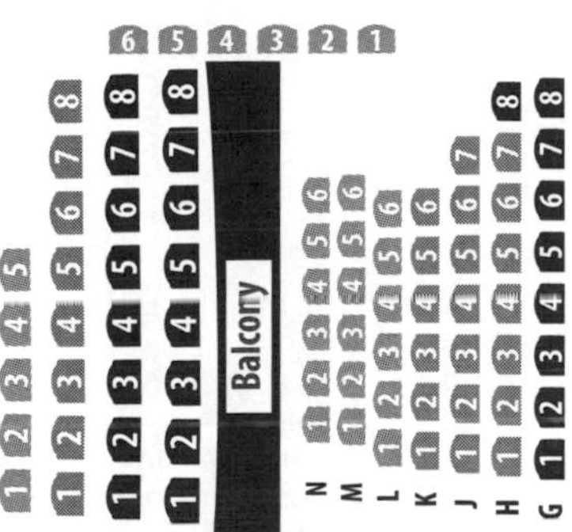

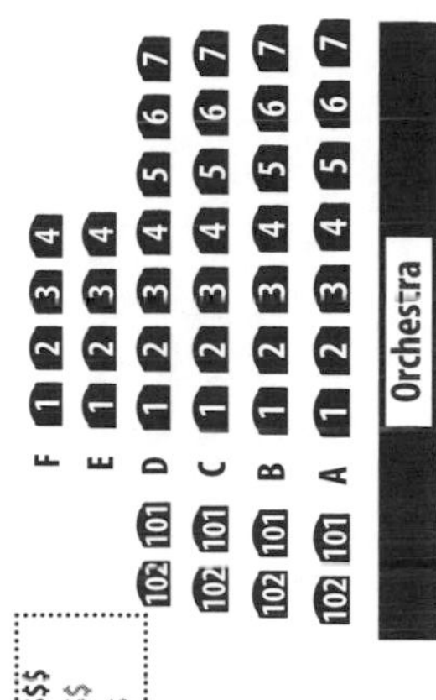

 6 to 28th St. & Park Ave. South
N,R to 28th St. & Broadway

 Excellent: 29th St. [bet. Lexington & 3rd Ave.]
Peter Operative: 26th St. [bet. 2nd & 3rd Ave.]

 M23, M101, M102

The Irish Repertory Theatre

132 West 22nd Street // New York, NY [between 6th & 7th Avenue]

Box Office: (212) 727-2737 [www.irishrepertorytheatre.com]

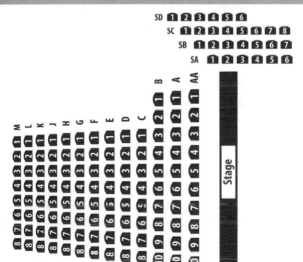

SD 1 2 3 4 5 6
SC 1 2 3 4 5 6 7 8
SB 1 2 3 4 5 6 7
SA 1 2 3 4 5 6

M 1 2 3 4 5 6 7 8
L 1 2 3 4 5 6 7 8
K 1 2 3 4 5 6 7 8
J 1 2 3 4 5 6 7 8
H 1 2 3 4 5 6 7 8
G 1 2 3 4 5 6 7 8
F 1 2 3 4 5 6 7 8
E 1 2 3 4 5 6 7 8
D 1 2 3 4 5 6 7 8
C 1 2 3 4 5 6 7 8
B 1 2 3 4 5 6 7 8 9 10
A 1 2 3 4 5 6 7 8 9 10
AA 1 2 3 4 5 6 7 8 9 10

Stage

 1,9,F to 23rd St.

 GMC: 7 West 21st Street [bet. 5th & 6th Ave.]
Kinney: 235 West 22nd Street

 M5, M6, M7, M10, M23

 Chelsea Map #70

John Houseman Theatre

450 West 42nd Street // New York, NY [between 9th & 10th Avenue]

Telecharge: (212) 239-6200 // Group Sales: (212) 302-7000

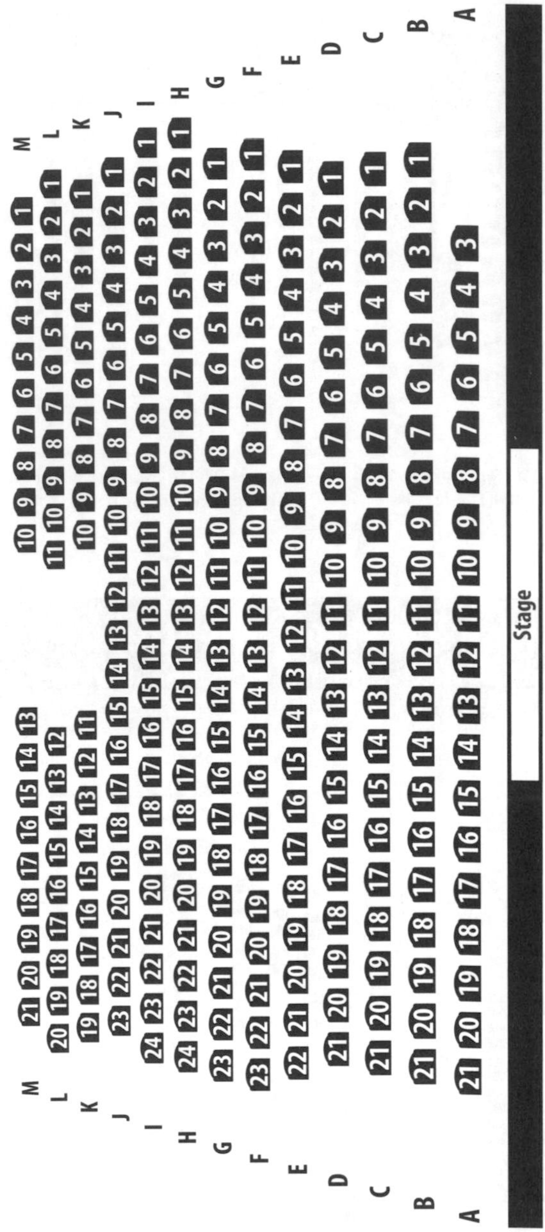

M	1–10, 13–21
L	1–11, 12–20
K	1–10, 11–19
J	1–23
I	1–24
H	1–24
G	1–23
F	1–23
E	1–22
D	1–21
C	1–21
B	1–21
A	3–21

Stage

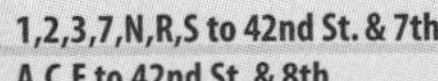
1,2,3,7,N,R,S to 42nd St. & 7th
A,C,E to 42nd St. & 8th

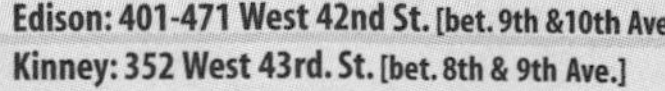
Edison: 401-471 West 42nd St. [bet. 9th &10th Ave.]
Kinney: 352 West 43rd. St. [bet. 8th & 9th Ave.]

M10, M11, M16, M42

Westside Map #50

José Quintero Theatre

534 West 42nd Street // New York, NY [between 10th & 11th Avenue]

Box Office: (212) 563.1684 [www.quinterotheatre.com]

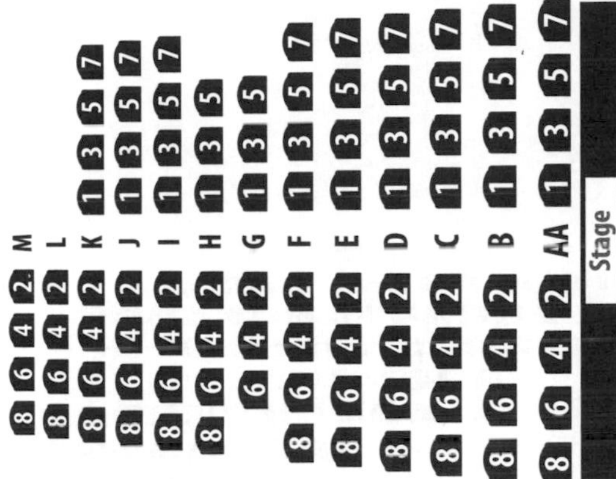

A,C,E to 42nd St. & 8th Ave.
N,R,S,1,2,3,7, to 42nd St. & 7th Ave.

Edison: 640 West 42nd Street

M11, M42

Westside Map #57

Intar Theatre

508 West 53rd Street // New York, NY [between 10th & 11th Avenue]

Ticket Central: (212) 279-4200

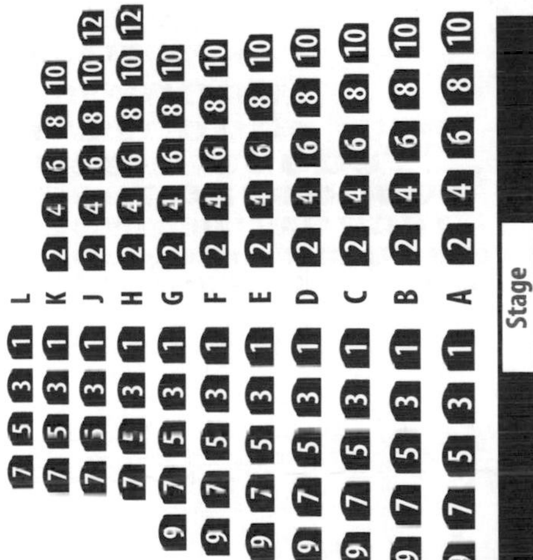

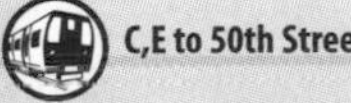

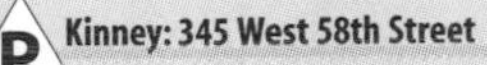

M11, M50

425 Lafayette Street // New York, NY [between Astor Place & 4th Street]

Telecharge: (212) 239-6200 // Group Sales: (212) 398-8383

[www.publictheater.org]

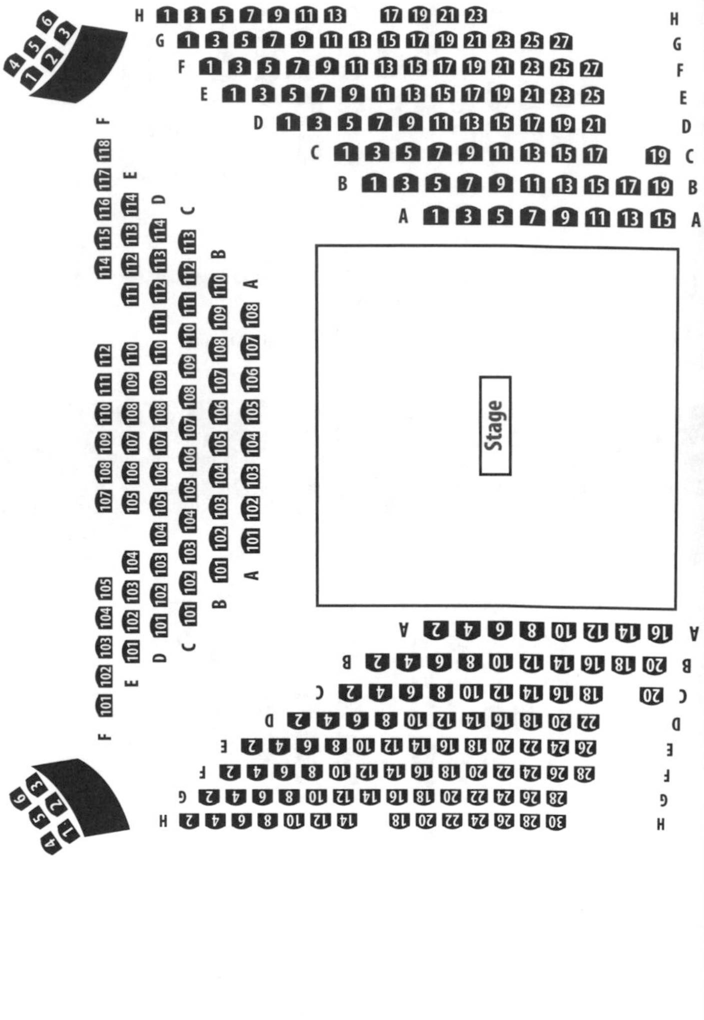

1 2 3 4 5 6

H 1 3 5 7 9 11 13 17 19 21 23 H
G 1 3 5 7 9 11 13 15 17 19 21 23 25 27 G
F 1 3 5 7 9 11 13 15 17 19 21 23 25 27 F
E 1 3 5 7 9 11 13 15 17 19 21 23 25 E
D 1 3 5 7 9 11 13 15 17 19 21 D
C 1 3 5 7 9 11 13 15 17 19 C
B 1 3 5 7 9 11 13 15 17 19 B
A 1 3 5 7 9 11 13 15 A

F 101 102 103 104 105 107 108 109 110 111 112 114 115 116 117 118 F
E 101 102 103 104 105 106 107 108 109 110 111 112 113 114 E
D 101 102 103 104 105 106 107 108 109 110 111 112 113 114 D
C 101 102 103 104 105 106 107 108 109 110 111 112 113 C
B 101 102 103 104 105 106 107 108 109 110 B
A 101 102 103 104 105 106 107 108 A

Stage

A 2 4 6 8 10 12 14 16 A
B 2 4 6 8 10 12 14 16 18 20 B
C 2 4 6 8 10 12 14 16 18 20 C
D 2 4 6 8 10 12 14 16 18 20 22 D
E 2 4 6 8 10 12 14 16 18 20 22 24 26 E
F 2 4 6 8 10 12 14 16 18 20 22 24 26 28 F
G 2 4 6 8 10 12 14 16 18 20 22 24 26 28 G
H 2 4 6 8 10 12 14 18 20 22 24 26 28 30 H

1 2 3 4 5 6

Anspacher Theater

6 to Astor Place // N,R to 8th Street
B,D,F,Q to Broadway & Lafayette

Stop & Park: 410-412 Lafayette Street

M2, M3, M5, M6, M8

East/West Village Map #84

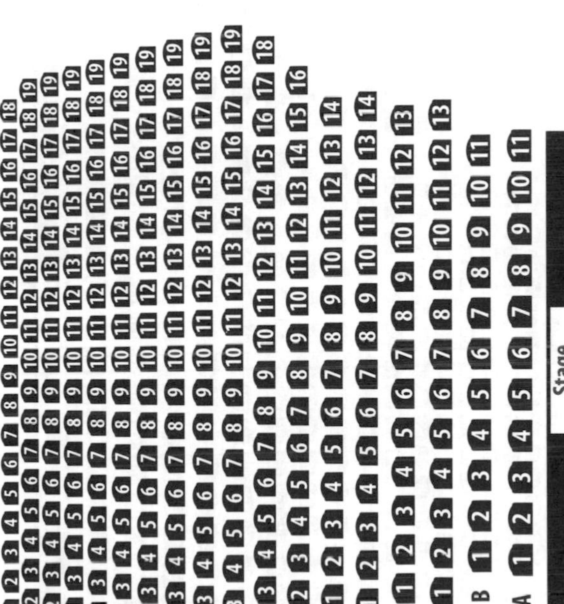

Newman Theater

Joyce Theater

175 8th Avenue // New York, NY [corner of 19th Street]

Box Office: (212) 242-0800 // Group Sales: (718) 499-9691

[www.joyce.org]

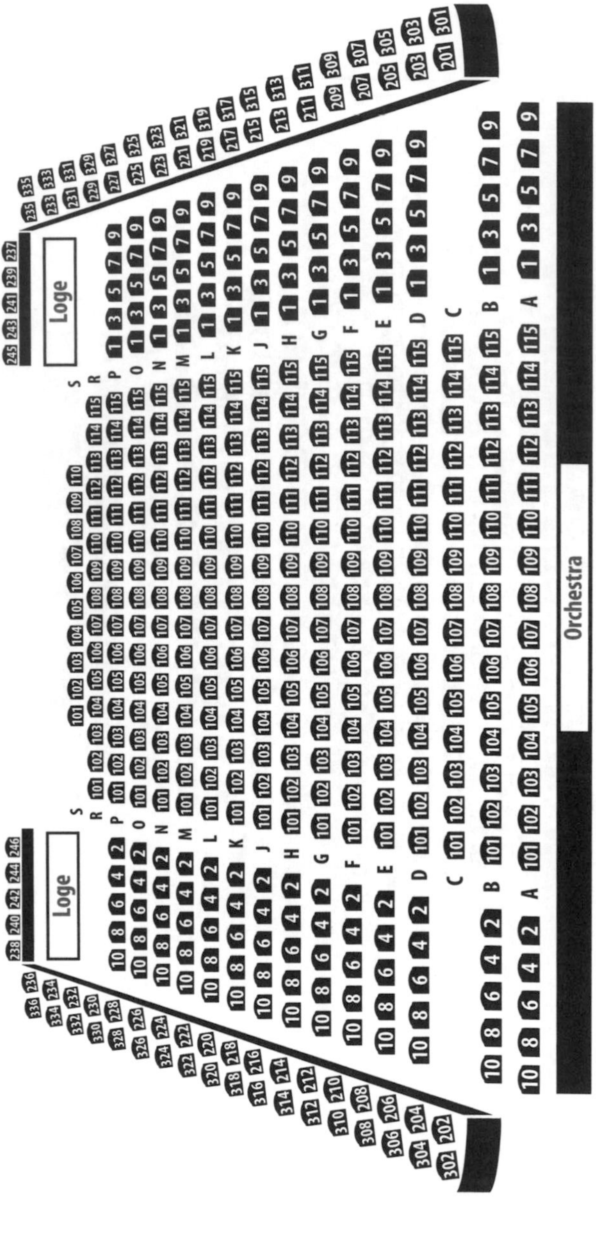

Loge

Loge

Orchestra

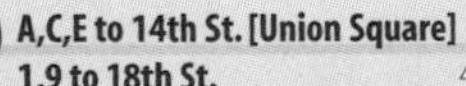

A,C,E to 14th St. [Union Square]
1,9 to 18th St.

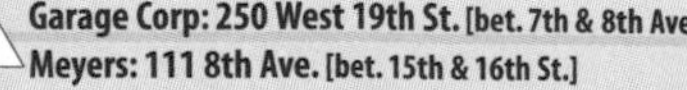

Garage Corp: 250 West 19th St. [bet. 7th & 8th Ave.]
Meyers: 111 8th Ave. [bet. 15th & 16th St.]

M10, M11

The Kaye Playhouse (Hunter College)

695 Park Avenue // New York, NY [68th St. between Park & Lexington Ave.]

Box Office: (212) 772-4448 [www.kayeplayhouse.org]

 6 to 68th St. or B, Q to Lexington Ave.

 Kinney: 301 East 66th St. [bet. 1st. & 2nd Ave.]
Kinney: 301 East 69th St. [bet. 1st & 2nd Ave.]

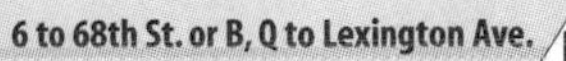

 M66, M98, M101, M102, M103

Laura Pels (Gramercy Theatre)

127 East 23rd Street // New York, NY [between Park Ave. S. & Lexington]

Box Office: (212) 719-1300 // Group Sales: (212) 777-4900

[www.roundabouttheatre.org]

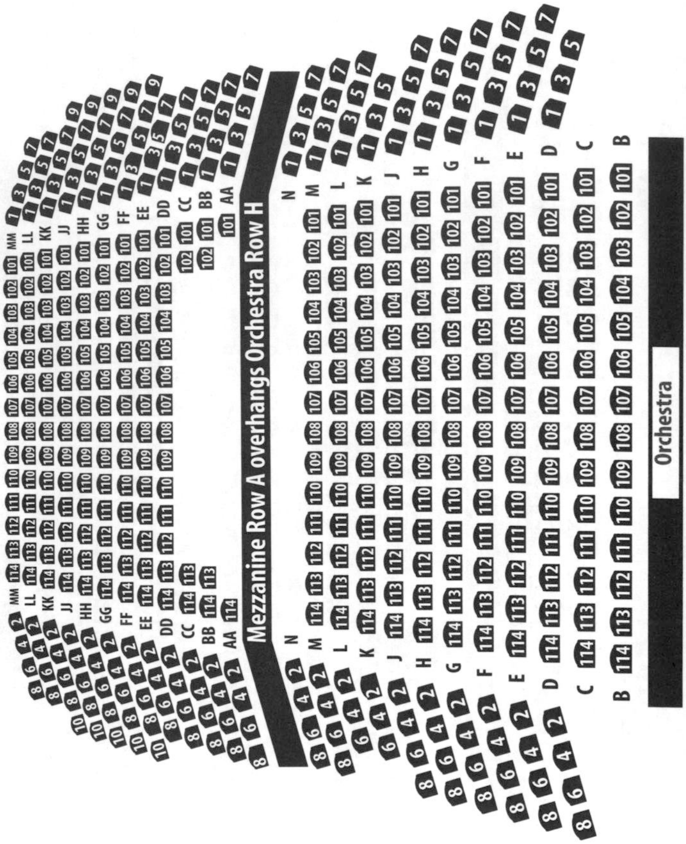

Mezzanine Row A overhangs Orchestra Row H

Orchestra

4, 5, 6, N, R, to 23rd St.

Kinney: 329 East 21st Street [bet. 1st & 2nd Ave.]

M1, M2, M3, M6, M7, M101, M102, M103

Lucille Lortel Theatre

121 Christopher Street // New York, NY [between Bleecker & Hudson]

Telecharge: (212) 239-6200

$$$$
$$$

 1,9 to Christopher Street

P GMC: 160 West 10th Street

 M8, M10

 East/West Village Map #78

Manhattan Ensemble Theater

55 Mercer Street // New York, NY [between Broome & Grand St.]

Telecharge: (212) 239-6200 [www.met.com]

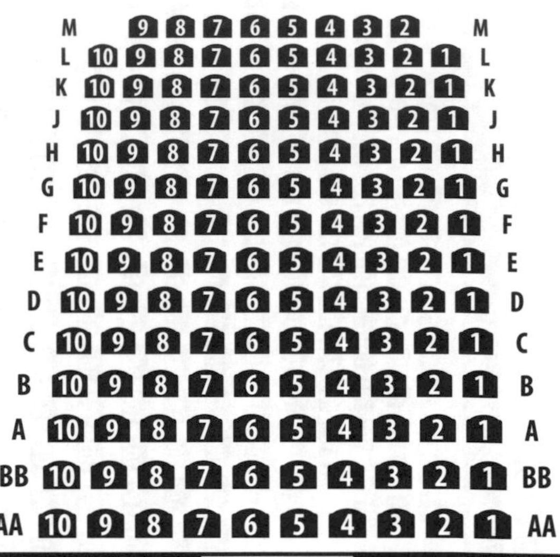

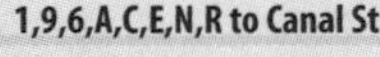

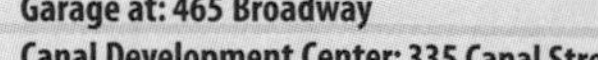

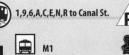

East/West Village Map #52

Manhattan Theatre Club

131 West 55th Street // New York, NY [between 6th & 7th Avenue]

City Tickets: (212) 581-1212 [www.manhattantheatreclub.com]

Stage

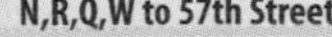

N,R,Q,W to 57th Street

GMC: 150 West 56th St. [bet. 6th & 7th Ave.]

M5, M6, M7, M30, M31, M57

Midtown Map #47

Minetta Lane Theatre

18 Minetta Lane // New York, NY [between 6th Avenue & MacDougal Street]

Ticketmaster: (212) 307-4100 // Box Office: (212) 420-8000

Group Sales: (212) 889-4300

Mezzanine

Mezzanine Row A overhangs Orchestra Row J

Orchestra

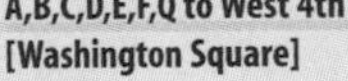

A,B,C,D,E,F,Q to West 4th St. [Washington Square]

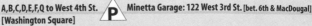

Minetta Garage: 122 West 3rd St. [bet. 6th & MacDougal]

M3, M5, M10

East/West Village Map #79

New York Theatre Workshop

79 East Fourth Street // New York, NY [between 2nd & 4th Avenue]

Box Office: (212) 460-5475 [www.nytw.org]

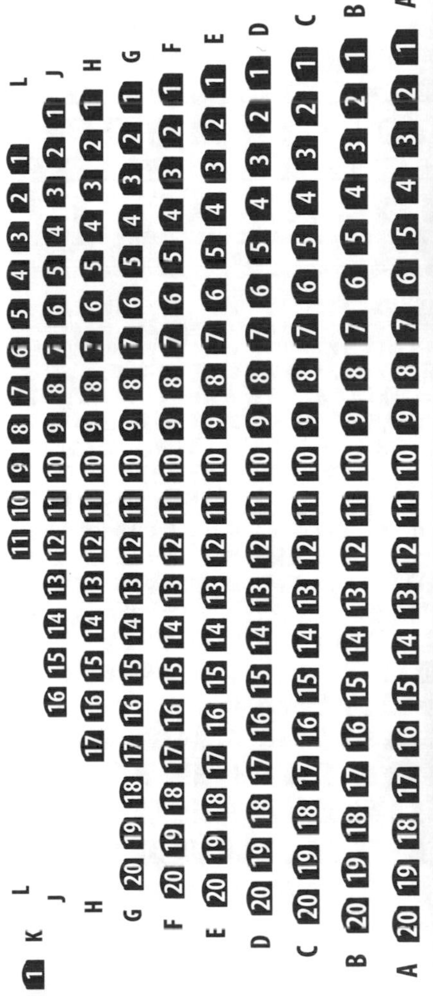

 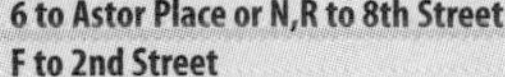
6 to Astor Place or N,R to 8th Street
F to 2nd Street

 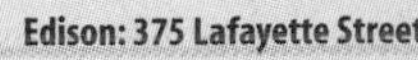
Edison: 375 Lafayette Street

M15, M21, M103

East/West Village Map #80

Orpheum Theatre

126 Second Avenue // New York, NY [corner of 8th Street]

Ticketmaster: (212) 307-4100 // Group Sales: (212) 302-7000

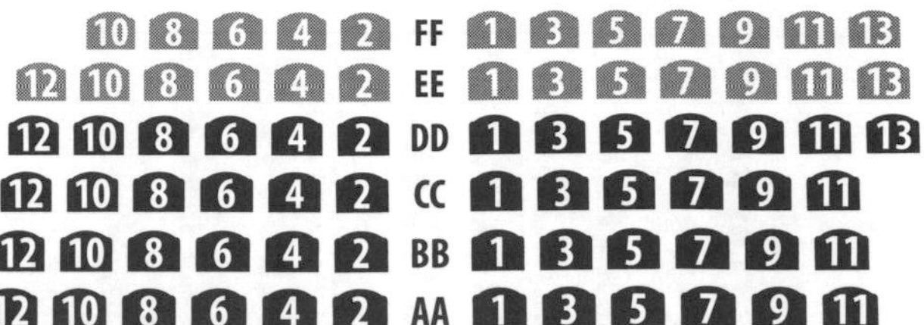

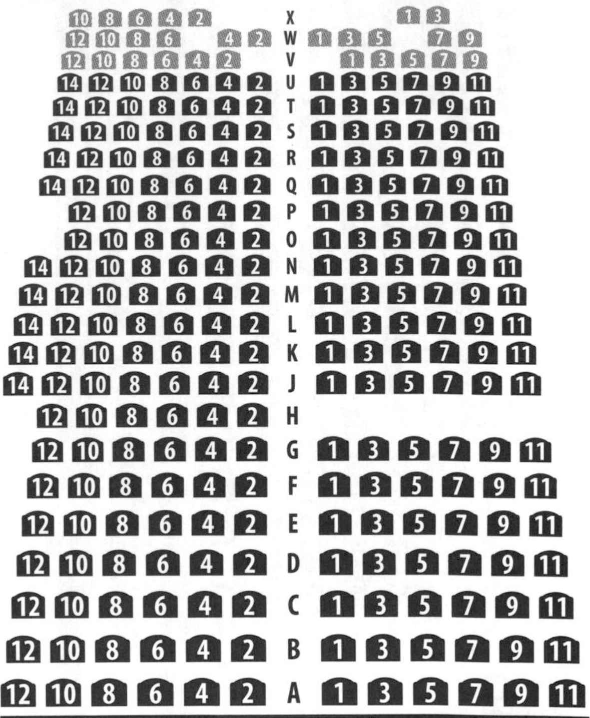

$$$$
$$$
$$

F to 2nd Avenue or N,R to 8th Street
6 to Astor Place

Kinney: 220 East 9th Street [bet. 2nd & 3rd Ave.]

M13, M15, M102, M103

East/West Village Map #81

The Pearl Theatre

80 St. Marks Place // New York, NY [between 1st & 2nd Avenue]

Box Office: (212) 598-9802 [www.pearltheatre.org]

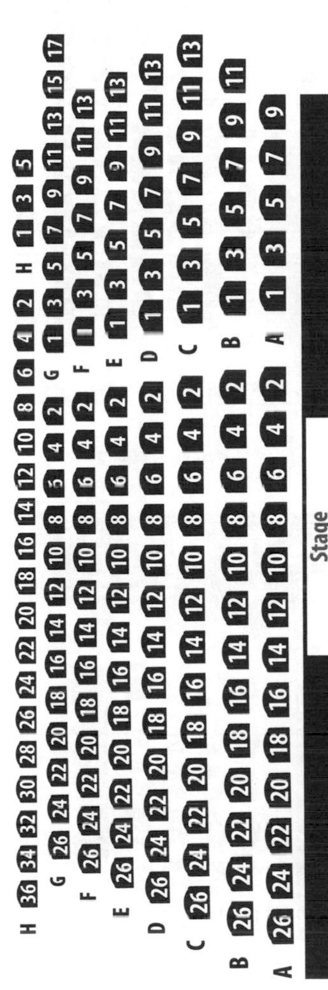

F to 2nd Avenue or 4,5,6 to Astor Place

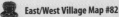

Edison: 204 Lafayette Street

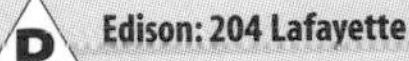

M1, M15

East/West Village Map #82

Player's Theater

115 MacDougal Street // New York, NY [between 3rd Ave. & Minetta Lane]

Box Office: (212) 254-5076

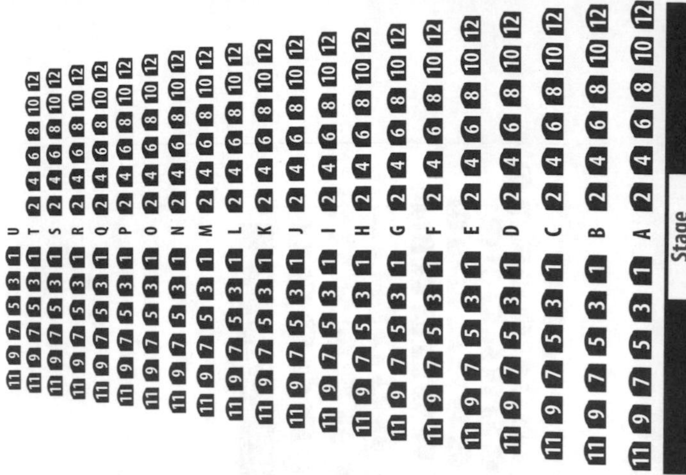

A,B,C,D,E,F,Q to West 4th St. [Washington Square]

Minetta Garage: 122 West 3rd St. [bet. 6th St. & MacDougal]

M5, M6, M10

East/West Village Map #83

Primary Stages Theatre

354 West 45th Street // New York, NY [between 8th & 9th Avenue]

Box Office: (212) 333-4052

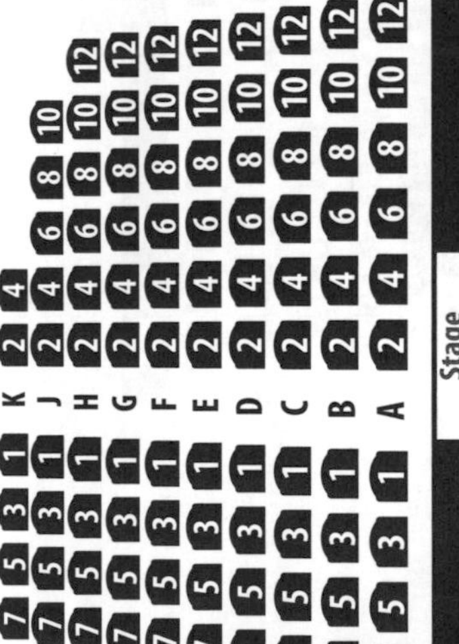

A,C,E to 42nd St. & 7th Ave.

Quik Park: 303 West 46th St. [bet. 8th & 9th Ave.]

M6, M7, M10, M42, M104

Westside Map #54

Playhouse 91

316 East 91st Street // New York, NY [between 1st & 2nd Avenue]

Ticketmaster: (212) 307-4100 // Box Office: (212) 831-2000

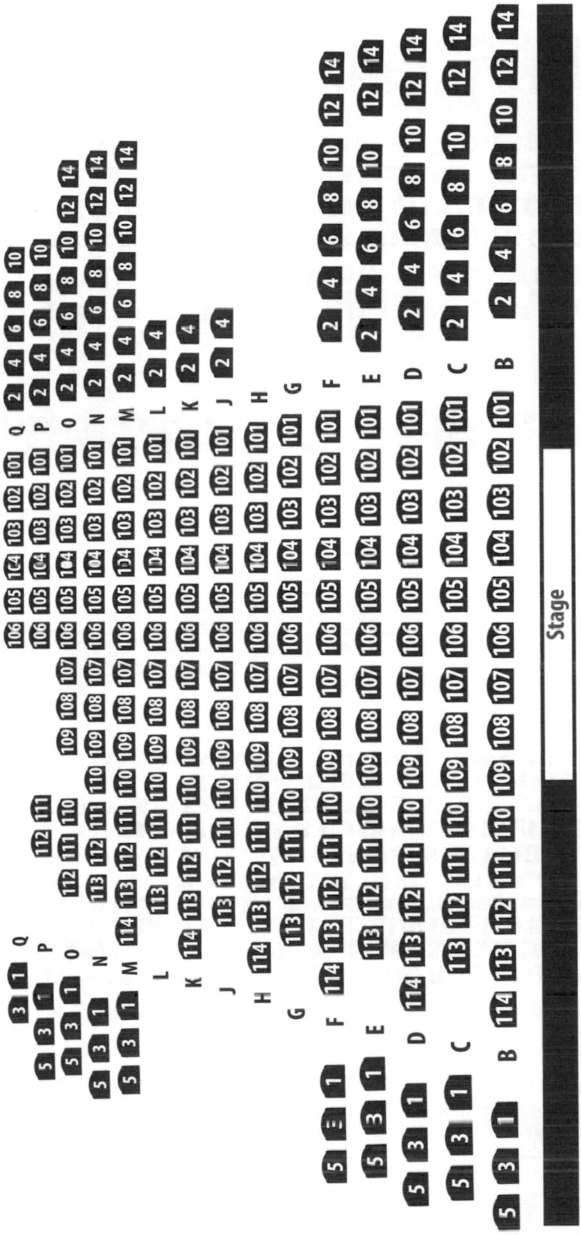

Stage

B: 5 3 1 — 114 113 112 111 110 109 108 107 106 105 104 103 102 101 — 2 4 6 8 10 12 14
C: 5 3 1 — 113 112 111 110 109 108 107 106 105 104 103 102 101 — 2 4 6 8 10 12 14
D: 5 3 1 — 114 113 112 111 110 109 108 107 106 105 104 103 102 101 — 2 4 6 8 10 12 14
E: 5 3 1 — 113 112 111 110 109 108 107 106 105 104 103 102 101 — 2 4 6 8 10 12 14
F: 5 3 1 — 114 113 112 111 110 109 108 107 106 105 104 103 102 101 — 2 4 6 8 10 12 14
G: 113 112 111 110 109 108 107 106 105 104 103 102 101
H: 114 113 112 111 110 109 108 107 106 105 104 103 102 101
J: 113 112 111 110 109 108 107 106 105 104 103 102 101 — 2 4
K: 114 113 112 111 110 109 108 107 106 105 104 103 102 101 — 2 4
L: 113 112 111 110 109 108 107 106 105 104 103 102 101 — 2 4
M: 5 3 1 — 114 113 112 111 110 109 108 107 106 105 104 103 102 101 — 2 4 6 8 10 12 14
N: 5 3 1 — 113 112 111 110 109 108 107 106 105 104 103 102 101 — 2 4 6 8 10 12 14
O: 5 3 1 — 112 111 110 109 108 107 106 105 104 103 102 101 — 2 4 6 8 10 12 14
P: 5 3 1 — 112 111 108 107 106 105 104 103 102 101 — 2 4 6 8 10
Q: 3 1 — 106 105 104 103 102 101 — 2 4 6 8 10

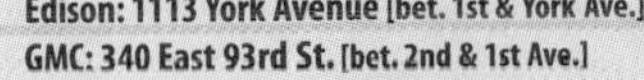

Edison: 1113 York Avenue [bet. 1st & York Ave.]
GMC: 340 East 93rd St. [bet. 2nd & 1st Ave.]

M15, M19, M31, M86, M101, M102

Playwrights Horizons

416 West 42nd Street // New York, NY [between 9th & 10th Avenue]

Ticketcentral: (212) 279-4200 // Box Office: (212) 564-1235

[www.playwrightshorizons.org]

Peter Jay Sharp

Row																	Row
H	16	15	14	13	12	11	10	9	8	7	6	5	4	3	2	1	H
G	16	15	14	13	12	11	10	9	8	7	6	5	4	3	2	1	G
F	16	15	14	13	12	11	10	9	8	7	6	5	4	3	2	1	F
E	16	15	14	13	12	11	10	9	8	7	6	5	4	3	2	1	E
D	16	15	14	13	12	11	10	9	8	7	6	5	4	3	2	1	D
C	16	15	14	13	12	11	10	9	8	7	6	5	4	3	2	1	C
B																	B
A																	A

Stage

Main Stage

Row																			Row
L	18	17	16	15	14	13	12	11	10	9	8	7	6	5	4	3	2	1	L
K	18	17	16	15	14	13	12	11	10	9	8	7	6	5	4	3	2	1	K
J	18	17	16	15	14	13	12	11	10	9	8	7	6	5	4	3	2	1	J
H	18	17	16	15	14	13	12	11	10	9	8	7	6	5	4	3	2	1	H
G	18	17	16	15	14	13	12	11	10	9	8	7	6	5	4	3	2	1	G
F	18	17	16	15	14	13	12	11	10	9	8	7	6	5	4	3	2	1	F
E	18	17	16	15	14	13	12	11	10	9	8	7	6	5	4	3	2	1	E
(boxes)	House Boxes Right									House Boxes Left									
D	18	17	16	15	14	13	12	11	10	9	8	7	6	5	4	3	2	1	D
C	18	17	16	15	14	13	12	11	10	9	8	7	6	5	4	3	2	1	C
B	18	17	16	15	14	13	12	11	10	9	8	7	6	5	4	3	2	1	B
A	18	17	16	15	14	13	12	11	10	9	8	7	6	5	4	3	2	1	A

Stage

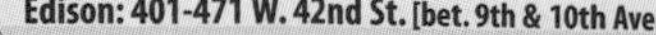

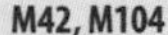

Westside Map #53

Promenade Theatre

2162 Broadway // New York, NY [corner of 78th Street]

Telecharge: (212) 239-6200 // Group Sales: (212) 239-6262

Stage

$$$$
$$$

1,9 to 79th Street

Kinney: 201 West 75th Street

Rapid Parking: 254 W. 79th St. [bet. Broadway & West End]

M7, M11, M79, M104

Samuel Beckett Theatre

410 West 42nd Street // New York, NY [between 9th & 10th Avenue]

Ticketcentral: (212) 279-4200

			Row						
	4	6	K						
2	4	6	J	1	3	5	7	9	11
2	4	6	H	1	3	5	7	9	11
2	4	6	G	1	3	5	7	9	11
2	4	6	F	1	3	5	7	9	11
2	4	6	E	1	3	5	7	9	11
2	4	6	D	1	3	5	7	9	11
2	4	6	C	1	3	5	7	9	11
2	4	6	B	1	3	5	7	9	11

Stage

A,C,E to 42nd St. & 8th Ave.

Edison: 640 West 43rd Street
Kinney: 264 West 42nd Street

M6, M10, M27, M50, M42

Westside Map #59

Signature Theatre

555 West 42nd Street // New York, NY [between 10th & 11th Avenue]

Box Office: (212) 244-7529 [www.signaturetheatre.org]

Row																					Row
H	121	120	119	118	117	116	115	114	113	112	111	110	109	108	107	106	105	104	103	102	H
G	121	120	119	118	117	116	115	114	113	112	111	110	109	108	107	106	105	104	103	102	G
F	121	120	119	118	117	116	115	114	113	112	111	110	109	108	107	106	105	104	103	102	F
E	121	120	119	118	117	116	115	114	113	112	111	110	109	108	107	106	105	104	103	102	E
D	121	120	119	118	117	116	115	114	113	112	111	110	109	108	107	106	105	104	103	102	D
C	121	120	119	118	117	116	115	114	113	112	111	110	109	108	107	106	105	104	103	102	C
B	121	120	119	118	117	116	115	114	113	112	111	110	109	108	107	106	105	104	103	102	B
A	121	120	119	118	117	116	115	114	113	112	111	110	109	108	107	106	105	104	103	102	A

Stage

A,C,E to 42nd St. & 8th Ave.
1,2,3,7,N,R,W,Q,S to 42nd St. & 7th Ave.

Edison: 640 West 42nd St.

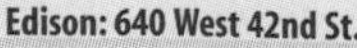

M42

Westside Map #56

Second Stage Theatre

307 West 43rd Street // New York, NY [corner of 8th Avenue]

Box Office: (212) 246-4422 // Group Sales: (212) 889-4300

[www.secondstagetheatre.com]

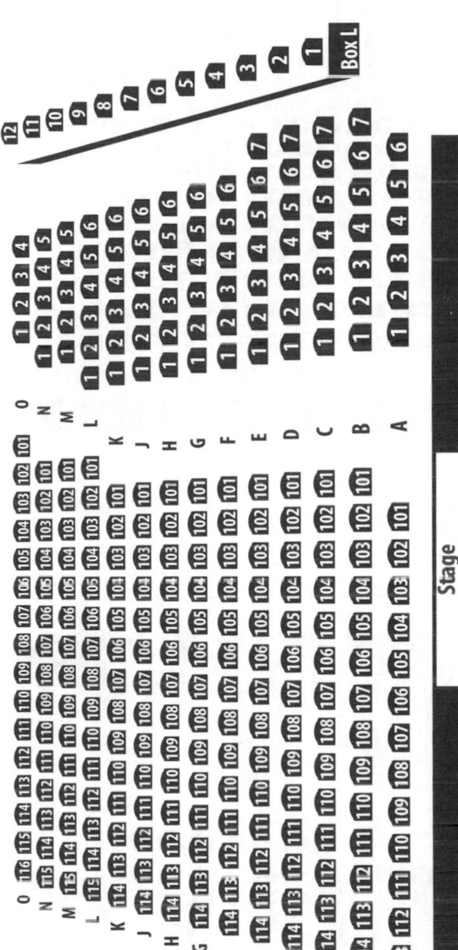

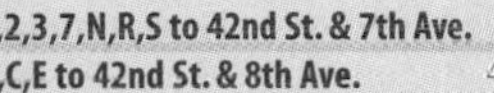

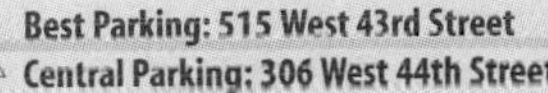

Best Parking: 515 West 43rd Street
Central Parking: 306 West 44th Street

M42

Westside Map #55

Soho Playhouse

15 Vandam Street // New York, NY [between 6th & 7th Avenue]

Telecharge: (212) 239-6200 // Group Sales: (212) 691-1555

P	11 9 7 5 3 1	2 4 6 8 10 12
O	11 9 7 5 3 1	2 4 6 8 10 12
N	11 9 7 5 3 1	2 4 6 8 10 12
M	11 9 7 5 3 1	2 4 6 8 10 12
L	11 9 7 5 3 1	2 4 6 8 10 12
K	11 9 7 5 3 1	2 4 6 8 10 12
J	11 9 7 5 3 1	2 4 6 8 10 12
I	11 9 7 5 3 1	2 4 6 8 10 12
H	11 9 7 5 3 1	2 4 6 8 10 12
G	11 9 7 5 3 1	2 4 6 8 10 12
F	11 9 7 5 3 1	2 4 6 8 10 12
E	11 9 7 5 3 1	2 4 6 8 10 12
D	11 9 7 5 3 1	2 4 6 8 10 12
C	11 9 7 5 3 1	2 4 6 8 10 12
B	11 9 7 5 3 1	2 4 6 8 10 12
A	11 9 7 5 3 1	2 4 6 8 10 12
BB	11 9 7 5 3 1	2 4 6 8 10 12
AA	9 7 5 3 1	2 4 6 8 10

Stage

$$$$
$$$
$$

1,9 to Houston Street
A,C,E to Spring Street

Edison: 215 East Houston Street

M5, M21

St. Luke's Church Theatre

308 West 46th Street // New York, NY [between 8th & 9th Avenue]

Telecharge: (212) 239-6200 // Group Sales: (212) 889-4300

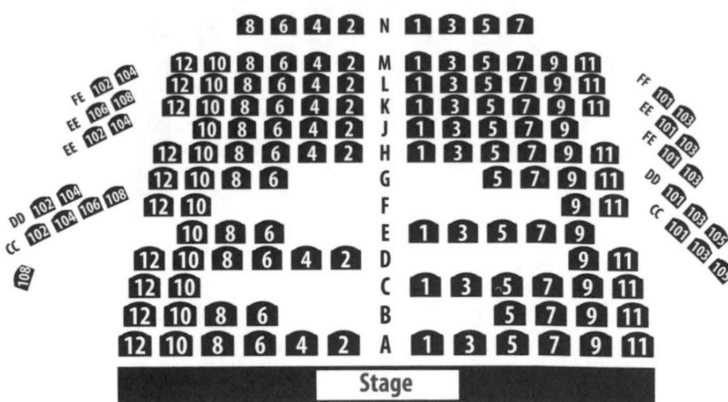

1,2,3,7,N,R,S to 42nd St. & 7th Ave.
A,C,E to 42nd St. & 8th Ave.

Quik Park: 303 West 46th St. [bet. 8th & 9th Ave.]

M6, M7, M10, M11, M42, M104

Westside Map #58

The Duke on 42nd Street

229 East 42nd Street // New York, NY [between 7th & 8th Avenue]

Ticketcentral: (212) 279-4200

8	6	4	2	K	112	111	110	109	108	107	106	105	104	103	102	101	K	1	3	5	7
8	6	4	2	J	112	111	110	109	108	107	106	105	104	103	102	101	J	1	3	5	7
8	6	4	2	H	112	111	110	109	108	107	106	105	104	103	102	101	H	1	3	5	7
8	6	4	2	G	112	111	110	109	108	107	106	105	104	103	102	101	G	1	3	5	7
8	6	4	2	F	112	111	110	109	108	107	106	105	104	103	102	101	F	1	3	5	7
8	6	4	2	E	112	111	110	109	108	107	106	105	104	103	102	101	E	1	3	5	7
8	6	4	2	D	112	111	110	109	108	107	106	105	104	103	102	101	D	1	3	5	7
8	6	4	2	C	112	111	110	109	108	107	106	105	104	103	102	101	C	1	3	5	7
8	6	4	2	B	112	111	110	109	108	107	106	105	104	103	102	101	B	1	3	5	7
8	6	4	2	A	112	111	110	109	108	107	106	105	104	103	102	101	A	1	3	5	7

Stage

 1,2,3,7 to 42nd Street & 7th Ave.

 Kinney: 264 West 42nd Street

 M10, M20, M42, M104

 Midtown Map #38

The Theatre at St. Clements

423 West 46th Street // New York, NY [between 9th & 10th Avenue]

Box Office: (212) 246-7277

I	1	2	3	4	5	6	7	8	9	10	11	12	13	14			I
H	1	2	3	4	5	6	7	8	9	10	11	12	13	14	15		H
G	1	2	3	4	5	6	7	8	9	10	11	12	13	14	15	16	G
F	1	2	3	4	5	6	7	8	9	10	11	12	13	14	15		F
E	1	2	3	4	5	6	7	8	9	10	11	12	13	14	15	16	E
D	1	2	3	4	5	6	7	8	9	10	11	12	13	14	15		D
C	1	2	3	4	5	6	7	8	9	10	11	12	13	14	15	16	C
B	1	2	3	4	5	6	7	8	9	10	11	12	13	14	15		B
A	1	2	3	4	5	6	7	8	9	10	11	12	13	14	15	16	A

Stage

 A,C,E to 50th St. & 8th Ave.
1,2,3,7,N to 42nd St. & 7th Ave.

 GMC: 257 West 47th St. [bet. Broadway & 8th Ave.]
Kinney: 253 West 47th St. [bet. Broadway & 8th Ave.]

 M10, M11, M42, M104

 Westside Map #57

Theater Four

424 West 55th Street // New York, NY [between 9th & 10th Avenue]

Telecharge: (212) 239-6200 // Group Sales: (212) 764-8745

F 105 104 103 102 101 F

E 113 112 111 110 109 108 105 106 105 104 103 102 101 E

D 108 107 106 105 104 103 102 101 D

109 C 108 107 106 105 104 103 102 101 C

111 110 B 109 108 107 106 105 104 103 102 101 B

A 104 103 102 101 A

Mezzanine

P 108 107 106 105 P

O 111 108 107 106 105 104 101 O

2 N 112 111 109 108 107 106 105 104 102 101 N 1 3

4 2 M 111 110 108 107 106 105 104 102 101 M 1 3

4 2 L 112 111 110 109 108 107 106 105 104 103 102 101 L 1 3

4 2 K 111 110 109 108 107 106 105 104 103 102 101 K 1 3

4 2 J 112 111 110 109 108 107 106 105 104 103 102 101 J 1 3

4 2 I 111 110 109 108 107 106 105 104 103 102 101 I 1 3

4 2 H 112 111 110 109 108 107 106 105 104 103 102 101 H 1 3

4 2 G 111 110 109 108 107 106 105 104 103 102 101 G 1 3

4 2 F 112 111 110 109 108 107 106 105 104 103 102 101 F 1 3

4 2 E 111 110 109 108 107 106 105 104 103 102 101 E 1 3

4 2 D 112 111 110 109 108 107 106 105 104 103 102 101 D 1 3

4 2 C 111 110 109 108 107 106 105 104 103 102 101 C 1 3

4 2 B 112 111 110 109 108 107 106 105 104 103 102 101 B 1 3

4 2 A 111 110 109 108 107 106 105 104 103 102 101 A 1 3

Orchestra

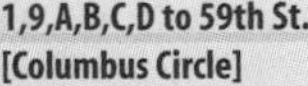

1,9,A,B,C,D to 59th St.
[Columbus Circle]

GMC: 622 West 57th Street [bet. 11th & 12th Ave.]
Kinney: 109 West 56th Street

M6, M7, M27, M50, M57

Union Square Theatre

100 East 17th Street // New York, NY [between Park Avenue & Irving Place]

Ticketmaster: (212) 307-4100 // Group Sales: (212) 889-4300

Mezzanine

Orchestra

$$$$

$$$

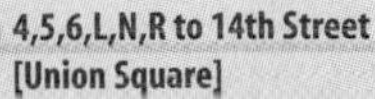

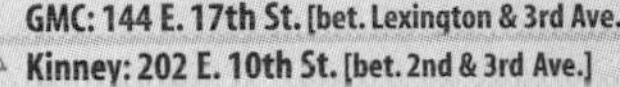

M1, M2, M3, M7, M14, M101, M102

Union Square Map #65

Variety Arts Theatre

110 Third Avenue // New York, NY [between 13th & 14th Street]

Telecharge: (212) 239-6200 // Group Sales: (800) 331-0472

LL 101 102 103 104 105 106 107 108 109 110 111 112 113 114 115 116 117 LL
KK 101 102 103 104 105 106 107 108 109 110 111 112 113 114 115 116 117 KK
JJ 101 102 103 104 105 106 107 108 109 110 111 112 113 114 115 116 117 JJ
HH 101 102 103 104 105 106 107 108 109 110 111 112 113 114 115 116 117 HH
GG 101 102 103 104 105 106 107 108 109 110 111 112 113 114 115 116 117 GG
FF 101 102 103 104 105 106 107 108 109 110 111 112 113 114 115 116 117 FF
EE 101 102 103 104 105 106 107 108 109 110 111 112 113 114 EE
8 6 4 2 DD 101 102 103 104 105 106 107 108 109 110 111 112 113 114 115 116 DD
8 6 4 2 CC 101 102 103 104 105 106 107 108 109 110 111 112 113 114 115 116 117 CC
8 6 4 2 BB 101 102 103 104 105 106 107 108 109 110 111 112 113 114 115 116 117 BB
8 6 4 2 AA 101 102 103 104 105 106 107 108 109 110 111 112 113 114 115 116 117 AA

Mezzanine Row AA overhangs Orchestra Row F

Q 104 105 106 107 108 Q
8 6 4 2 P 104 105 106 107 108 109 P 1 3 5 7
8 6 4 2 O 101 102 103 104 105 106 107 108 109 110 111 112 113 114 O 1 3 5 7
8 6 4 2 N 101 102 103 104 105 106 107 108 109 110 111 112 113 114 N 1 3 5 7
8 6 4 2 M 101 102 103 104 105 106 107 108 109 110 111 112 113 114 M 1 3 5 7
8 6 4 2 L 101 102 103 104 105 106 107 108 109 110 111 112 113 114 L 1 3 5 7
8 6 4 2 K 101 102 103 104 105 106 107 108 109 110 111 112 113 114 K 1 3 5 7
8 6 4 2 J 101 102 103 104 105 106 107 108 109 110 111 112 113 114 J 1 3 5 7
8 6 4 2 H 101 102 103 104 105 106 107 108 109 110 111 112 113 114 H 1 3 5 7
8 6 4 2 G 101 102 103 104 105 106 107 108 109 110 111 112 113 114 G 1 3 5 7
8 6 4 2 F 101 102 103 104 105 106 107 108 109 110 111 112 113 114 F 1 3 5 7
8 6 4 2 E 101 102 103 104 105 106 107 108 109 110 111 112 113 114 E 1 3 5 7
8 6 4 2 D 101 102 103 104 105 106 107 108 109 110 111 112 113 114 D 1 3 5 7
8 6 4 2 C 101 102 103 104 105 106 107 108 109 110 111 112 113 114 C 1 3 5 7
8 6 4 2 B 101 102 103 104 105 106 107 108 109 110 111 112 113 114 B 1 3 5 7
8 6 4 2 A 101 102 103 104 105 106 107 108 109 110 111 112 113 114 A 1 3 5 7

Orchestra

4,5,6,L,N,R to 14th St.
[Union Square]

GMC: 144 East 17th St. [bet. Irving Place & 3rd Ave.]
Kinney: 311 East 11th St. [bet. 1st & 2nd Ave.]

M101, M102, M103

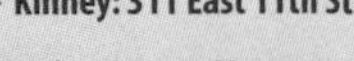

Union Square Map #66

Vineyard's Dimson Theatre

108 East 15th Street // New York, NY [between Union Square & Irving Place]

Box Office: (212) 353-0303 [www.vineyardtheatre.org]

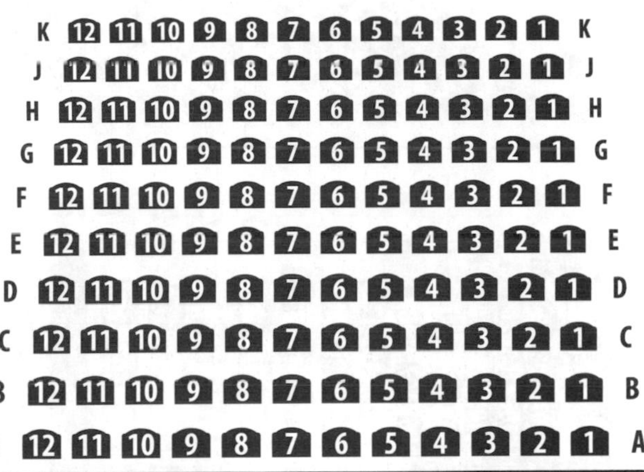

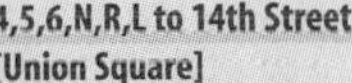
4,5,6,N,R,L to 14th Street [Union Square]

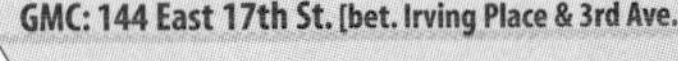
GMC: 144 East 17th St. [bet. Irving Place & 3rd Ave.]

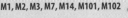

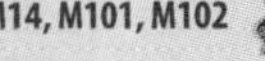
M1, M2, M3, M7, M14, M101, M102

Union Square Map #67

Westside Theatre

407 West 43rd Street // New York, NY [between 9th & 10th Avenue]

Telecharge: (212) 239-6200 // Group Sales: (212) 889-4300

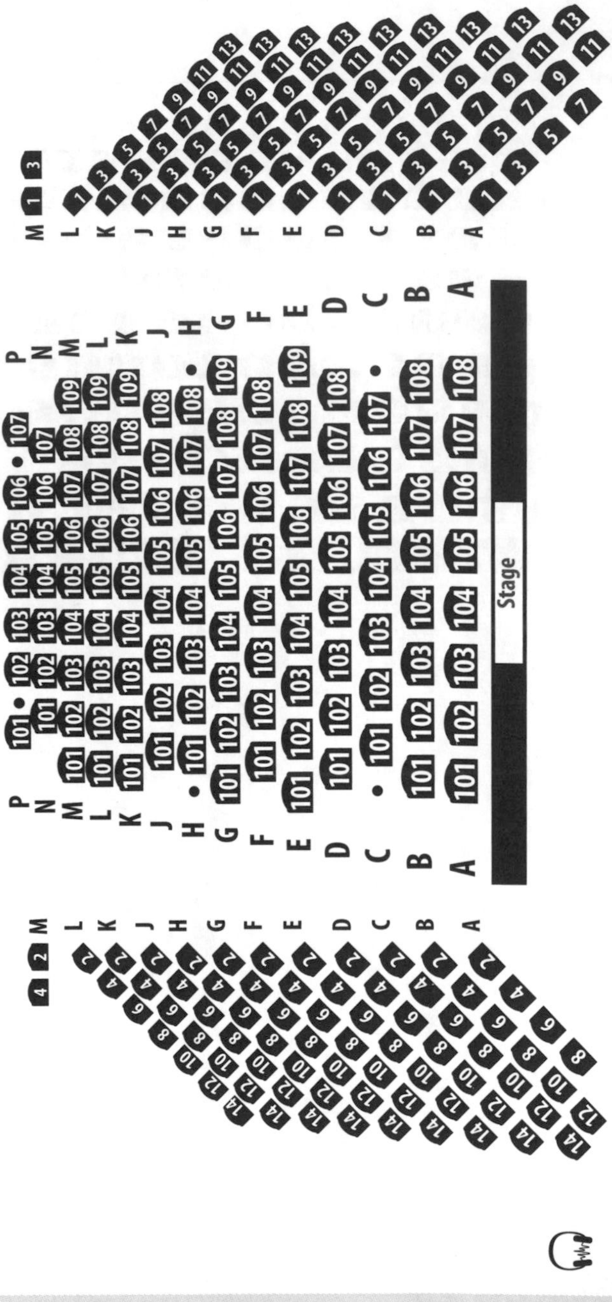

Stage

Downstairs

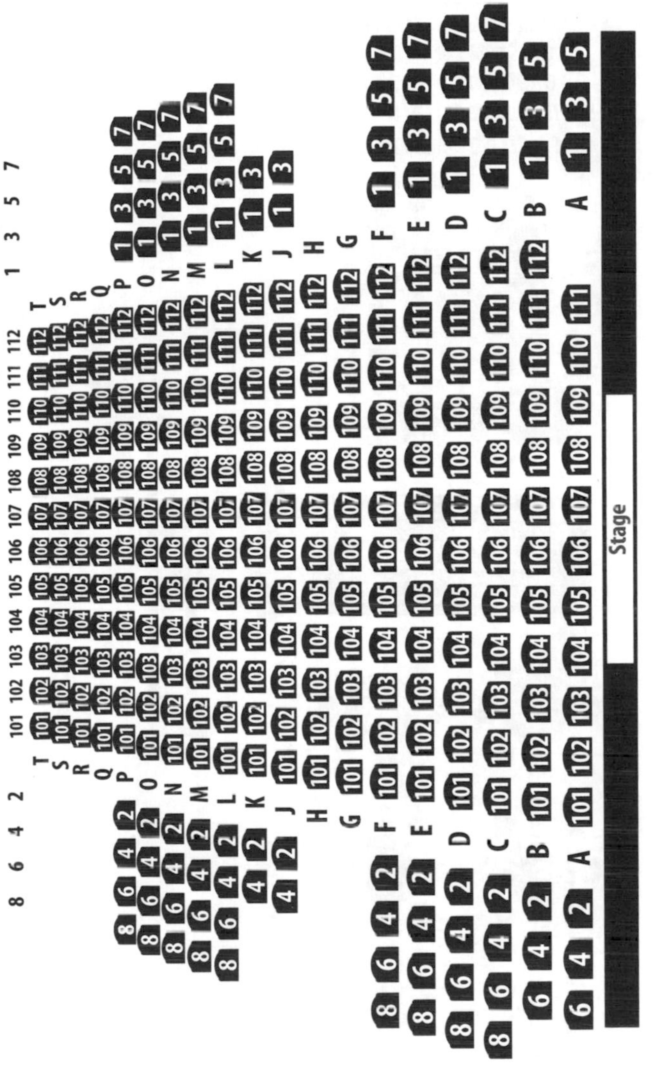

Stage

Upstairs

150 Broadway // New York, NY [between 43rd Street & Broadway]

Box Office: (212) 398-3439 // Group Sales: (212) 971-7205

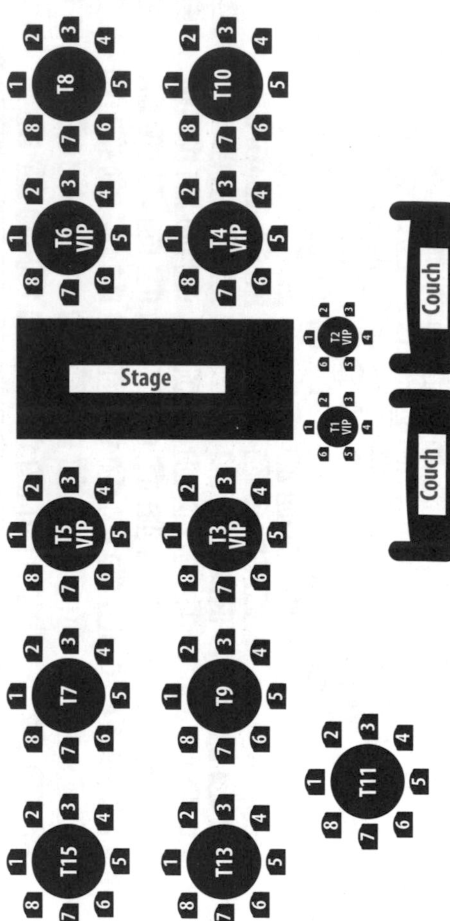

A,C,E to 42nd St. & 8th Ave.
1,2,3,N,R to 42nd St. & 7th Ave.

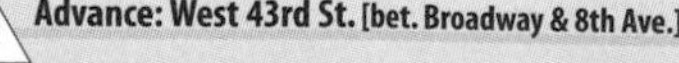

Advance: West 43rd St. [bet. Broadway & 8th Ave.]

M104, M10, M27, M42

Midtown Map #46

York Theatre Company (St. Peter's Church)

619 Lexington Avenue // New York, NY [corner of 54th Street]

Box Office: (212) 935-5820 [www.yorktheatreco.org]

2	K	1 3
16 14 12 10 8 6 4 2	J	1 3 5 7 9 11 13 15
16 14 12 10 8 6 4 2	H	1 3 5 7 9 11 13 15
16 14 12 10 8 6 4 2	G	1 3 5 7 9 11 13 15
16 14 12 10 8 6 4 2	F	1 3 5 7 9 11 13 15
16 14 12 10 8 6 4 2	E	1 3 5 7 9 11 13 15
16 14 12 10 8 6 4 2	D	1 3 5 7 9 11 13 15
16 14 12 10 8 6 4 2	C	1 3 5 7 9 11 13 15
16 14 12 10 8 6 4 2	B	1 3 5 7 9 11 13 15
16 14 12 10 8 6 4 2	A	1 3 5 7 9 11 13 15

Stage

E,F,V to Lexington or 6 to 51st Street
N,R,W,4,5 to Lexington & 59th Street

GMC: 229 East 55th St. [bet. 2nd & 3rd Ave.]

M27, M31, M50, M57, M101, M102, M103

47th Street Theatre

304 West 47th Street // New York, NY [between 8th & 9th Avenue]

Telecharge: (212) 239-6200

R	2 3 4 5 6 7 8 9 10	R
Q	2 3 4 5 6 7 8 9	Q
P	1 2 3 4 5 6 7 8 9 10	P
N	1 2 3 4 5 6 7 8 9 10	N
M	1 2 3 4 5 6 7 8 9 10	M

13 11 9 7 5 3 1

Balcony

10 8 6 4 2	L	1 3 5 7 9 11
12 10 8 6 4 2	K	1 3 5 7 9 11
12 10 8 6 4 2	J	1 3 5 7 9 11
12 10 8 6 4 2	H	1 3 5 7 9 11
12 10 8 6 4 2	G	1 3 5 7 9 11
12 10 8 6 4 2	F	1 3 5 7 9 11
12 10 8 6 4 2	E	1 3 5 7 9 11
12 10 8 6 4 2	D	1 3 5 7 9 11
12 10 8 6 4 2	C	1 3 5 7 9 11
12 10 8 6 4 2	B	1 3 5 7 9 11
12 10 8 6 4 2	A	1 3 5 7 9 11

Orchestra

C,E to 50th Street

Kinney: 155 West 48th St. [bet. 6th & 7th Ave.]

M11, M50

Westside Map #61

concert halls

"I'm not interested in having an orchestra sound like itself. I want it to sound like the composer."

—Leonard Bernstein

92nd St. Y/Kaufman Center
Apollo Theater
Beacon Theatre
Brooklyn Academy of Music
  Harvey Theater
  Howard Gilman Opera House
Carnegie Hall
Carnegie Hall (Weill Recital)
Florence Gould Hall
City Center Main Stage
Julliard School
  Drama Workshop
  Paul Recital Hall
  The Julliard Theater
Lincoln Center
  Alice Tully Hall
  Avery Fisher Hall
  Metropolitan Opera House
  Mitzi E. Newhouse Theatre
  New York State Theater
  Vivian Beaumont Theater
Manhattan School of Music
  John C. Borden Auditorium
Merkin Concert Hall
New Jersey Performing Arts Center
PNC Bank Arts Center
Radio City Music Hall
Staller Center for the Performing Arts
  Main Stage
  Recital Hall
Symphony Space
  Leonard Nimoy Thalia
  Peter Jay Sharp
Tilles Center for the Performing Arts
  Concert/Orchestra
  Dance/Broadway
Tommy Hilfiger at Jones Beach Theater
Town Hall
Tribeca Performing Arts Center
  Theater One
  Theater Two
Westbury Music Fair

92nd Street Y (Kaufmann Concert Hall)

1395 Lexington Ave. // New York, NY [between 91st & 92nd Street]

Y-Charge: (212) 415-5500 // Group Sales: (212) 415-5447

[www.92ndsty.org]

Balcony

▼ Orchestra ▼

Balcony Row A overhangs Orchestra Row S

Apollo Theater

253 West 125th Street // Harlem, NY [between 7th & 8th Avenue]

Box Office: (212) 531-5305 // Information Line: (212) 749-5838

[www.apollotheater.org] [www.itsshowtimeattheapollo.com]

Upper Mezzanine

Lower Mezzanine

Mezzanine Row A overhangs Orchestra Row H

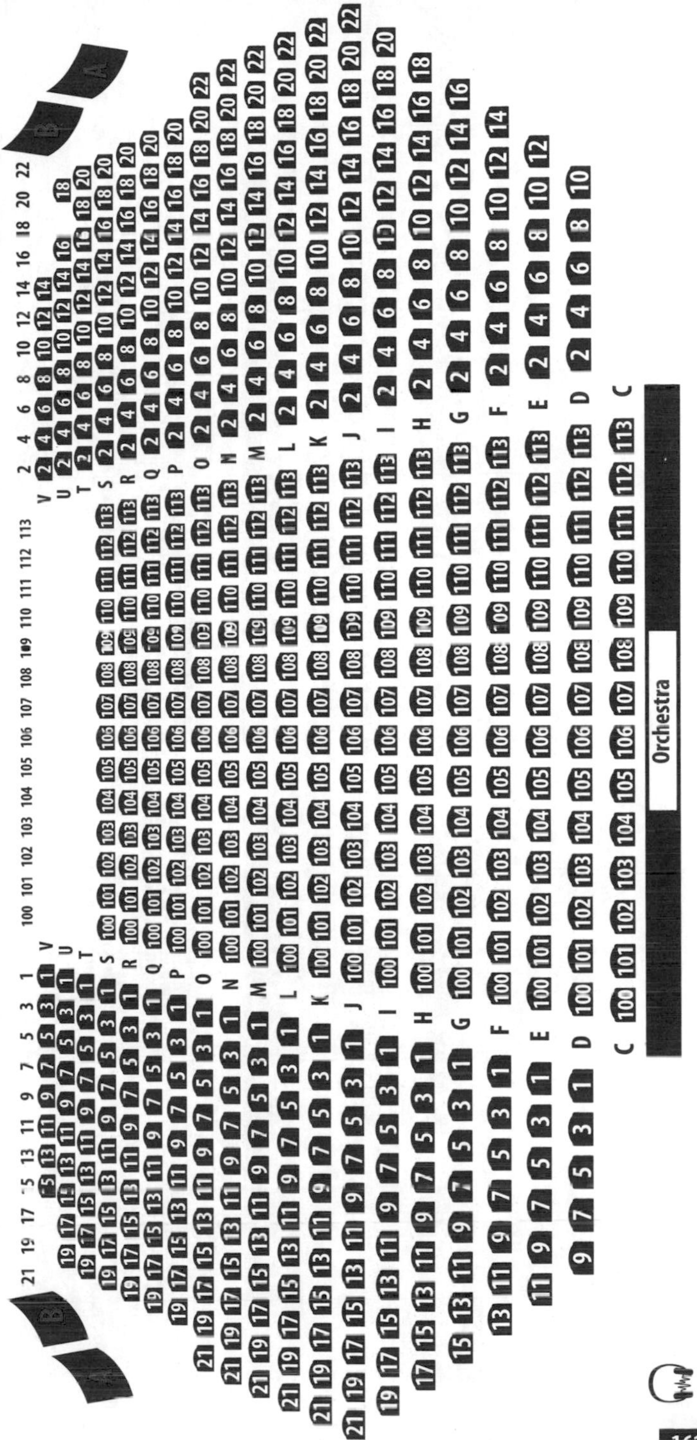

A,B,C,D,2,3 to 125th Street
Metro North to 125th Street

Central Parking

M10, M100, M101, BX15

Orchestra

Beacon Theatre

2124 Broadway // New York, NY [between 74th & 75th Street]

Box Office: (212) 496-7070

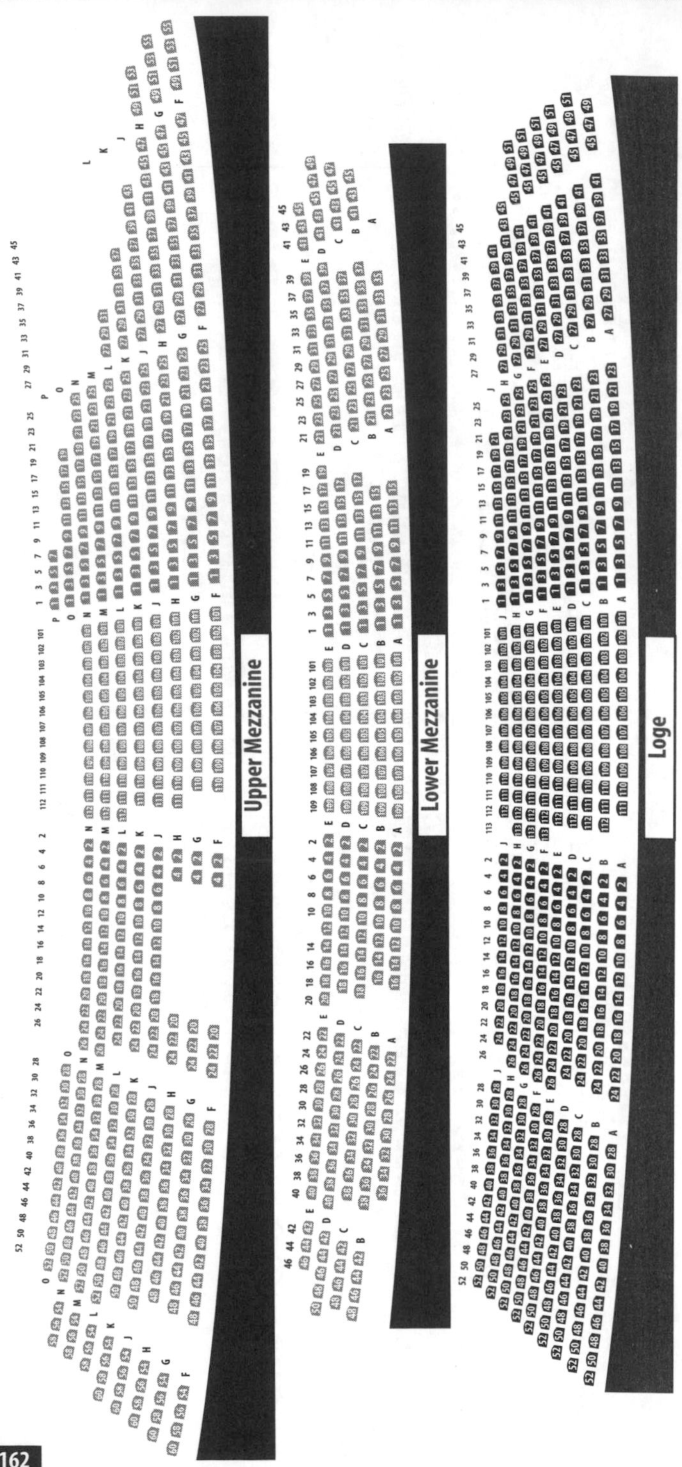

Upper Mezzanine

Lower Mezzanine

Loge

Orchestra

$$$$

$$$

Brooklyn Academy of Music (Harvey Theater

30 Lafayette Avenue // Brooklyn, NY

Ticketmaster: (212) 307-4100 [www.bam.org

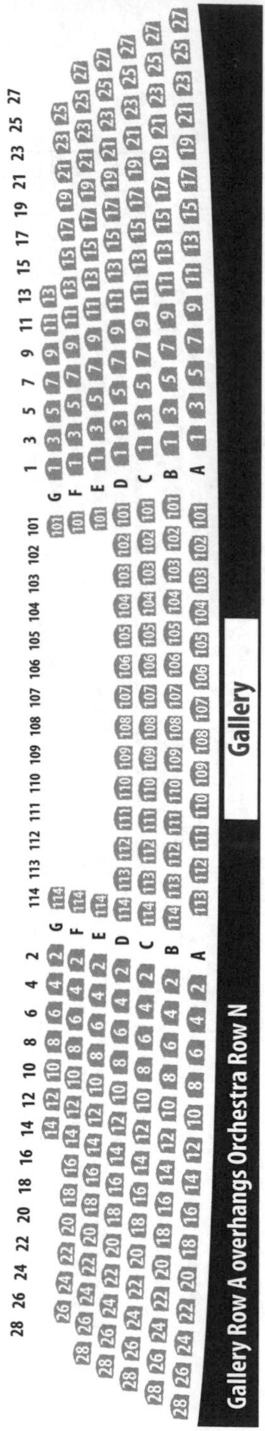

Gallery

Gallery Row A overhangs Orchestra Row N

1,2,4,5,M,N,Q,R,W to Atlantic Ave.
C to Lafayette St. or G to Fulton St.

P Edison Park East. Ashland Place

Call BAM Bus at [718] 636-4100

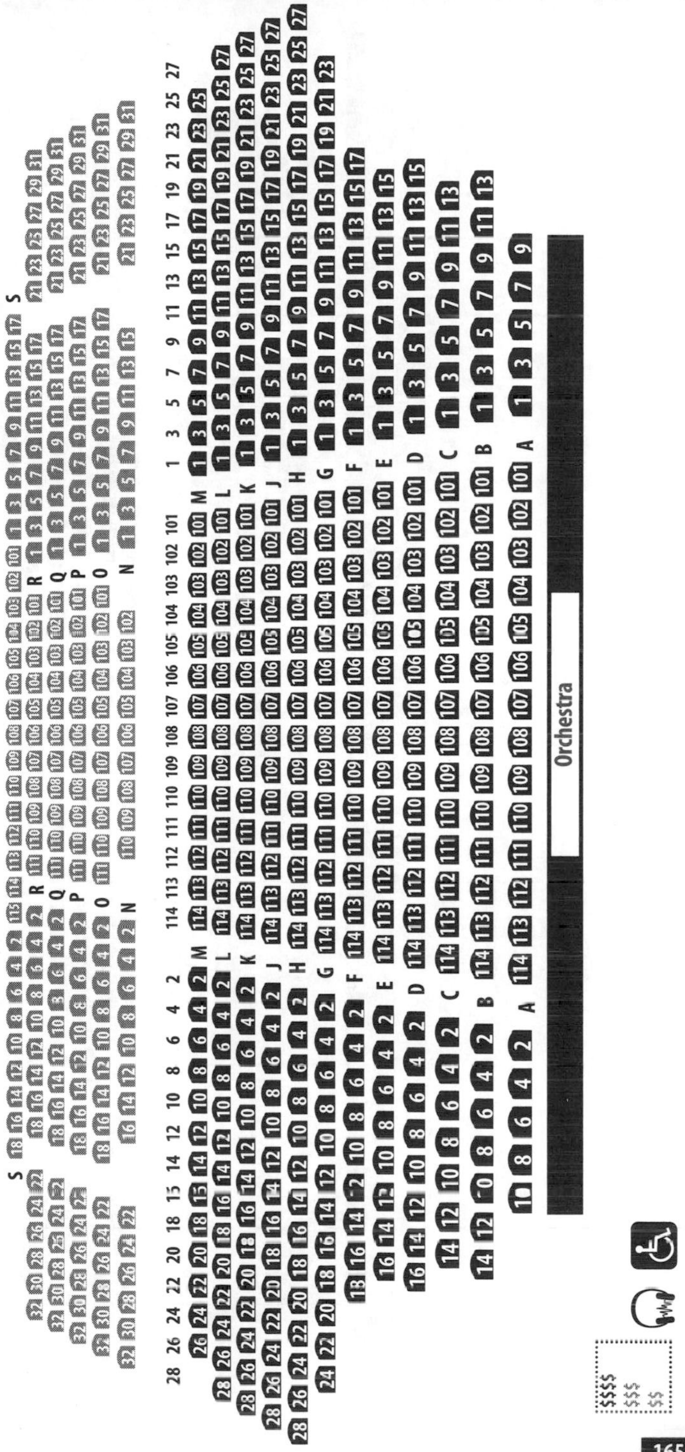

Orchestra

$$$$
$$$
$$

Brooklyn Academy of Music (Opera House)

30 Lafayette Avenue // Brooklyn, NY

Ticketmaster: (212) 307-4100 [www.bam.org]

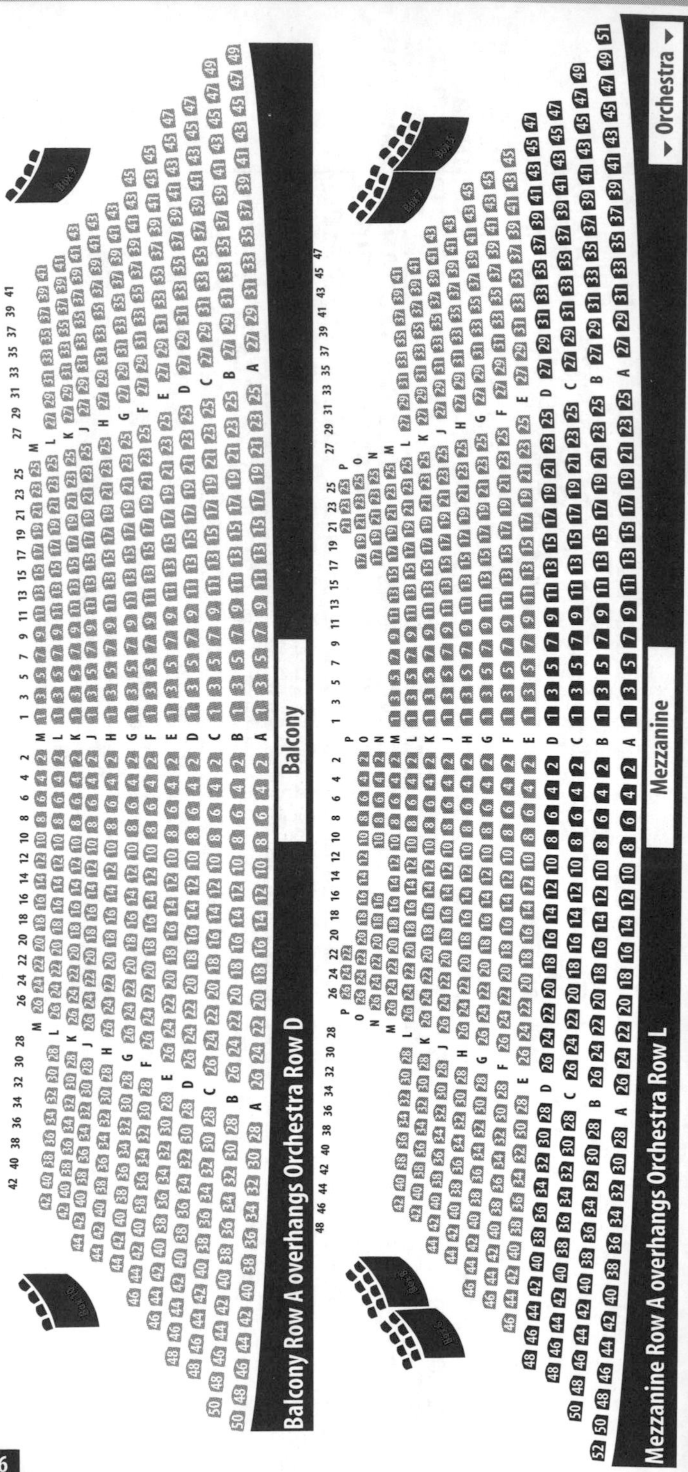

Balcony

Balcony Row A overhangs Orchestra Row D

Mezzanine

Mezzanine Row A overhangs Orchestra Row L

▼ Orchestra ▼

1,2,4,5,M,N,Q,R,W to Atlantic Ave.
C to Lafayette St. or G to Fulton St.

Edison Park East: Ashland Place

Call BAM Bus at [718] 636-4100

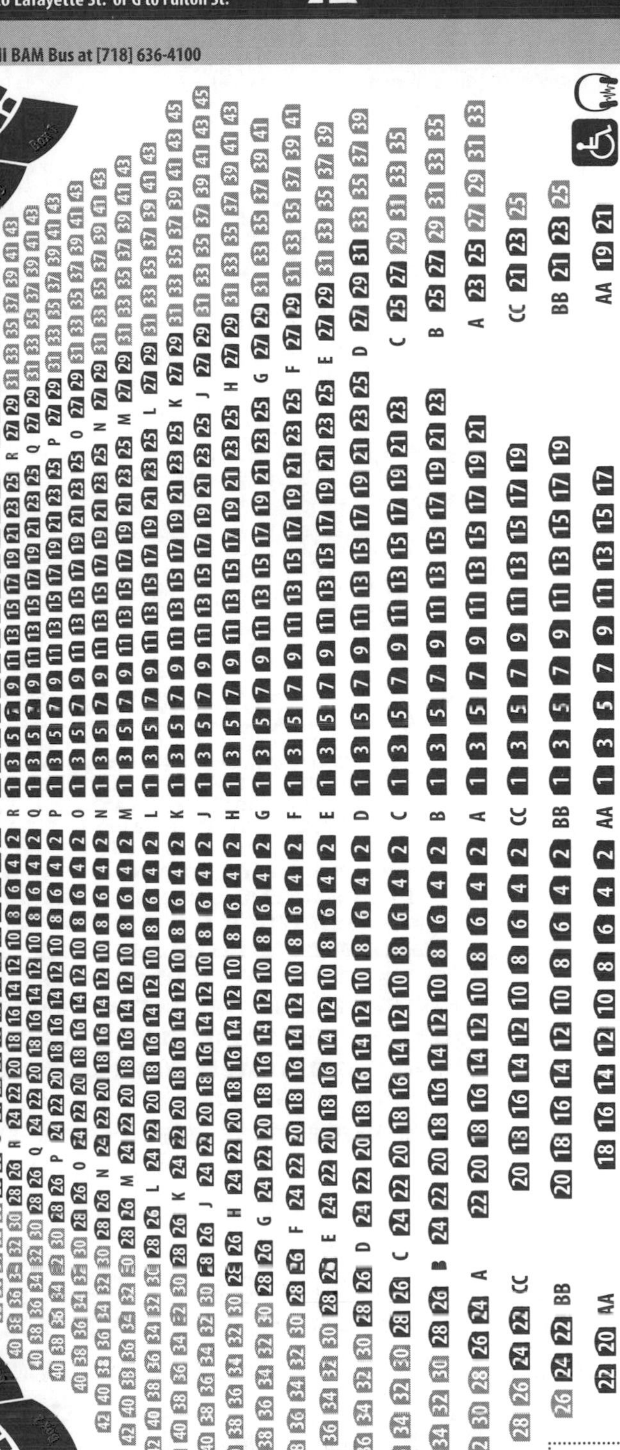

Carnegie Hall

881 Seventh Avenue // New York, NY [at 57th Street]

Box Office: (212) 247-7800 // Group Sales: (212) 903-9705

[www.carnegiehall.org]

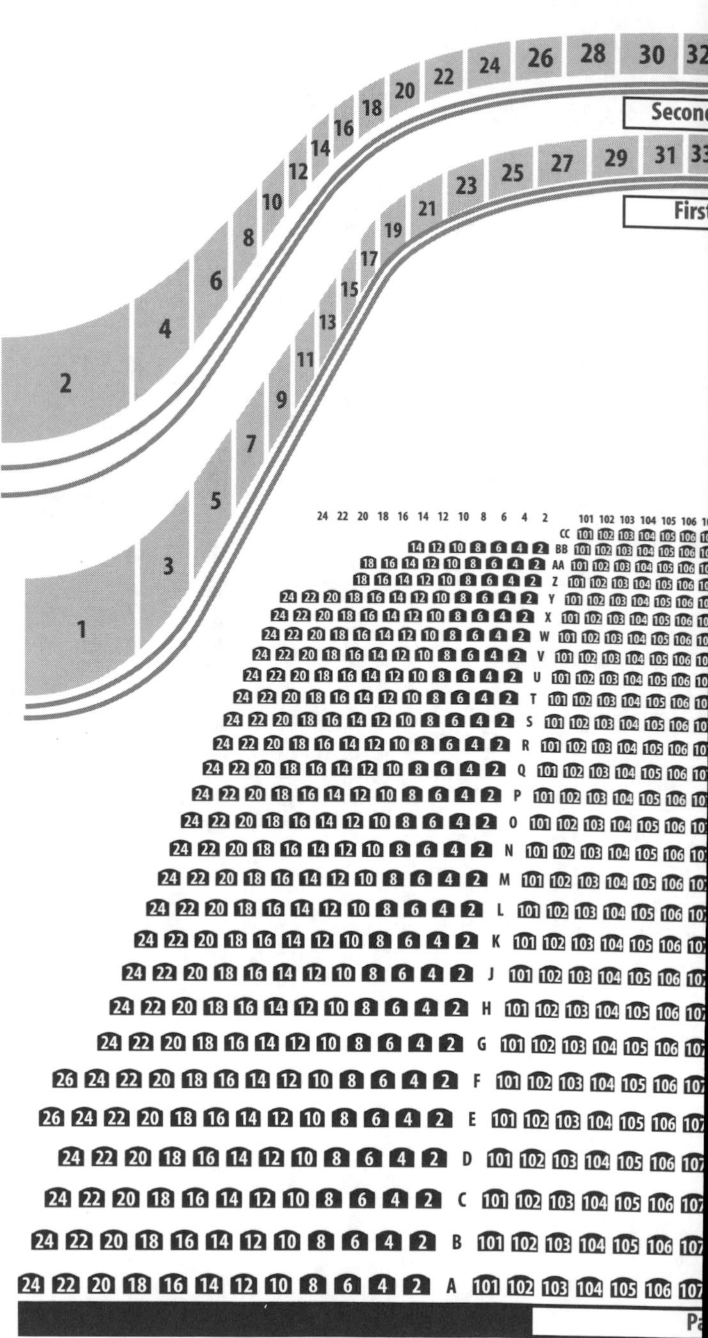

32 34 36 38 40 42 44 46 48 50 52 54 56 58 60 62

Tier

33 35 37 39 41 43 45 47 49 51 53 55 57 59 61 63 65

Tier

108 109 110 111 112 113 114 1 3 5 7 9 11 13 15 17 19 21 23
108 109 110 111 112 113 CC
108 109 110 111 112 113 114 BB 1 3 5 7 9 11 13
108 109 110 111 112 113 114 AA 1 3 5 7 9 11 13 15 17
108 109 110 111 112 113 114 Z 1 3 5 7 9 11 13 15 17
108 109 110 111 112 113 114 Y 1 3 5 7 9 11 13 15 17 19 21 23
108 109 110 111 112 113 114 X 1 3 5 7 9 11 13 15 17 19 21 23
108 109 110 111 112 113 114 W 1 3 5 7 9 11 13 15 17 19 21 23
108 109 110 111 112 113 114 V 1 3 5 7 9 11 13 15 17 19 21 23
108 109 110 111 112 113 114 U 1 3 5 7 9 11 13 15 17 19 21 23
108 109 110 111 112 113 114 T 1 3 5 7 9 11 13 15 17 19 21 23
108 109 110 111 112 113 114 S 1 3 5 7 9 11 13 15 17 19 21 23
108 109 110 111 112 113 114 R 1 3 5 7 9 11 13 15 17 19 21 23
108 109 110 111 112 113 114 Q 1 3 5 7 9 11 13 15 17 19 21 23
108 109 110 111 112 113 114 P 1 3 5 7 9 11 13 15 17 19 21 23
108 109 110 111 112 113 114 O 1 3 5 7 9 11 13 15 17 19 21 23
108 109 110 111 112 113 114 N 1 3 5 7 9 11 13 15 17 19 21 23
108 109 110 111 112 113 114 M 1 3 5 7 9 11 13 15 17 19 21 23
108 109 110 111 112 113 114 L 1 3 5 7 9 11 13 15 17 19 21 23
108 109 110 111 112 113 114 K 1 3 5 7 9 11 13 15 17 19 21 23
108 109 110 111 112 113 114 J 1 3 5 7 9 11 13 15 17 19 21 23
108 109 110 111 112 113 114 H 1 3 5 7 9 11 13 15 17 19 21 23
108 109 110 111 112 113 114 G 1 3 5 7 9 11 13 15 17 19 21 23
108 109 110 111 112 113 114 F 1 3 5 7 9 11 13 15 17 19 21 23 25
108 109 110 111 112 113 114 E 1 3 5 7 9 11 13 15 17 19 21 23 25
108 109 110 111 112 113 114 D 1 3 5 7 9 11 13 15 17 19 21 23
108 109 110 111 112 113 114 C 1 3 5 7 9 11 13 15 17 19 21 23
108 109 110 111 112 113 114 B 1 3 5 7 9 11 13 15 17 19 21 23
108 109 110 111 112 113 114 A 1 3 5 7 9 11 13 15 17 19 21 23

uet

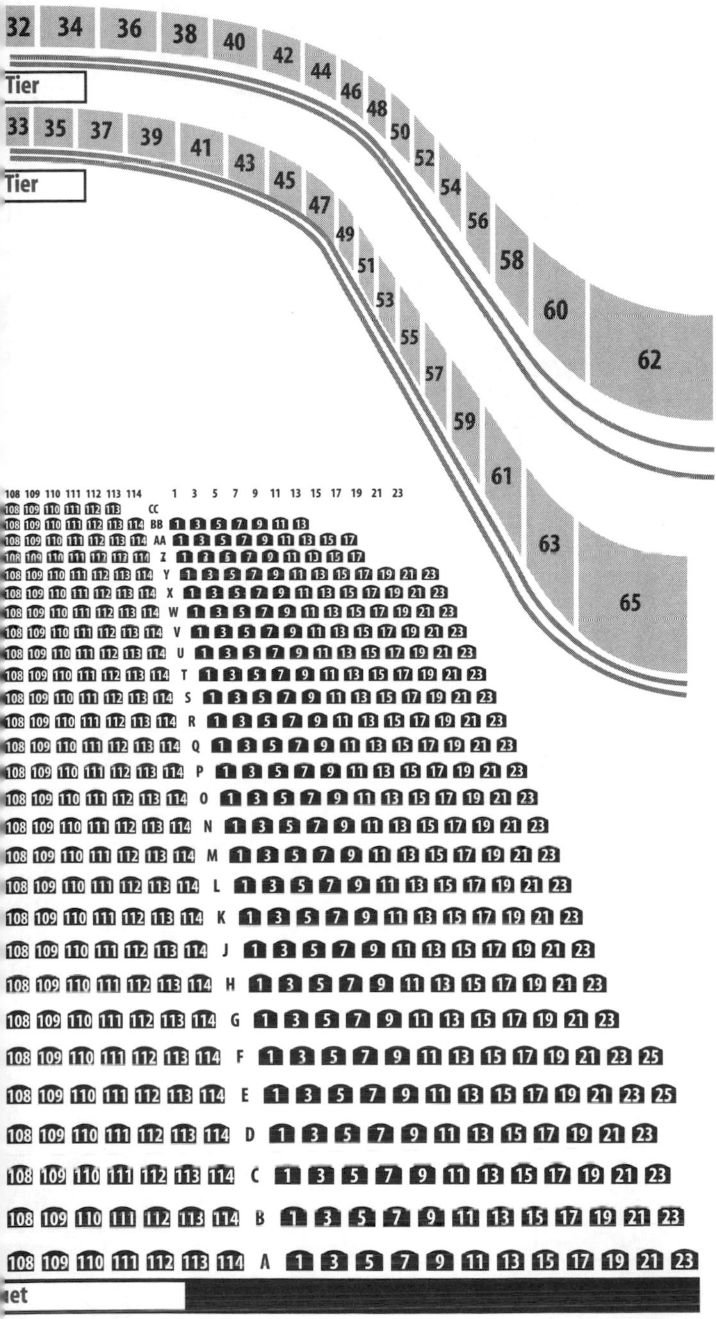

See color chart on next page for price categories

Carnegie Hall (Upper Levels)

881 Seventh Avenue // New York, NY [at 57th Street]

Box Office: (212) 247-7800 // Group Sales: (212) 903-9705

Rear

Front

Dress

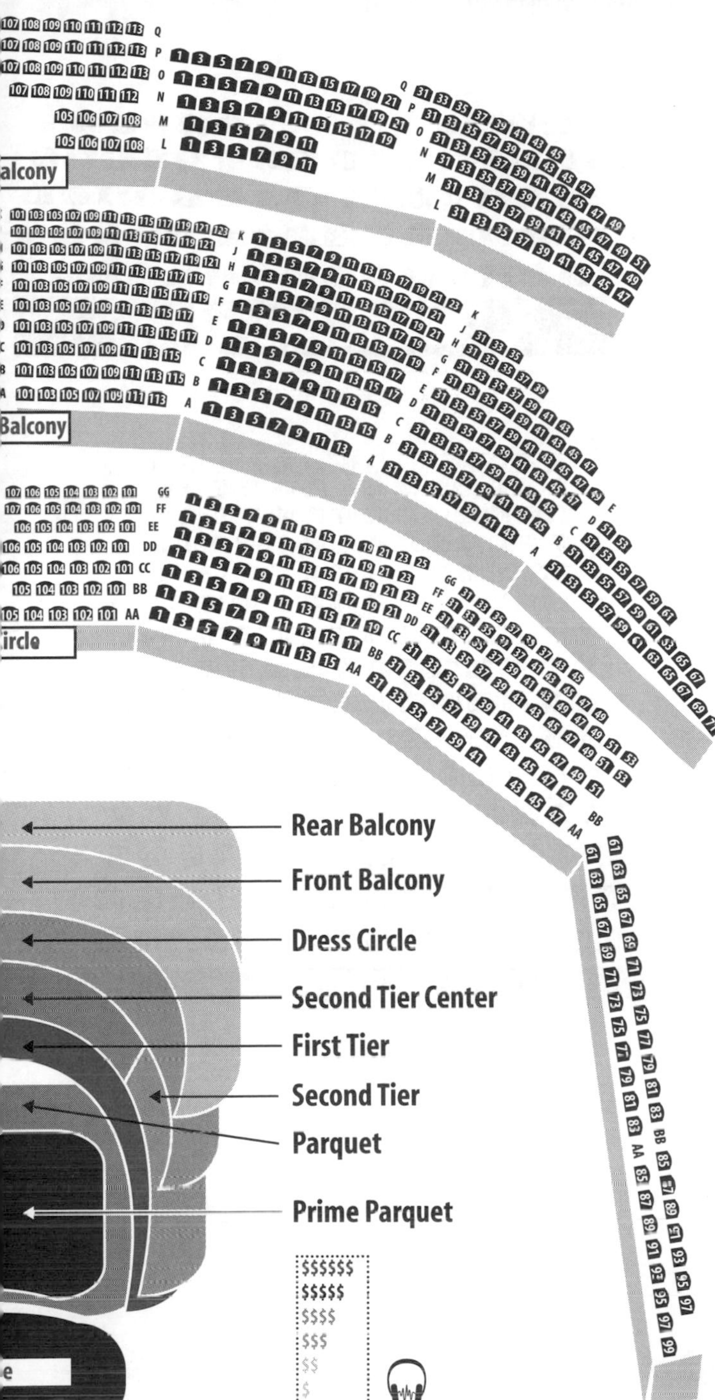
Balcony
Balcony
Circle
Rear Balcony
Front Balcony
Dress Circle
Second Tier Center
First Tier
Second Tier
Parquet
Prime Parquet
$$$$$$
$$$$$
$$$$
$$$
$$
$

Carnegie Hall (Weill Recital)

881 Seventh Avenue // New York, NY [at 57th Street]

Box Office: (212) 247-7800 // Group Sales: (212) 903-9705

[www.carnegiehall.org]

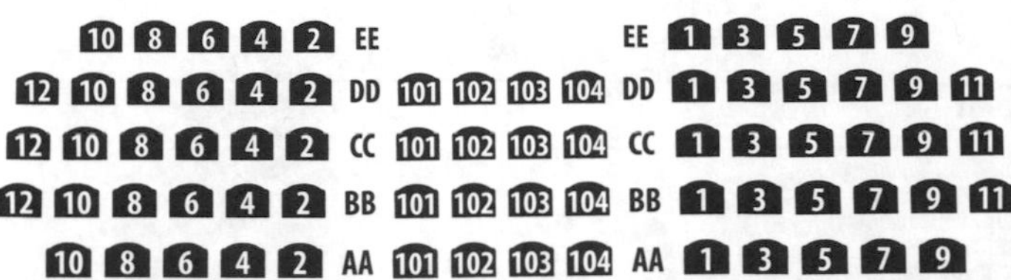

Balcony

101 102 103 104 105 106 107 108 109 110 111 112 113 114

O 101 102 103 104 105 106 107 108 109 110 111 112 113 114 O

N 101 102 103 104 105 106 107 108 109 110 111 112 113 114 N

M 101 102 103 104 105 106 107 108 109 110 111 112 113 114 M

L 101 102 103 104 105 106 107 108 109 110 111 112 113 114 L

K 101 102 103 104 105 106 107 108 109 110 111 112 113 114 K

J 101 102 103 104 105 106 107 108 109 110 111 112 113 114 J

H 101 102 103 104 105 106 107 108 109 110 111 112 113 114 H

G 101 102 103 104 105 106 107 108 109 110 111 112 113 114 G

F 101 102 103 104 105 106 107 108 109 110 111 112 113 114 F

E 101 102 103 104 105 106 107 108 109 110 111 112 113 114 E

D 101 102 103 104 105 106 107 108 109 110 111 112 113 114 D

C 101 102 103 104 105 106 107 108 109 110 111 112 113 114 C

B 101 102 103 104 105 106 107 108 109 110 111 112 113 114 B

A 101 102 103 104 105 106 107 108 109 110 111 112 113 114 A

Orchestra

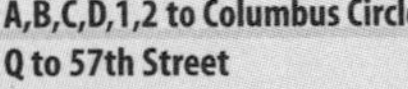

A,B,C,D,1,2 to Columbus Circle
Q to 57th Street

GMC: 200 Central Park South

M5, M6, M7, M10, M30, M31, M57, M104

Florence Gould Hall (French Institute)

55 East 59th Street // New York, NY [between Park and Madison Avenue]

Box Office: (212) 355-6160

Row	Seats	Row
R	112 111 110 109 108 107 106 105 104 103 102 101	R
P	109 108 107 106 105 104 103 102 101	P
O	110 109 108 107 106 105 104 103 102 101	O
N	121 120 119 118 117 116 115 114 113 112 111 110 109 108 107 106 105 104 103 102 101	N
M	120 119 118 117 116 115 114 113 112 111 110 109 108 107 106 105 104 103 102 101	M
L	121 120 119 118 117 116 115 114 113 112 111 110 109 108 107 106 105 104 103 102 101	L
K	120 119 118 117 116 115 114 113 112 111 110 109 108 107 106 105 104 103 102 101	K
J	121 120 119 118 117 116 115 114 113 112 111 110 109 108 107 106 105 104 103 102 101	J
H	120 119 118 117 116 115 114 113 112 111 110 109 108 107 106 105 104 103 102 101	H
G	121 120 119 118 117 116 115 114 113 112 111 110 109 108 107 106 105 104 103 102 101	G
F	120 119 118 117 116 115 114 113 112 111 110 109 108 107 106 105 104 103 102 101	F
E	121 120 119 118 117 116 115 114 113 112 111 110 109 108 107 106 105 104 103 102 101	E
D	120 119 118 117 116 115 114 113 112 111 110 109 108 107 106 105 104 103 102 101	D
C	121 120 119 118 117 116 115 114 113 112 111 110 109 108 107 106 105 104 103 102 101	C
B	120 119 118 117 116 115 114 113 112 111 110 109 108 107 106 105 104 103 102 101	B
A	121 120 119 118 117 116 115 114 113 112 111 110 109 108 107 106 105 104 103 102 101	A

Balcony

Row	Seats	Row
FF	120 119 118 117 116 115 114 113 112 111 110 109 108 107 106 105 104 103 102 101	FF
EE	117 116 115 114 113 112 111 110 109 108 107 106 105 104 103 102 101	EE
DD	118 117 116 115 114 113 112 111 110 109 108 107 106 105 104 103 102 101	DD
CC	120 119 118 117 116 115 114 113 112 111 110 109 108 107 106 105 104 103 102 101	CC
BB	118 117 116 115 114 113 112 111 110 109 108 107 106 105 104 103 102 101	BB
AA	109 108 107 106 105 104 103 102 101	AA

Orchestra

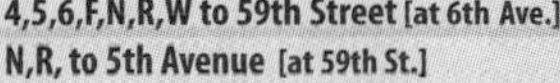
4,5,6,F,N,R,W to 59th Street [at 6th Ave.]
N,R, to 5th Avenue [at 59th St.]

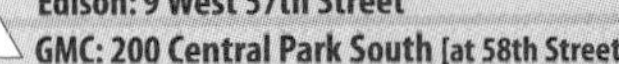
Edison: 9 West 57th Street
GMC: 200 Central Park South [at 58th Street]

M1, M2, M3, M4, M31, M57

City Center

131 West 55th Street // New York, NY [between 6th & 7th Avenue]

City Tix: (212) 581-1212 [www.citycenter.org]

28 26 24 22 20 18 16 14 12 10 8 6 4 2 | 114 113 112 111 110 109 108 107 106 105 104 103 102 101 | 1 3 5 7 9 11 13 15 17 19 21 23 25 27

F 28 26 24 22 20 18 16 14 12 10 8 6 4 2 F 114 113 112 111 110 109 108 107 106 105 104 103 102 101 F 1 3 5 7 9 11 13 15 17 19 21 23 25 27 F

E 28 26 24 22 20 18 16 14 12 10 8 6 4 2 E 114 113 112 111 110 109 108 107 106 105 104 103 102 101 E 1 3 5 7 9 11 13 15 17 19 21 23 25 27 E

D 26 24 22 20 18 16 14 12 10 8 6 4 2 D 114 113 112 111 110 109 108 107 106 105 104 103 102 101 D 1 3 5 7 9 11 13 15 17 19 21 23 25 D

208 206 204 202 C 24 22 20 18 16 14 12 10 8 6 4 2 C 114 113 112 111 110 109 108 107 106 105 104 103 102 101 C 1 3 5 7 9 11 13 15 17 19 21 23 C 201 203 205 207

210 208 206 204 202 B 22 20 18 16 14 12 10 8 6 4 2 B 114 113 112 111 110 109 108 107 106 105 104 103 102 101 B 1 3 5 7 9 11 13 15 17 19 21 B 201 203 205 207 209

210 208 206 204 202 A 18 16 14 12 10 8 6 4 2 A 114 113 112 111 110 109 108 107 106 105 104 103 102 101 A 1 3 5 7 9 11 13 15 17 A 201 203 205 207 209

Grand Tier Row A overhangs Orchestra Row H

First Balcony / Grand Tier

Upper Levels shown on next page

Orchestra Pit

$$$$
$$$
$$
$

Rear Gallery

Second Balcony / Front Gallery

Front Gallery Row A overhangs First Balcony Row E

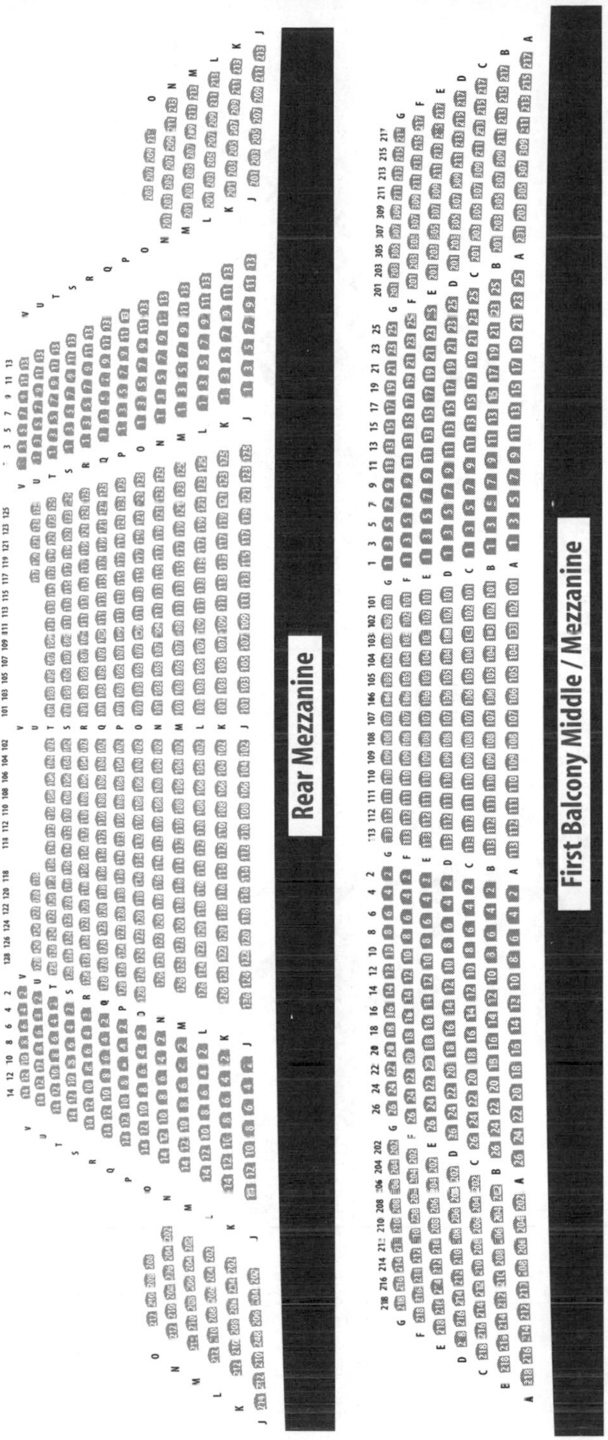

Rear Mezzanine

First Balcony Middle / Mezzanine

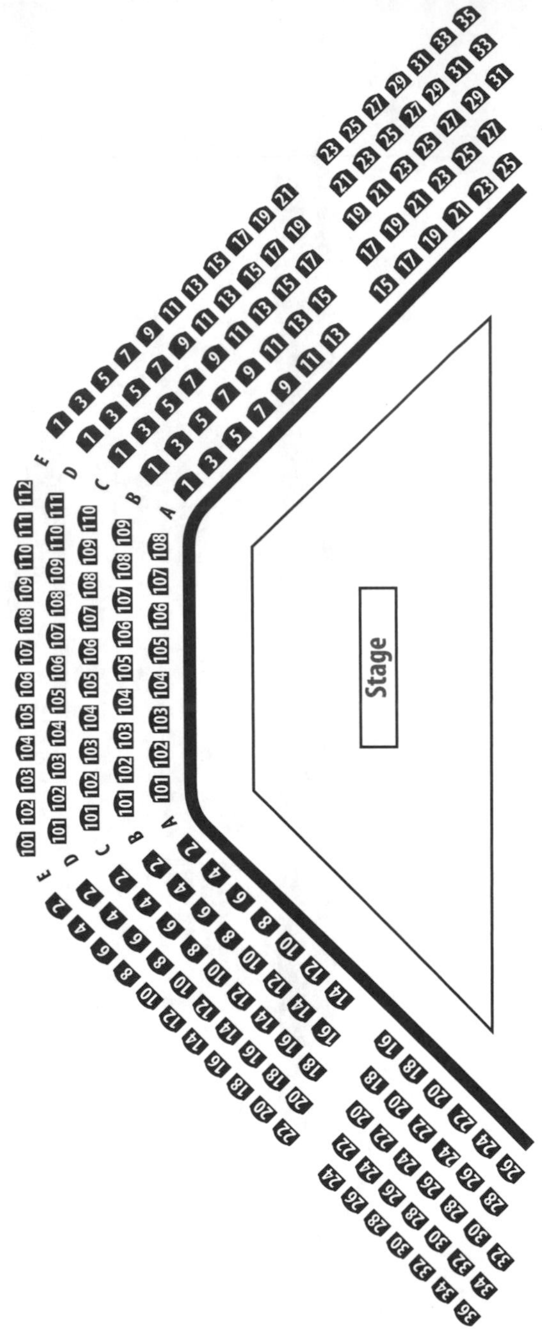

Drama Workshop

Stage

Rows A–L

Paul Recital Hall

The Julliard School (The Julliard Theater)

60 Lincoln Center Plaza // New York, NY [between Columbus & Amsterdam]

Box Office: (212) 769-7406 **[www.julliard.edu]**

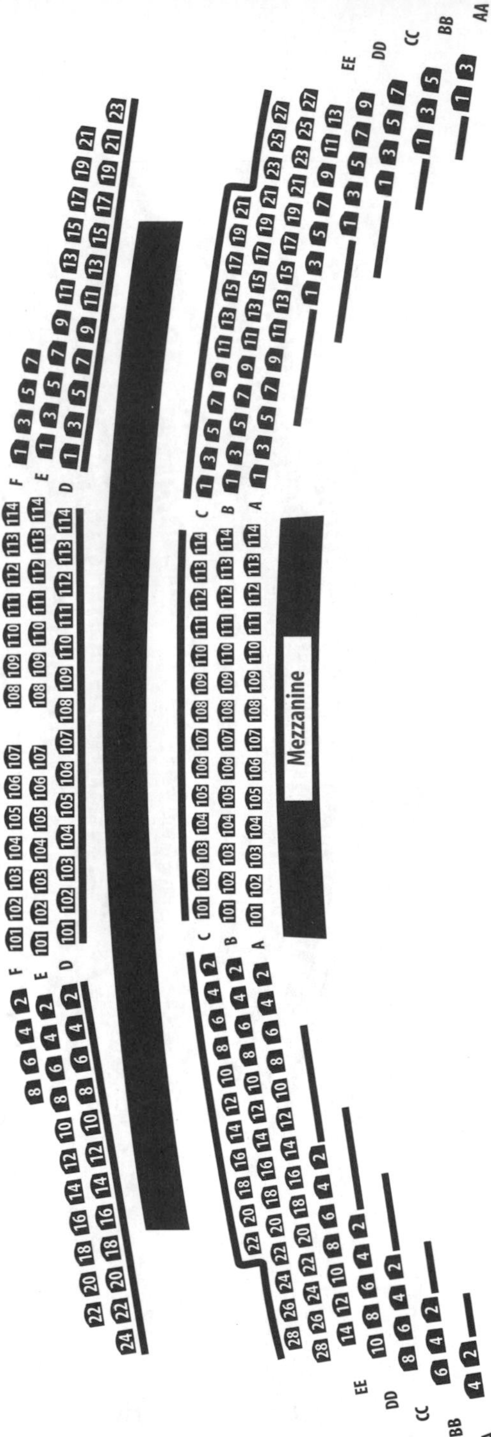

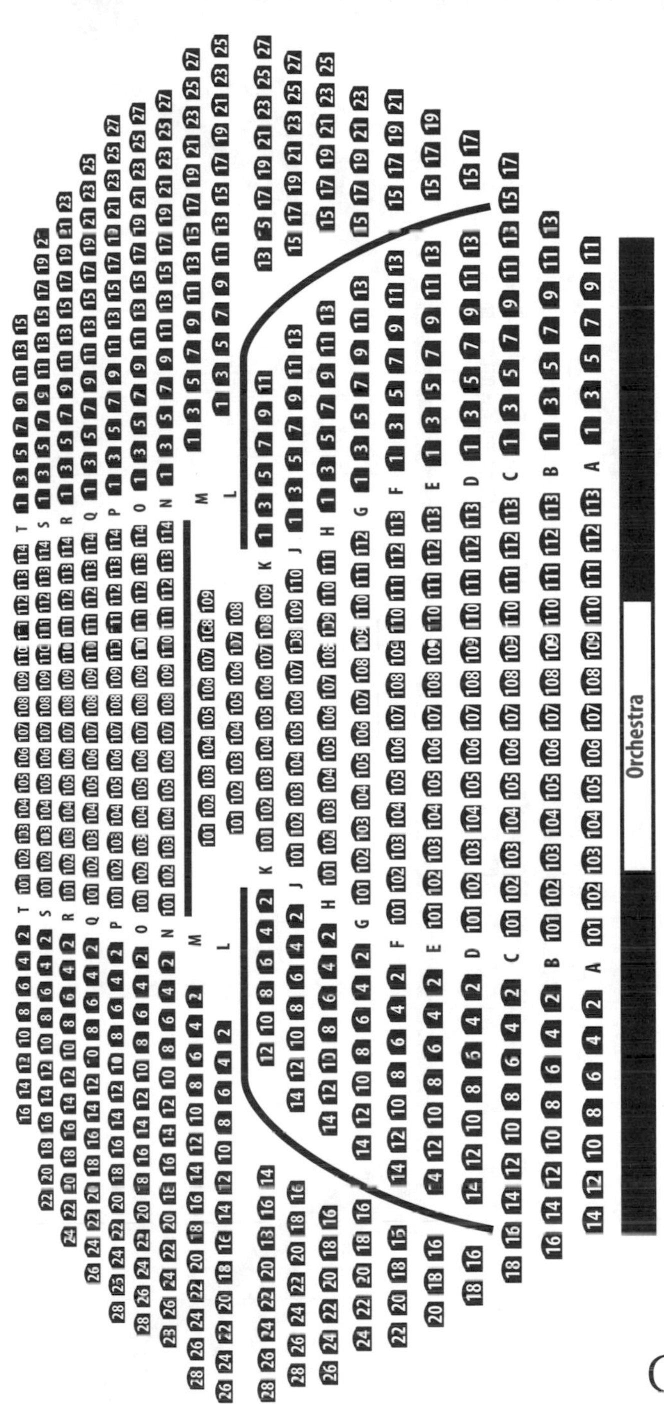

Orchestra

Lincoln Center (Alice Tully Hall)

1941 Broadway // New York, NY [Broadway at 65th Avenue]

Centercharge: (212) 721-6500 Box Office: (212) 875-5050

[www.lincolncenter.org]

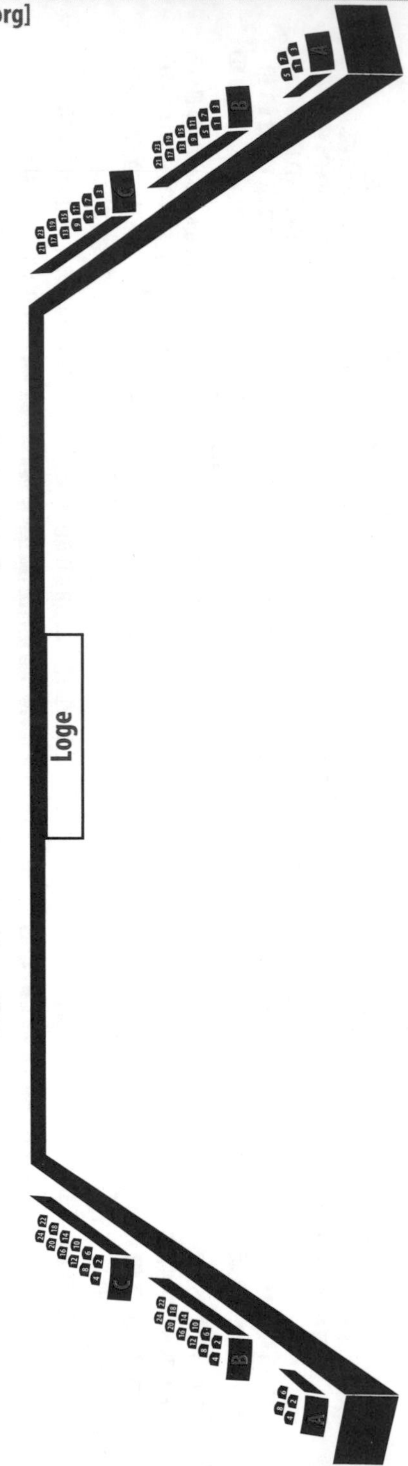

Orchestra

Lincoln Center (Avery Fisher Hall)

10 Lincoln Center Plaza // New York, NY] [Broadway at 65th Avenue]

Centercharge: (212) 721-6500 // Box Office: (212) 875-5030

[www.newyorkphilharmonic.org]

Boxes

Tier 3 [Center]

Boxes

Tier 2 [Center]

Boxes

Tier 1 [Center]

Left Box Tiers on next page

Right Box Tiers on next page

Row	Seats	Row	Seats	Row	Seats
EE	24 22 20 18 16 14 12 10 8 6 4 2	EE	116 115 114 113 112 111 110 109 108 107 106 105 104 103 102 101	EE	1 3 5 7 9 11 13 15 17 19 21 23
DD	24 22 20 18 16 14 12 10 8 6 4 2	DD	116 115 114 113 112 111 110 109 108 107 106 105 104 103 102 101	DD	1 3 5 7 9 11 13 15 17 19 21 23
CC	24 22 20 18 16 14 12 10 8 6 4 2	CC	116 115 114 113 112 111 110 109 108 107 106 105 104 103 102 101	CC	1 3 5 7 9 11 13 15 17 19 21 23
BB	24 22 20 18 16 14 12 10 8 6 4 2	BB	116 115 114 113 112 111 110 109 108 107 106 105 104 103 102 101	BB	1 3 5 7 9 11 13 15 17 19 21 23
AA	24 22 20 18 16 14 12 10 8 6 4 2	AA	116 115 114 113 112 111 110 109 108 107 106 105 104 103 102 101	AA	1 3 5 7 9 11 13 15 17 19 21 23
Z	24 22 20 18 16 14 12 10 8 6 4 2	Z	116 115 114 113 112 111 110 109 108 107 106 105 104 103 102 101	Z	1 3 5 7 9 11 13 15 17 19 21 23
Y	24 22 20 18 16 14 12 10 8 6 4 2	Y	116 115 114 113 112 111 110 109 108 107 106 105 104 103 102 101	Y	1 3 5 7 9 11 13 15 17 19 21 23
X	24 22 20 18 16 14 12 10 8 6 4 2	X	116 115 114 113 112 111 110 109 108 107 106 105 104 103 102 101	X	1 3 5 7 9 11 13 15 17 19 21 23
W	24 22 20 18 16 14 12 10 8 6 4 2	W	116 115 114 113 112 111 110 109 108 107 106 105 104 103 102 101	W	1 3 5 7 9 11 13 15 17 19 21 23
V	24 22 20 18 16 14 12 10 8 6 4 2	V	116 115 114 113 112 111 110 109 108 107 106 105 104 103 102 101	V	1 3 5 7 9 11 13 15 17 19 21 23
U	24 22 20 18 16 14 12 10 8 6 4 2	U	116 115 114 113 112 111 110 109 108 107 106 105 104 103 102 101	U	1 3 5 7 9 11 13 15 17 19 21 23
T	24 22 20 18 16 14 12 10 8 6 4 2	T	116 115 114 113 112 111 110 109 108 107 106 105 104 103 102 101	T	1 3 5 7 9 11 13 15 17 19 21 23
S	24 22 20 18 16 14 12 10 8 6 4 2	S	116 115 114 113 112 111 110 109 108 107 106 105 104 103 102 101	S	1 3 5 7 9 11 13 15 17 19 21 23
R	24 22 20 18 16 14 12 10 8 6 4 2	R	116 115 114 113 112 111 110 109 108 107 106 105 104 103 102 101	R	1 3 5 7 9 11 13 15 17 19 21 23
Q	26 24 22 20 18 16 14 12 10 8 6 4 2	Q	116 115 114 113 112 111 110 109 108 107 106 105 104 103 102 101	Q	1 3 5 7 9 11 13 15 17 19 21 23 25
P	26 24 22 20 18 16 14 12 10 8 6 4 2	P	116 115 114 113 112 111 110 109 108 107 106 105 104 103 102 101	P	1 3 5 7 9 11 13 15 17 19 21 23 25
O	26 24 22 20 18 16 14 12 10 8 6 4 2	O	116 115 114 113 112 111 110 109 108 107 106 105 104 103 102 101	O	1 3 5 7 9 11 13 15 17 19 21 23 25
N	26 24 22 20 18 16 14 12 10 8 6 4 2	N	116 115 114 113 112 111 110 109 108 107 106 105 104 103 102 101	N	1 3 5 7 9 11 13 15 17 19 21 23 25
M	26 24 22 20 18 16 14 12 10 8 6 4 2	M	116 115 114 113 112 111 110 109 108 107 106 105 104 103 102 101	M	1 3 5 7 9 11 13 15 17 19 21 23 25
L	26 24 22 20 18 16 14 12 10 8 6 4 2	L	116 115 114 113 112 111 110 109 108 107 106 105 104 103 102 101	L	1 3 5 7 9 11 13 15 17 19 21 23 25
K	26 24 22 20 18 16 14 12 10 8 6 4 2	K	116 115 114 113 112 111 110 109 108 107 106 105 104 103 102 101	K	1 3 5 7 9 11 13 15 17 19 21 23 25
J	26 24 22 20 18 16 14 12 10 8 6 4 2	J	116 115 114 113 112 111 110 109 108 107 106 105 104 103 102 101	J	1 3 5 7 9 11 13 15 17 19 21 23 25
H	26 24 22 20 18 16 14 12 10 8 6 4 2	H	116 115 114 113 112 111 110 109 108 107 106 105 104 103 102 101	H	1 3 5 7 9 11 13 15 17 19 21 23 25
G	26 24 22 20 18 16 14 12 10 8 6 4 2	G	116 115 114 113 112 111 110 109 108 107 106 105 104 103 102 101	G	1 3 5 7 9 11 13 15 17 19 21 23 25
F	26 24 22 20 18 16 14 12 10 8 6 4 2	F	116 115 114 113 112 111 110 109 108 107 106 105 104 103 102 101	F	1 3 5 7 9 11 13 15 17 19 21 23 25
E	26 24 22 20 18 16 14 12 10 8 6 4 2	E	116 115 114 113 112 111 110 109 108 107 106 105 104 103 102 101	E	1 3 5 7 9 11 13 15 17 19 21 23 25
D	26 24 22 20 18 16 14 12 10 8 6 4 2	D	116 115 114 113 112 111 110 109 108 107 106 105 104 103 102 101	D	1 3 5 7 9 11 13 15 17 19 21 23 25
C	26 24 22 20 18 16 14 12 10 8 6 4 2	C	116 115 114 113 112 111 110 109 108 107 106 105 104 103 102 101	C	1 3 5 7 9 11 13 15 17 19 21 23 25
B	18 16 14 12 10 8 6 4 2	B	116 115 114 113 112 111 110 109 108 107 106 105 104 103 102 101	B	1 3 5 7 9 11 13 15 17
A		A	116 115 114 113 112 111 110 109 108 107 106 105 104 103 102 101	A	

Orchestra

Lincoln Center (Avery Fisher Hall)

10 Lincoln Center Plaza // New York, NY [Broadway at 65th Avenue]

Centercharge: (212) 721-6500 // Box Office: (212) 875-5050

[www.newyorkphilharmonic.org]

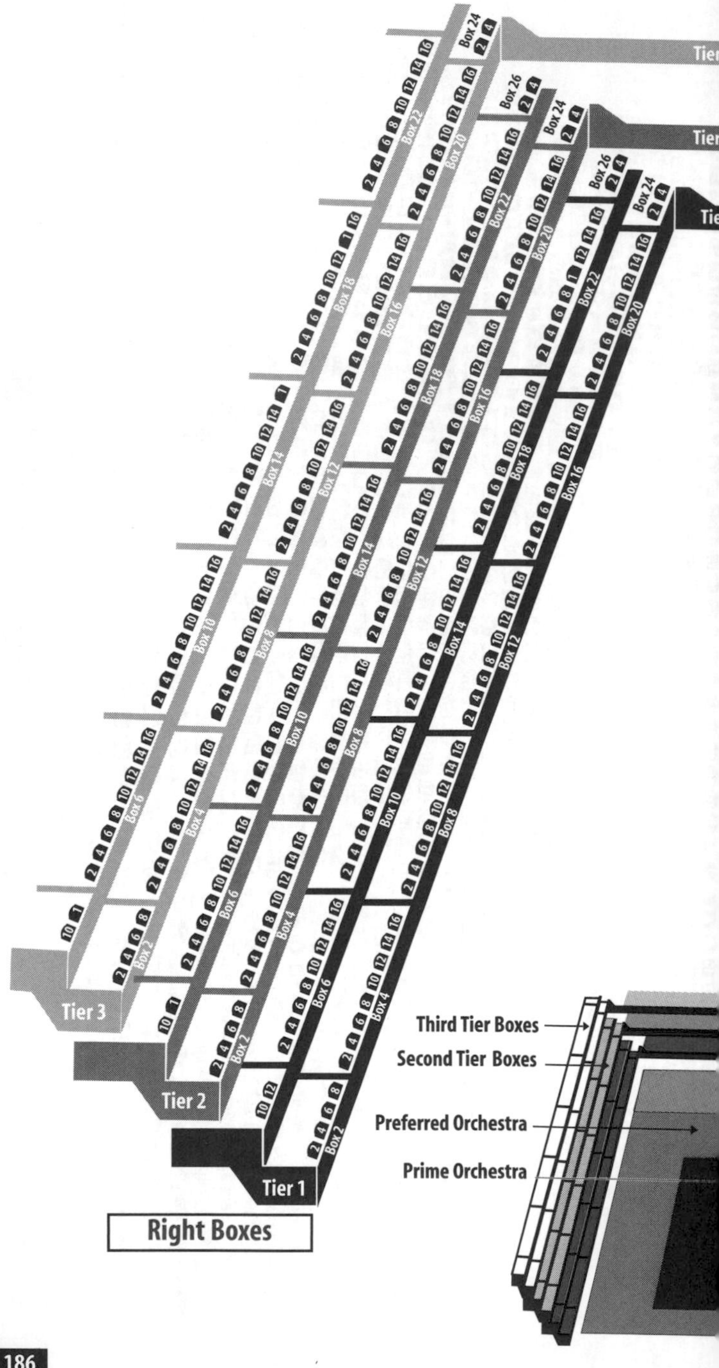

Great Performer Group: (212) 875-5475

NY Philharmonic Group Sales: (212) 875-5672

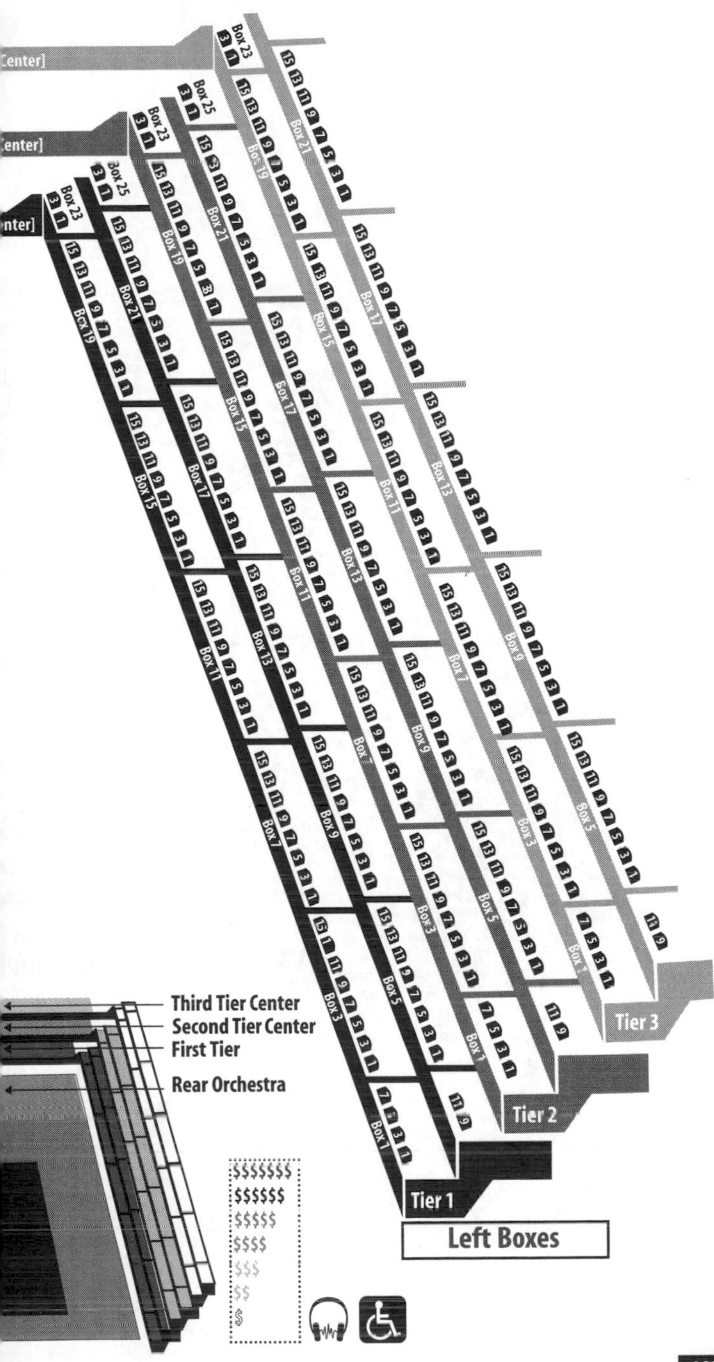

Lincoln Center (Metropolitan Opera House)

30 Lincoln Center Plaza // New York, NY [at Columbus bet. 62nd & 65th St.]

Box Office: (212) 362-6000 // Group Sales: (212) 501-3410

[www.metopera.org] [www.abt.org]

STANDING ROOM

See color chart on next page for price categories

Lincoln Center (Metropolitan Opera House)

30 Lincoln Center Plaza // New York, NY [at Columbus bet. 62nd & 65th St.]

Box Office: (212) 362-6000 // Group Sales: (212) 501-3410

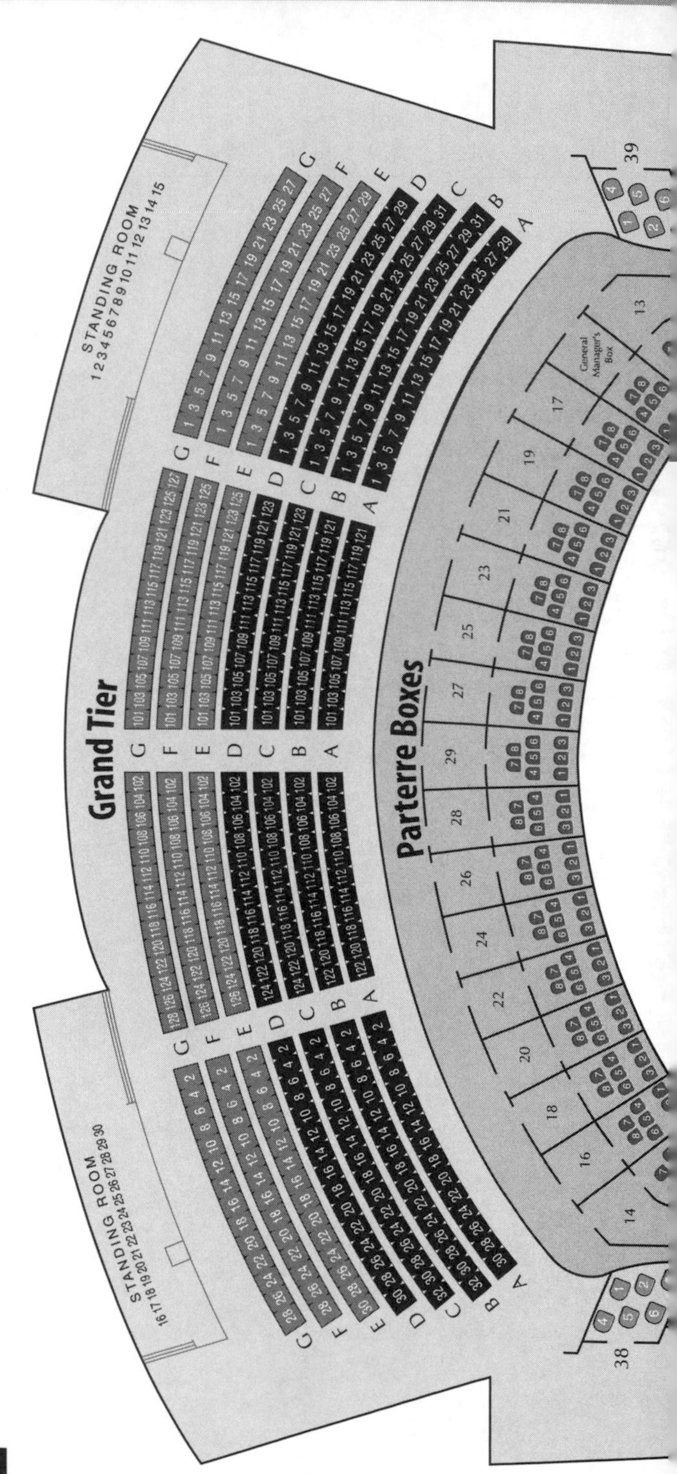

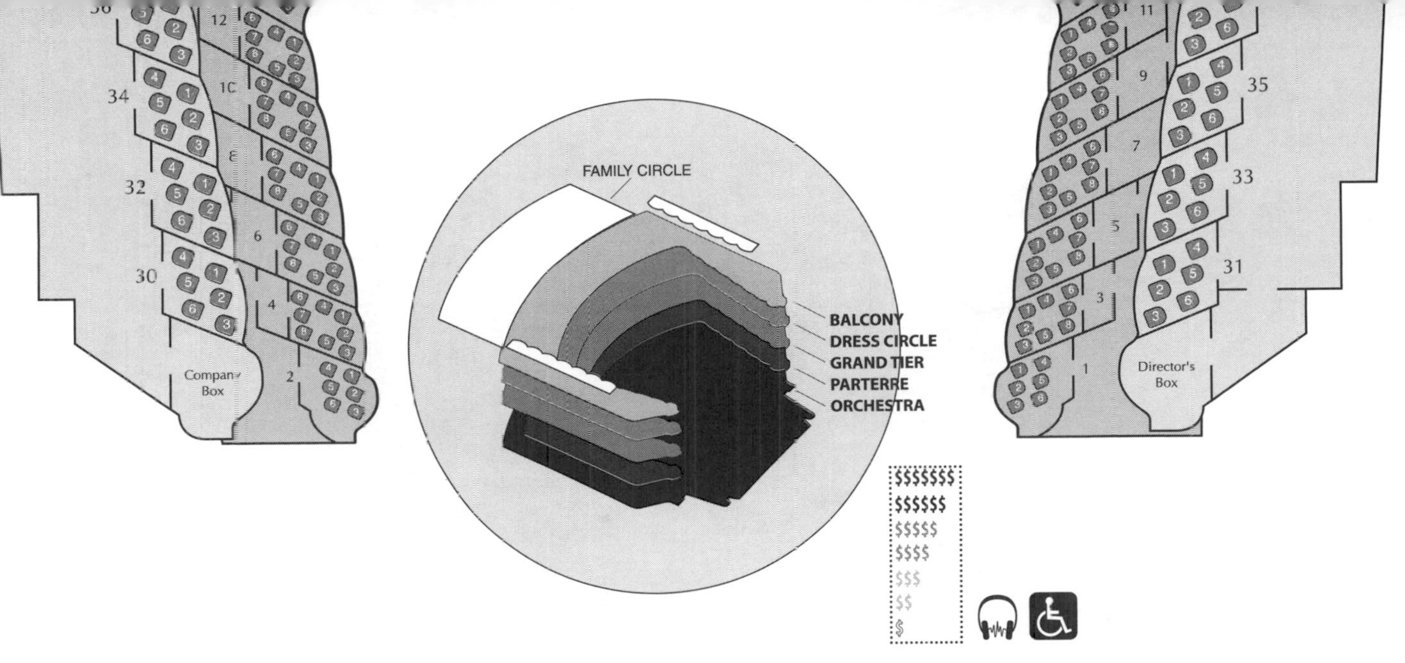
FAMILY CIRCLE
BALCONY
DRESS CIRCLE
GRAND TIER
PARTERRE
ORCHESTRA
$$$$$$$
$$$$$$
$$$$$
$$$$
$$$
$$
$
Director's Box
Company Box

Lincoln Center (Metropolitan Opera House)

30 Lincoln Center Plaza // New York, NY [at Columbus bet. 62nd & 65th St.]

Box Office: (212) 362-6000 // Group Sales: (212) 501-3410

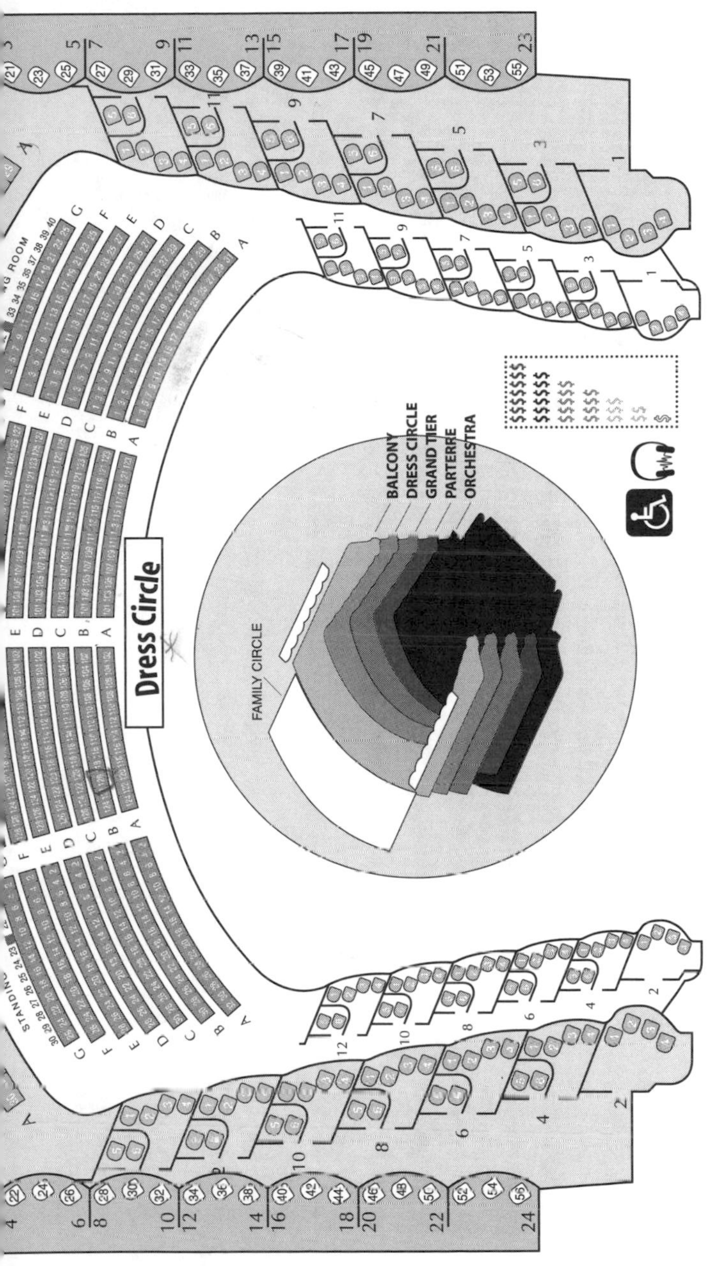
Dress Circle
STANDING ROOM
FAMILY CIRCLE
BALCONY
DRESS CIRCLE
GRAND TIER
PARTERRE
ORCHESTRA
$$$$$$$
$$$$$$
$$$$$
$$$$
$$$
$$
$

Lincoln Center (Mitzi E. Newhouse Theater)

150 West 65th Street // New York, NY [between Broadway & Amsterdam]

Telecharge: (212) 239-6200 // Group Sales: (212) 889-4300

[www.lincolncenter.org]

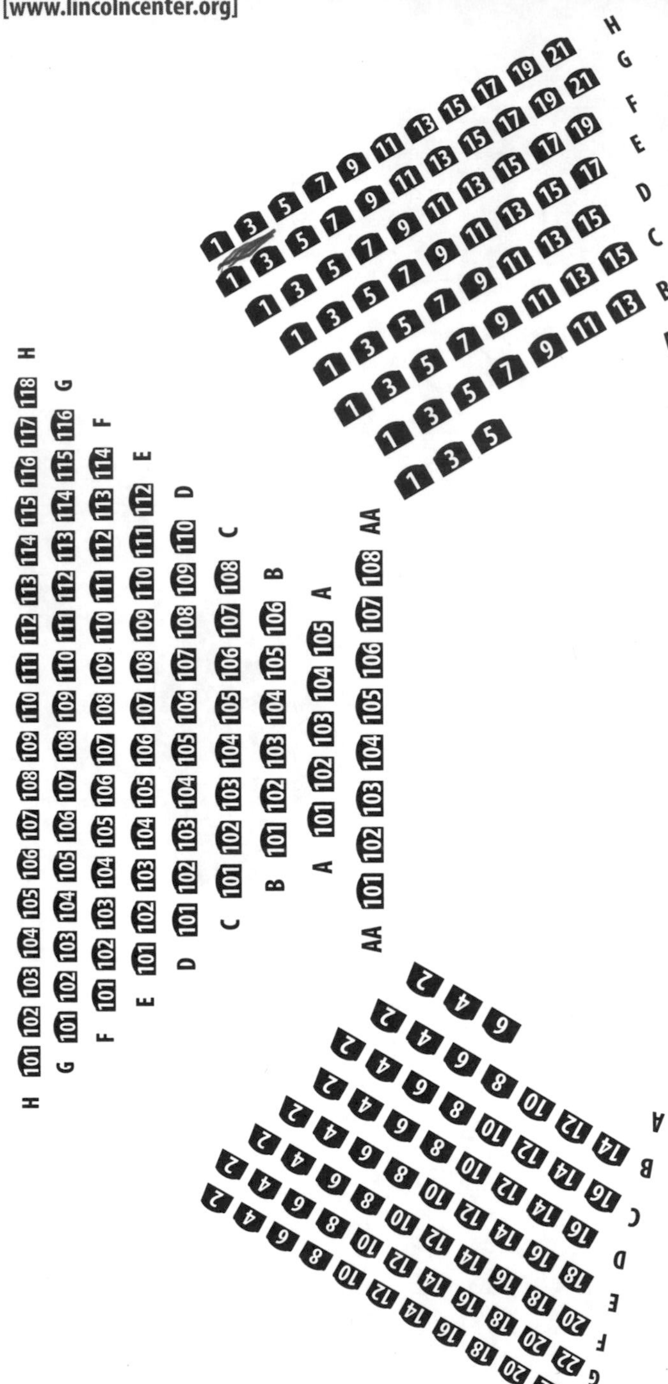

H 31 33 35 37 39

G 31 33 35 37 39 41

F 31 33 35 37 39 41 43

E 31 33 35 37 39 41 43

D 31 33 35 37 39 41 43

C 31 33 35 37 39 41 43

B 31 33 35 37 39 41

A

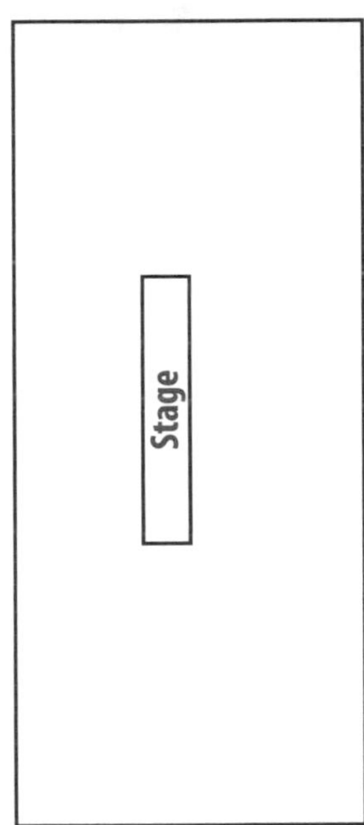

A 30 32 34 36

B 30 32 34 36 38 40 42

C 30 32 34 36 38 40 42

D 30 32 34 36 38 40 42

E 30 32 34 36 38 40 42

F 30 32 34 36 38 40 42

G 30 32 34 36 38 40

H 30 32 34 36 38 40

Lincoln Center (New York State Theater)

20 Lincoln Center Plaza // New York, NY [at Columbus Avenue & 63rd Street]

Box Office: (212) 870-5570

[www.nycballet.org] [www.nycopera.com]

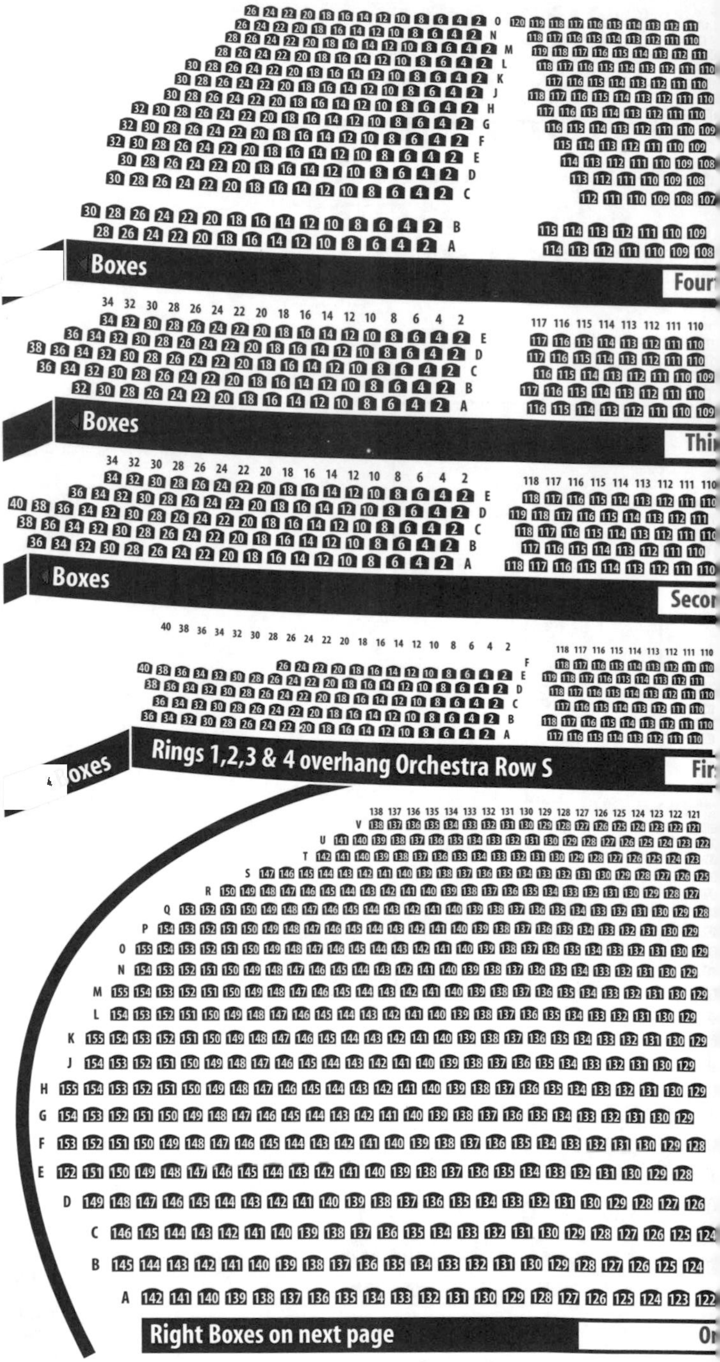

Boxes

Four

Boxes

Thi

Boxes

Secon

Boxes

Rings 1,2,3 & 4 overhang Orchestra Row S

Firs

Right Boxes on next page

Or

1,2,9 to 66th St. [Lincoln Center]

Lincoln Center Park & Lock. W...
[bet. Amsterdam & Broadway]

M5, M7, M10, M11, M66, M104

Lincoln Center Map #85

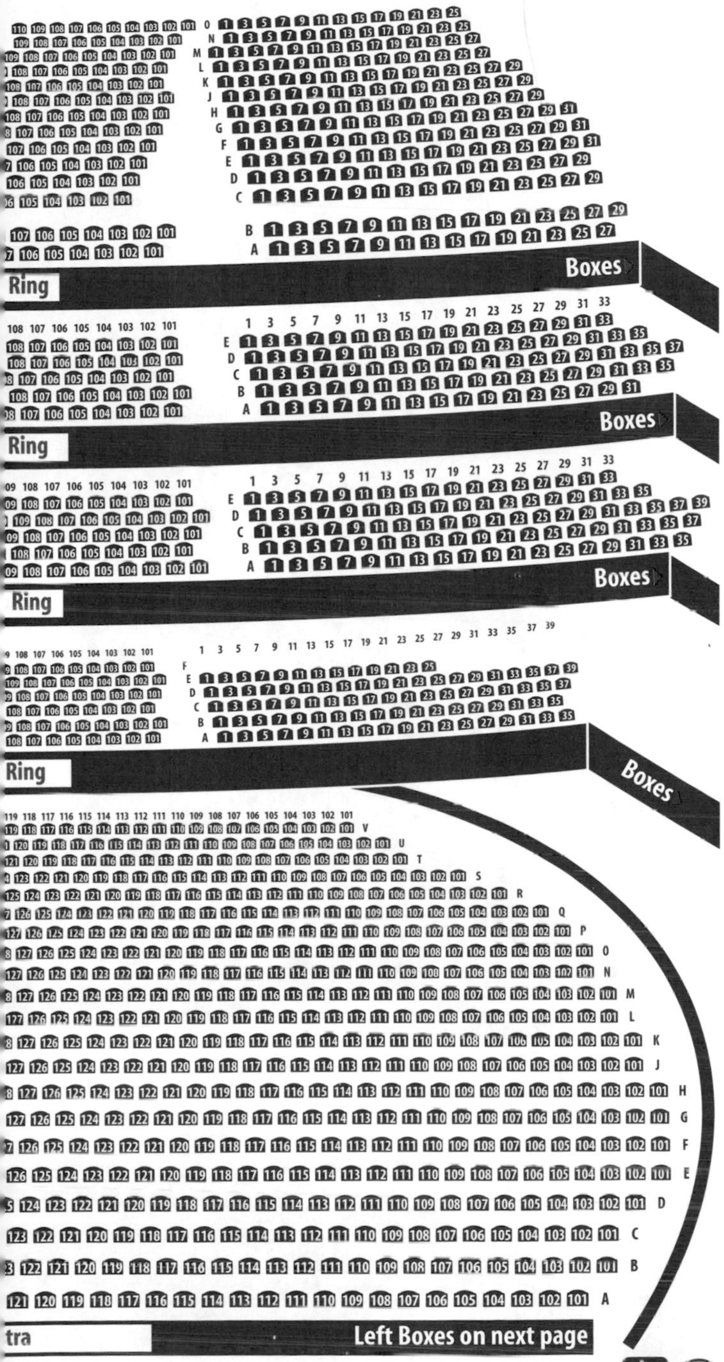

Boxes
Ring
Boxes
Ring
Boxes
Ring
Boxes
Ring
tra
Left Boxes on next page

See color chart on next page for price categories

Lincoln Center (New York State Theater)

20 Lincoln Center Plaza // New York, NY [at Columbus Avenue & 63rd Street]

Box Office: (212) 870-5570

[www.nycballet.org] [www.nycopera.com]

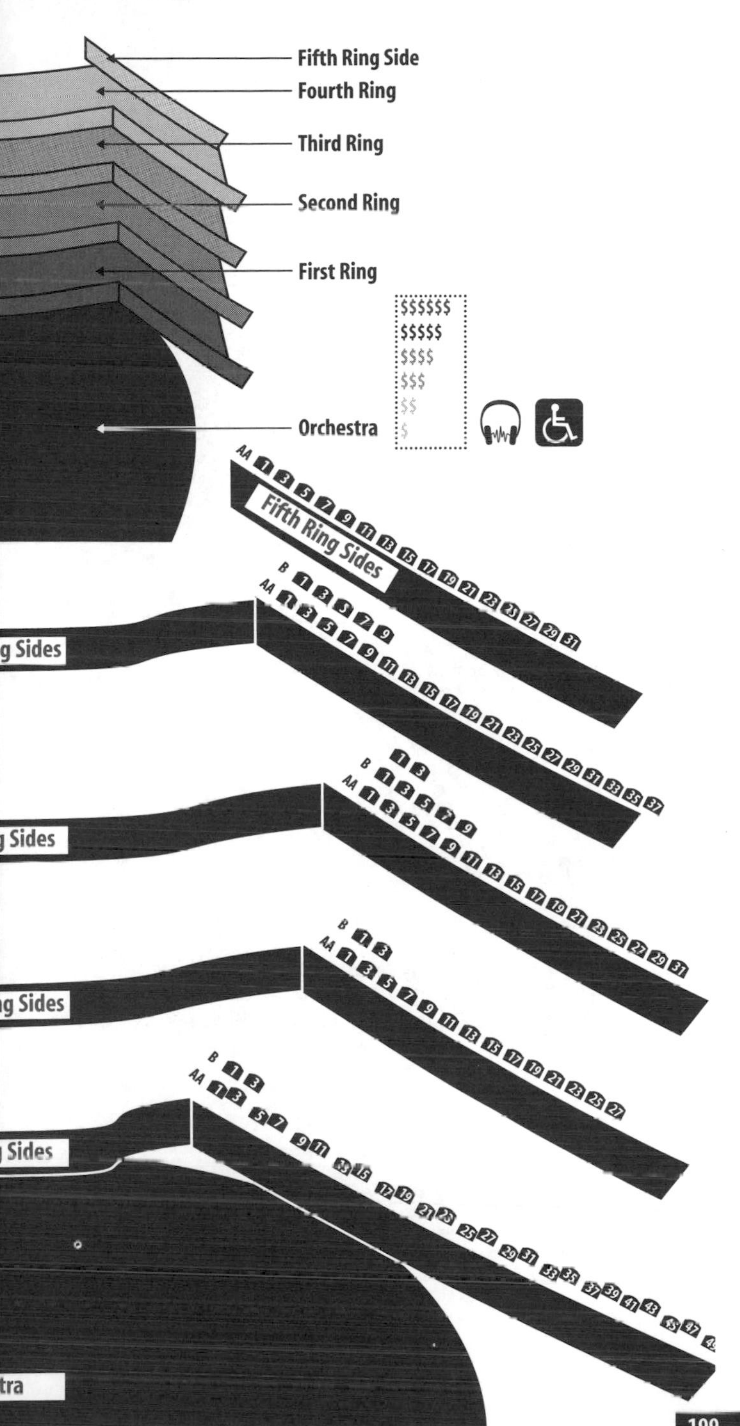
Fifth Ring Side
Fourth Ring
Third Ring
Second Ring
First Ring
Orchestra
$$$$$$
$$$$$
$$$$
$$$
$$
$
Fifth Ring Sides
g Sides
g Sides
ng Sides
g Sides
tra

Lincoln Center (Vivian Beaumont Theater)

150 West 65th Street // New York, NY [between Broadway & Amsterdam]

Telecharge: (212) 239-6200 // Group Sales: (212) 889-4300

[www.lincolncenter.org]

Lincoln Center Park & Lock: West 65th St. [bet. Amsterdam & Broadway]

M5, M7, M10, M11, M66, M104

Lincoln Center Map #89

Loge

Orchestra

Manhattan School of Music

120 Claremont Avenue // New York, NY [between Broadway & 122nd Street]

Box Office:(212) 749-2802 ext. 4428 **[www.msmnyc.edu]**

John C. Borden Auditorium

1 to 116th St. [Columbia Univ.]
Walk North on Broadway to 122nd St.

GMC. 122nd St. [bet. Amsterdam & Broadway]

M4, M104

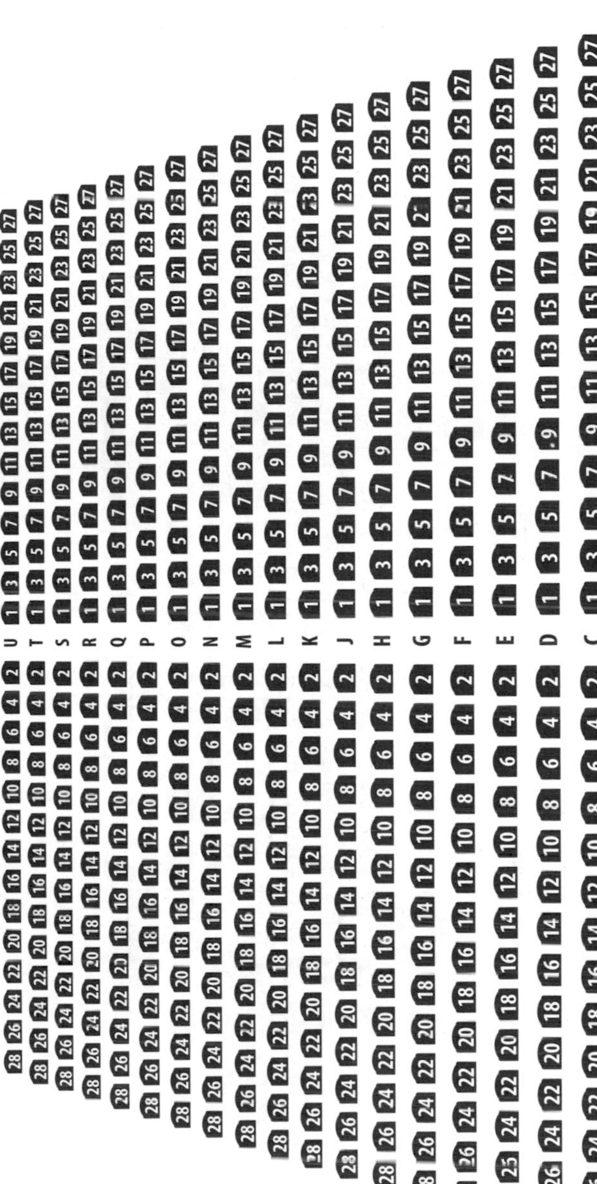

Merkin Concert Hall (Abraham Goodman House)

129 West 67th Street // New York, NY [between Broadway & Amsterdam]

Box Office: (212) 501-3330 [www.ekcc.org]

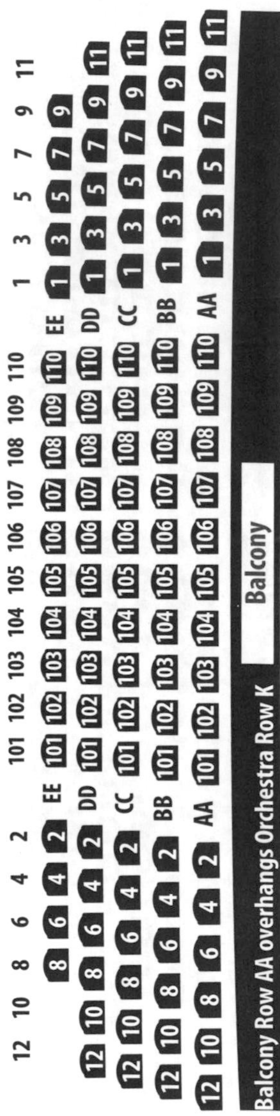

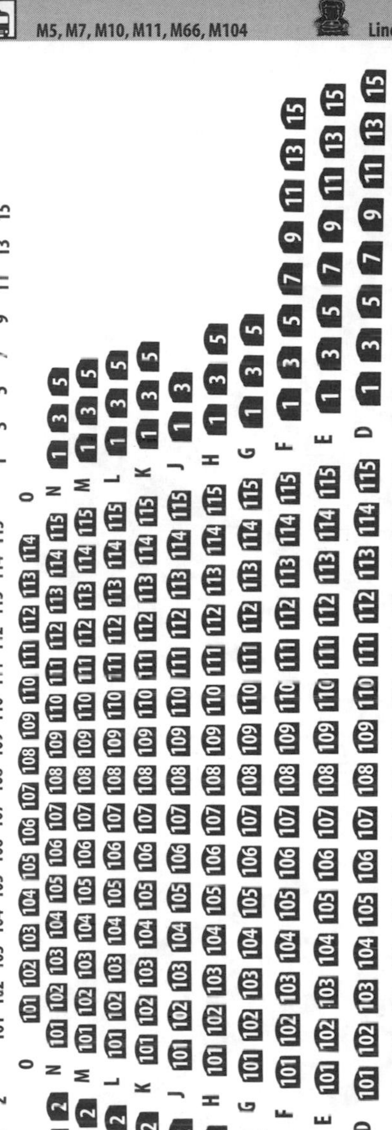
Orchestra

NJPAC (Prudential Hall)

One Center Street // Newark, NJ

Box Office: (888) GO-NJPAC Group Sales: (800) 223-7565

[www.njpac.org]

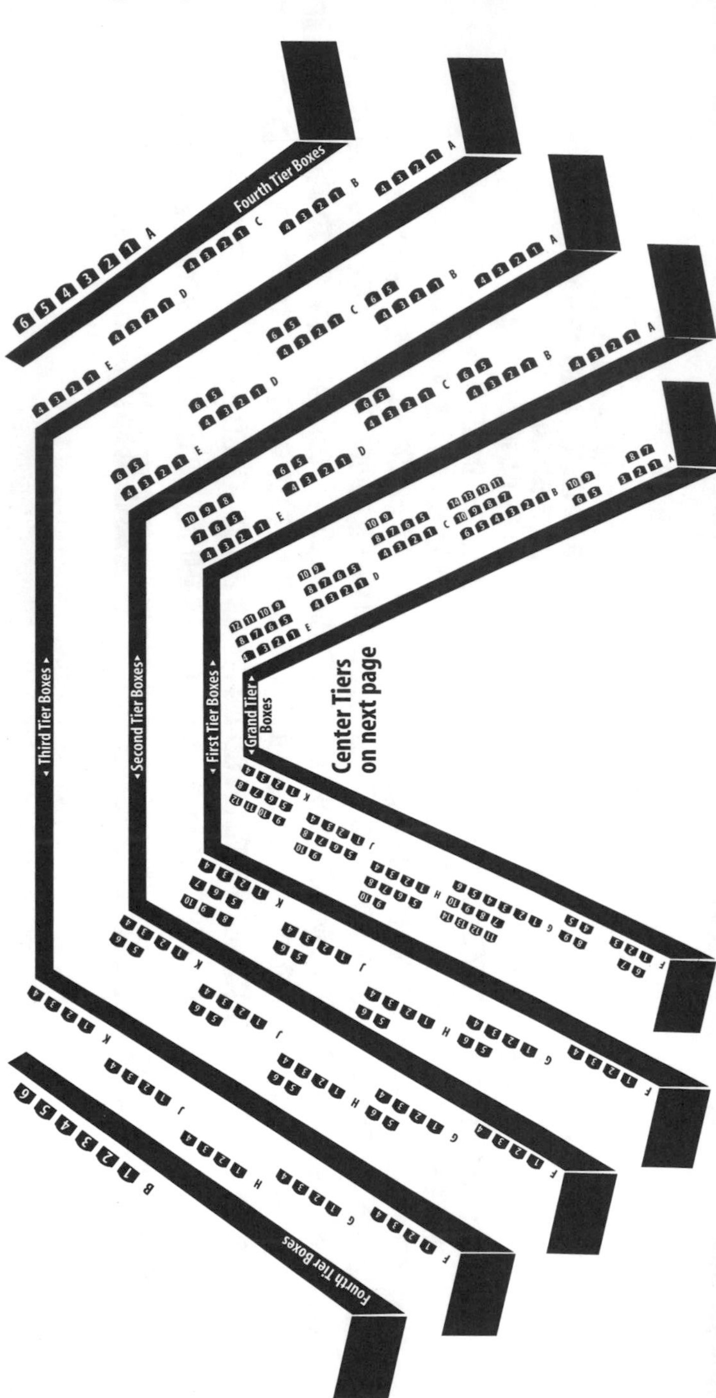

NJ Tpke South to Exit 15W [Rte. 280] to Exit 15A to Rte. 21 South

Garage: Under Military Park [across from NJPAC]

PATH Train to Newark's Penn Station and Loop Bus to NJPAC

Orchestra

NJPAC (Prudential Hall)

One Center Street // Newark, NJ

Box Office: (888) GO-NJPAC   Group Sales: (800) 223-7565

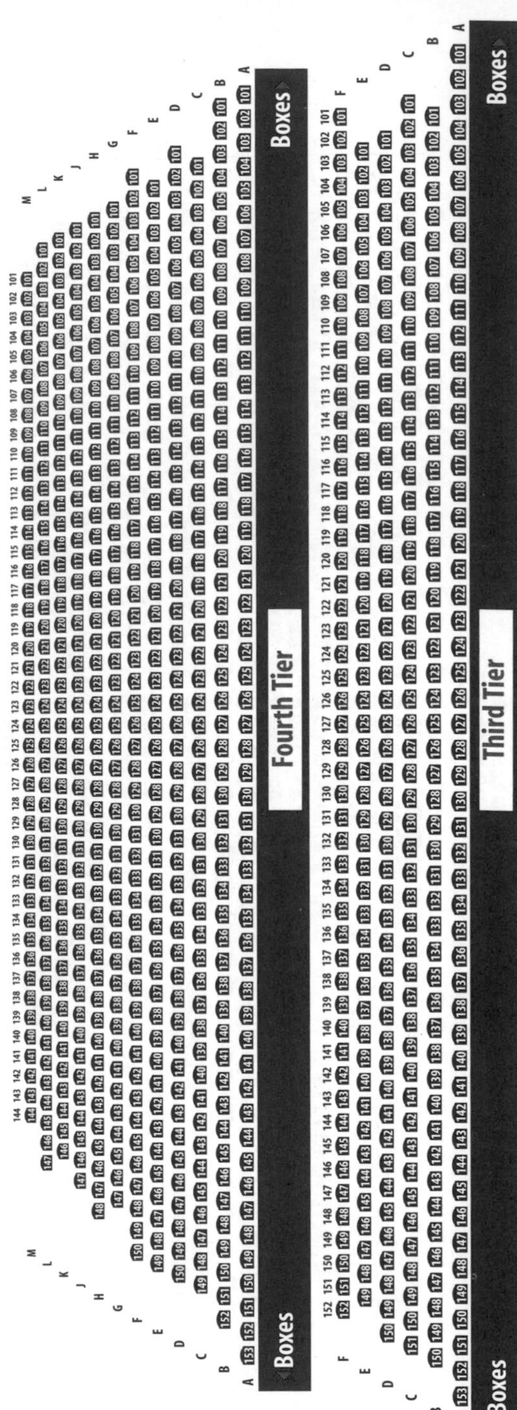

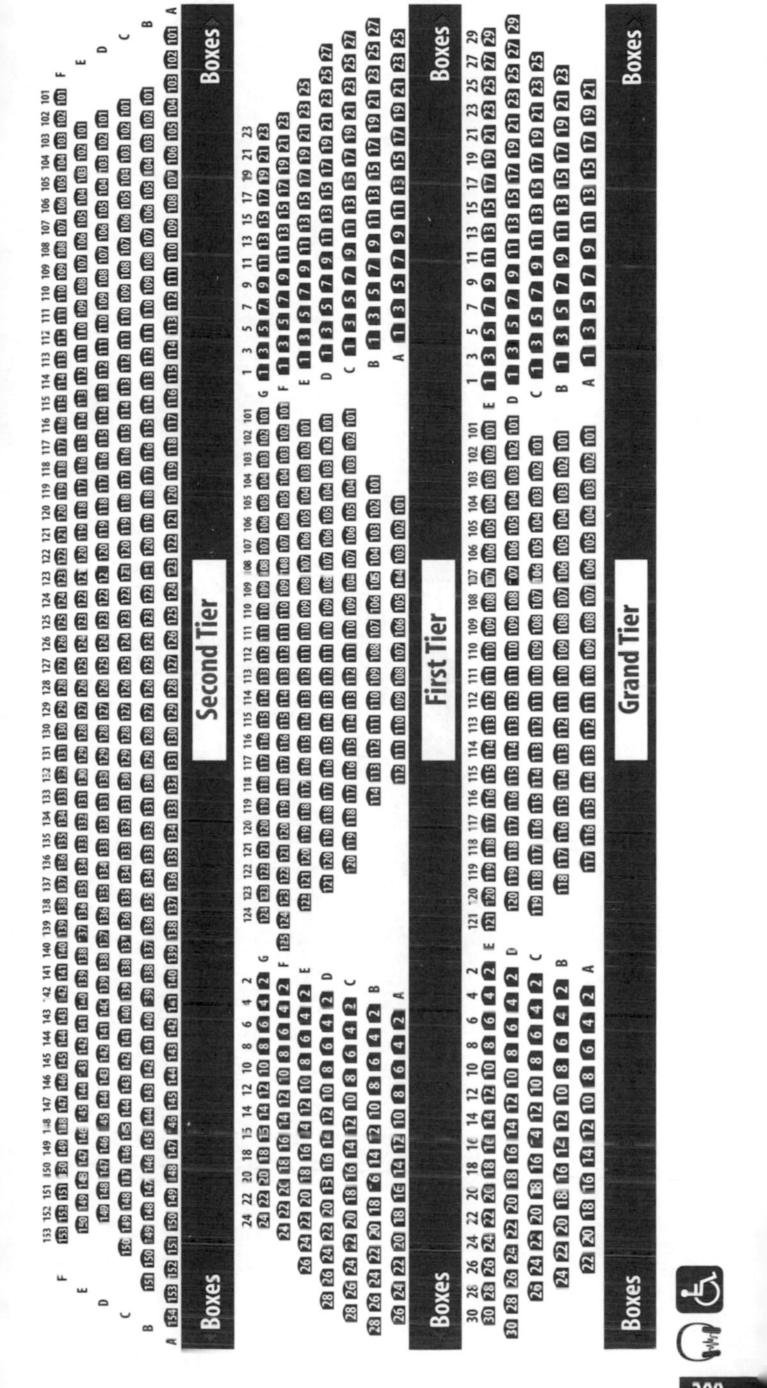

Boxes

Second Tier

Boxes

Boxes

First Tier

Boxes

Boxes

Grand Tier

Boxes

PNC Bank Arts Center

Telegraph Hill // Holmdel, NJ

Ticketmaster: [201] 507-8900

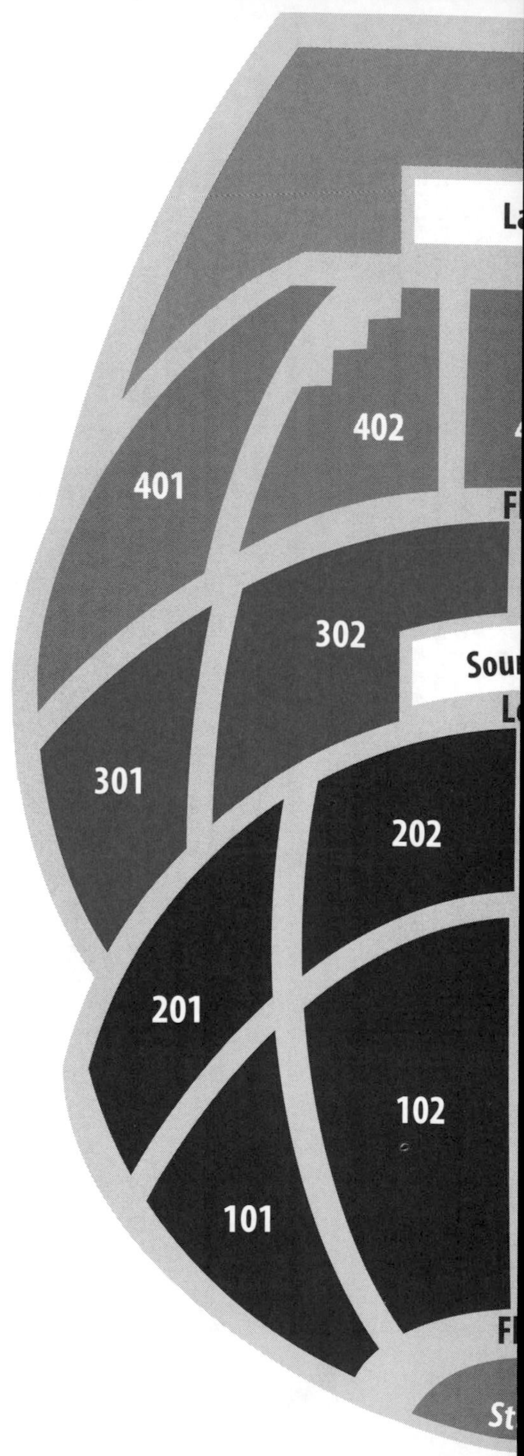

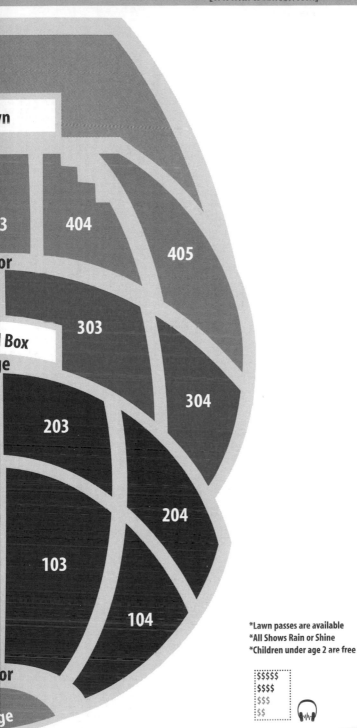

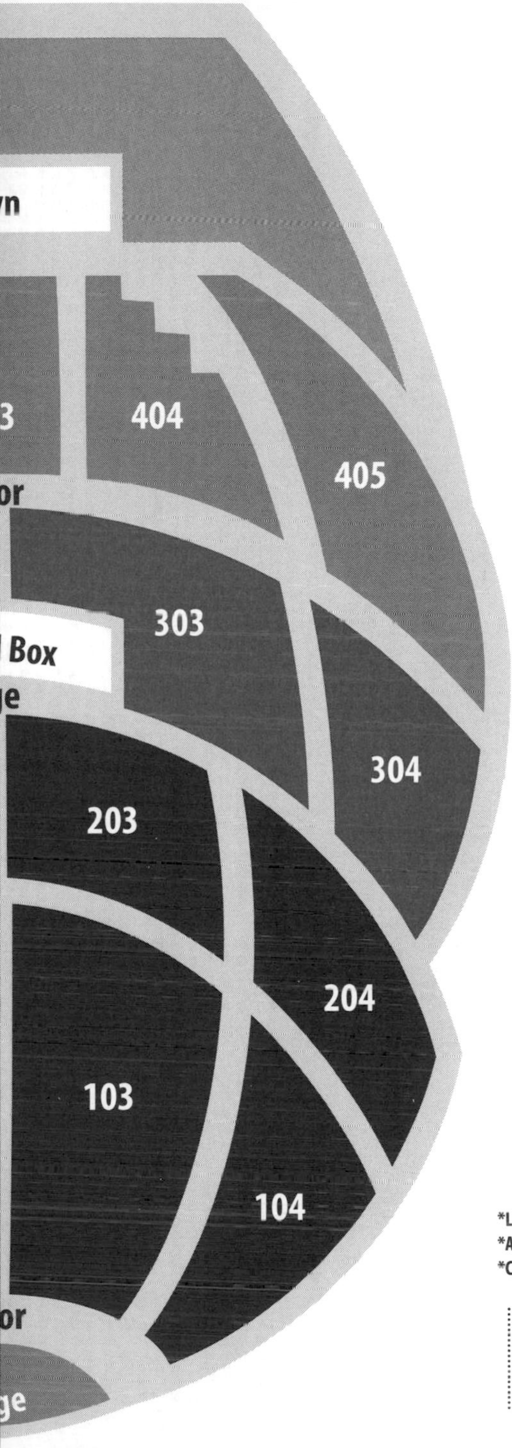

*Lawn passes are available
*All Shows Rain or Shine
*Children under age 2 are free

$$$$$
$$$$
$$$
$$

Radio City Music Hall

1260 Avenue of Americas // New York, NY [at 50th Street]

Ticketmaster: (212) 307-7171 // Group Sales: (212) 265-6100

[www.radiocity.com]

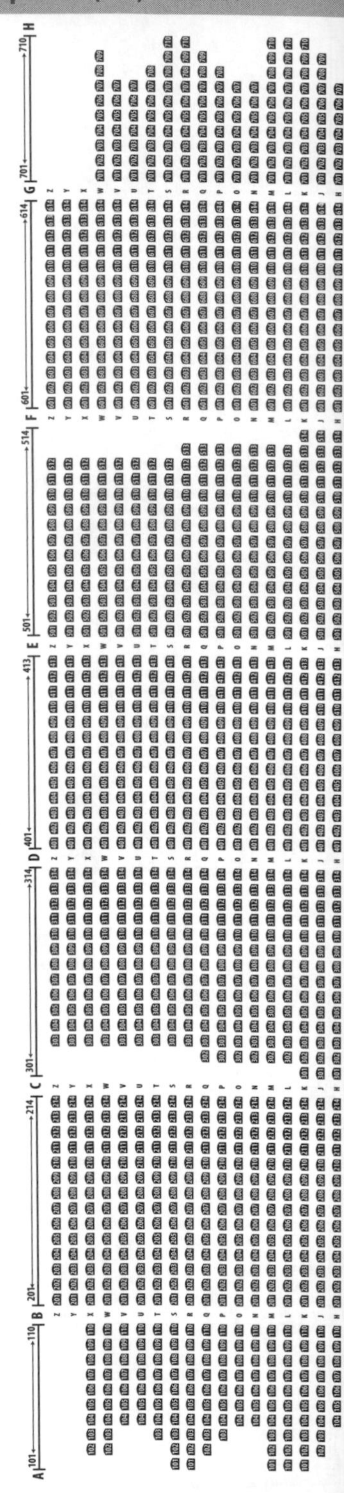

B,D,F to 50th St. [Rockefeller Center]

GMC: 218 W. 50th St. [bet. Broadway & 8th Ave.]
Kinney: 155 W. 48th St. [bet. 6th & 7th St.]

M5, M6, M7, M27, M50

Midtown Map #43

Orchestra

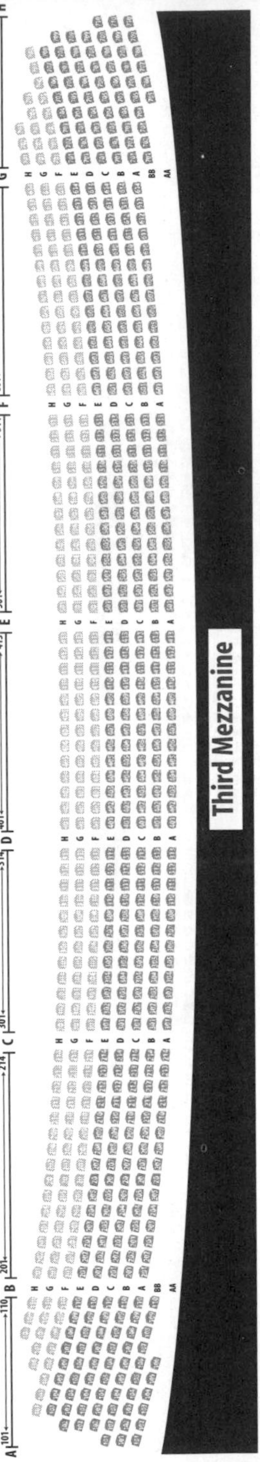

Radio City Music Hall (Upper Levels)

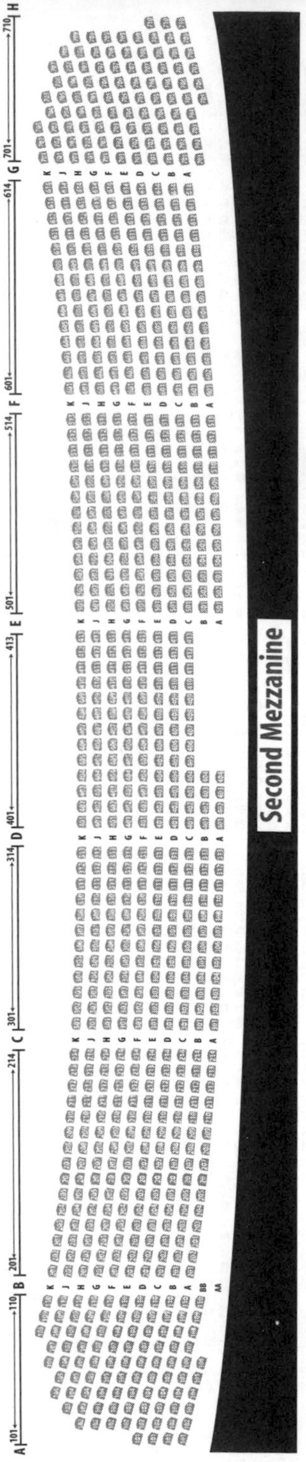

Third Mezzanine

Second Mezzanine

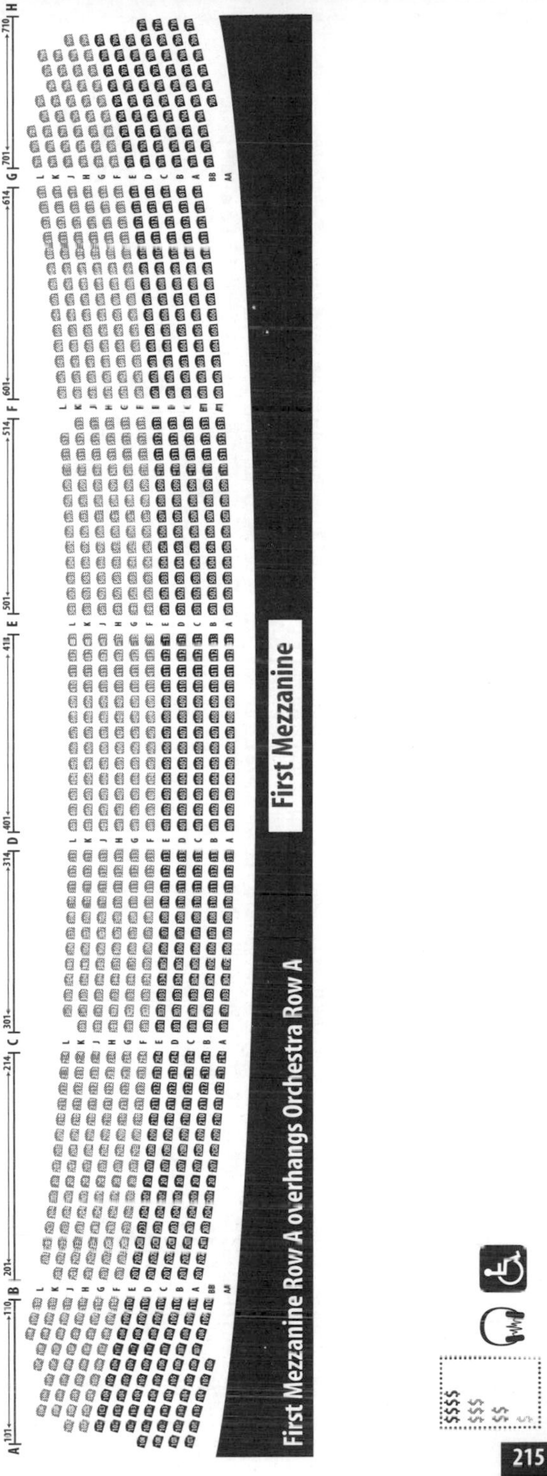

A 101–110 B 201–214 C 301–314 D 401–418 E 501–514 F 601–614 G 701–710 H

First Mezzanine Row A overhangs Orchestra Row A

First Mezzanine

$$$$
$$$
$$
$

Staller Center for the Arts

State University of New York // Stony Brook, NY

Box Office: (631) 632-ARTS

Stage

Main Stage

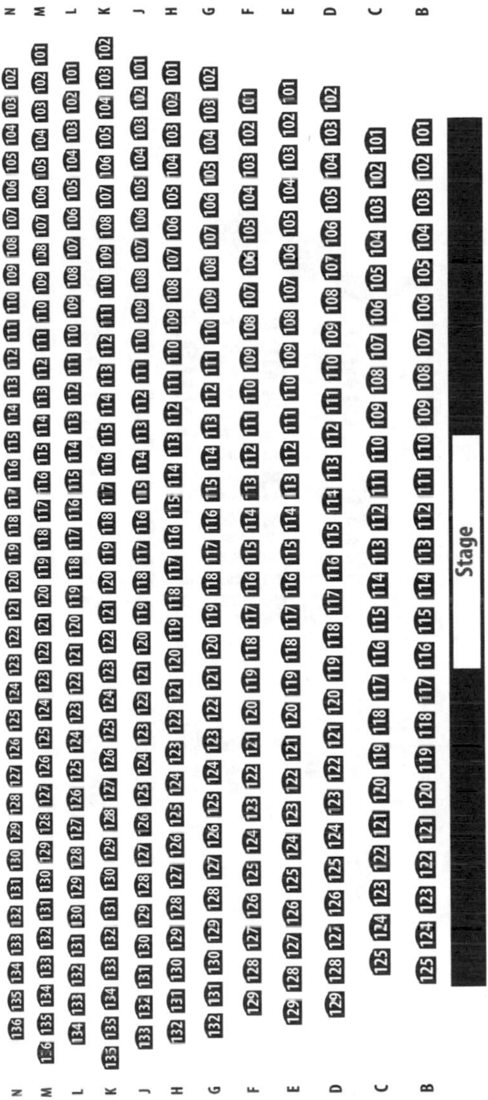

Stage

Recital Hall

2537 Broadway // New York, NY [corner of 95th Street]

Box Office: (212) 864-5400 // Group Sales: (212) 864-1414 ext. 220

[www.symphonyspace.org]

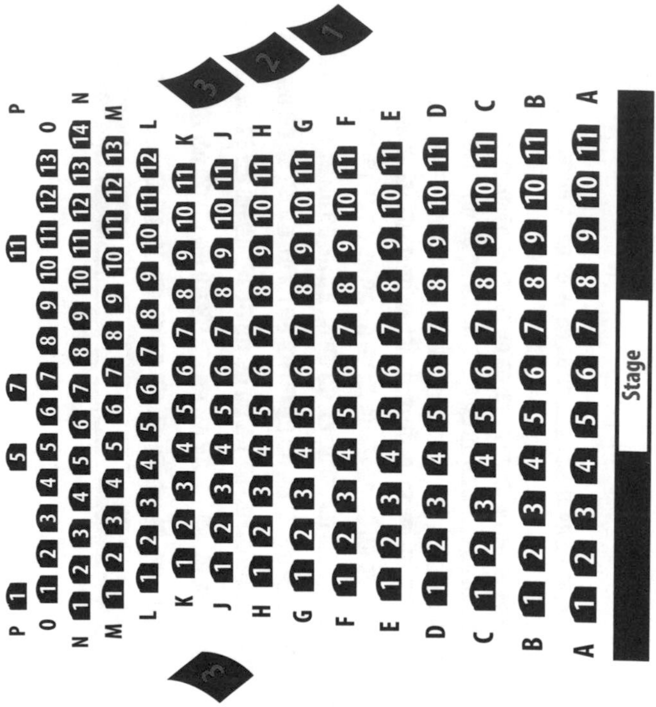

Row	Seats	Row
P	1 5 7 11	P
O	1 2 3 4 5 6 7 8 9 10 11 12 13	O
N	1 2 3 4 5 6 7 8 9 10 11 12 13 14	N
M	1 2 3 4 5 6 7 8 9 10 11 12 13	M
L	1 2 3 4 5 6 7 8 9 10 11 12	L
K	1 2 3 4 5 6 7 8 9 10 11	K
J	1 2 3 4 5 6 7 8 9 10 11	J
H	1 2 3 4 5 6 7 8 9 10 11	H
G	1 2 3 4 5 6 7 8 9 10 11	G
F	1 2 3 4 5 6 7 8 9 10 11	F
E	1 2 3 4 5 6 7 8 9 10 11	E
D	1 2 3 4 5 6 7 8 9 10 11	D
C	1 2 3 4 5 6 7 8 9 10 11	C
B	1 2 3 4 5 6 7 8 9 10 11	B
A	1 2 3 4 5 6 7 8 9 10 11	A

3 2 1

3

Stage

Leonard Nimoy Thalia

B,C,1,2,3 to 96th Street

Kinney: 711 West End Ave. [entrance on 95th St.]
PAO: 214 West 95th St. [bet. Amsterdam & Broadway]

M96, M104, M106

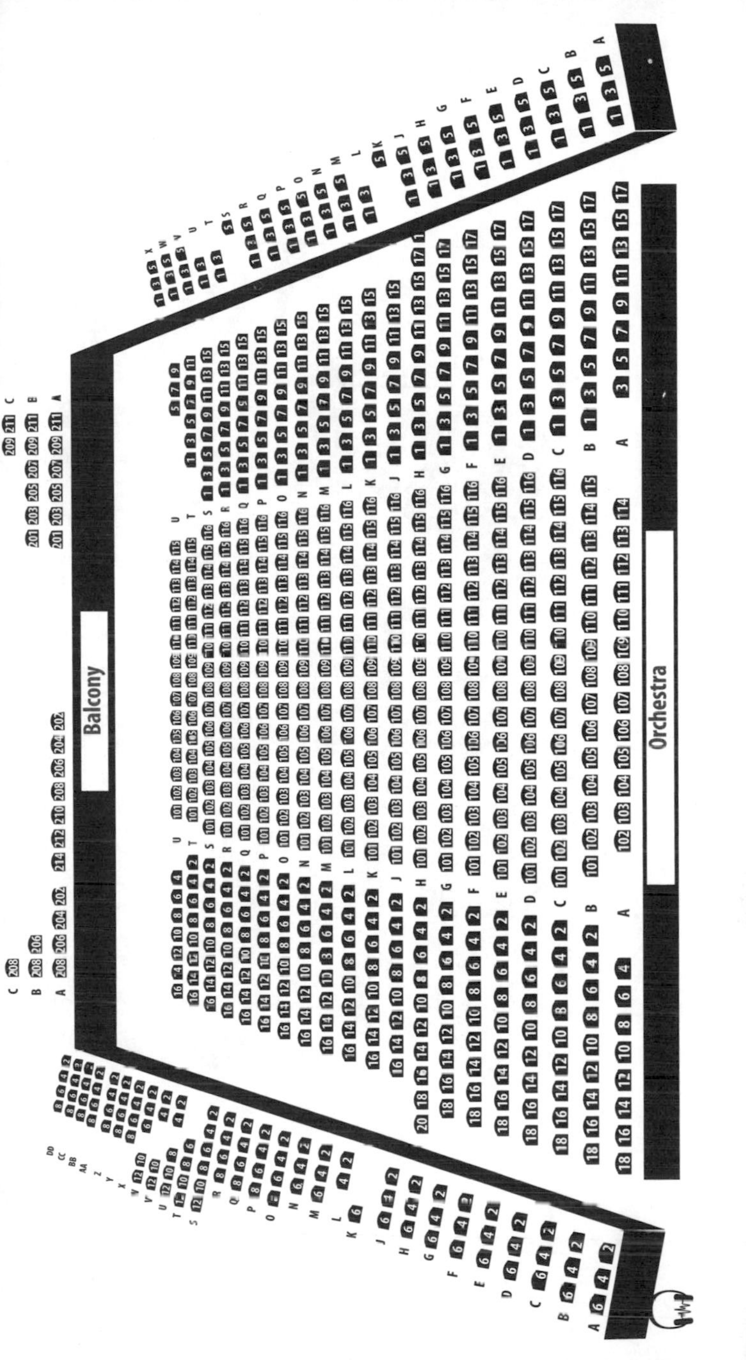

Balcony

Orchestra

Peter Jay Sharp

Tilles Center For the Performing Arts

Long Island University [C.W. Post Campus] // Greenvale, NY

Tilles Charge: (516) 299-3100 **[www.tillescenter.org]**

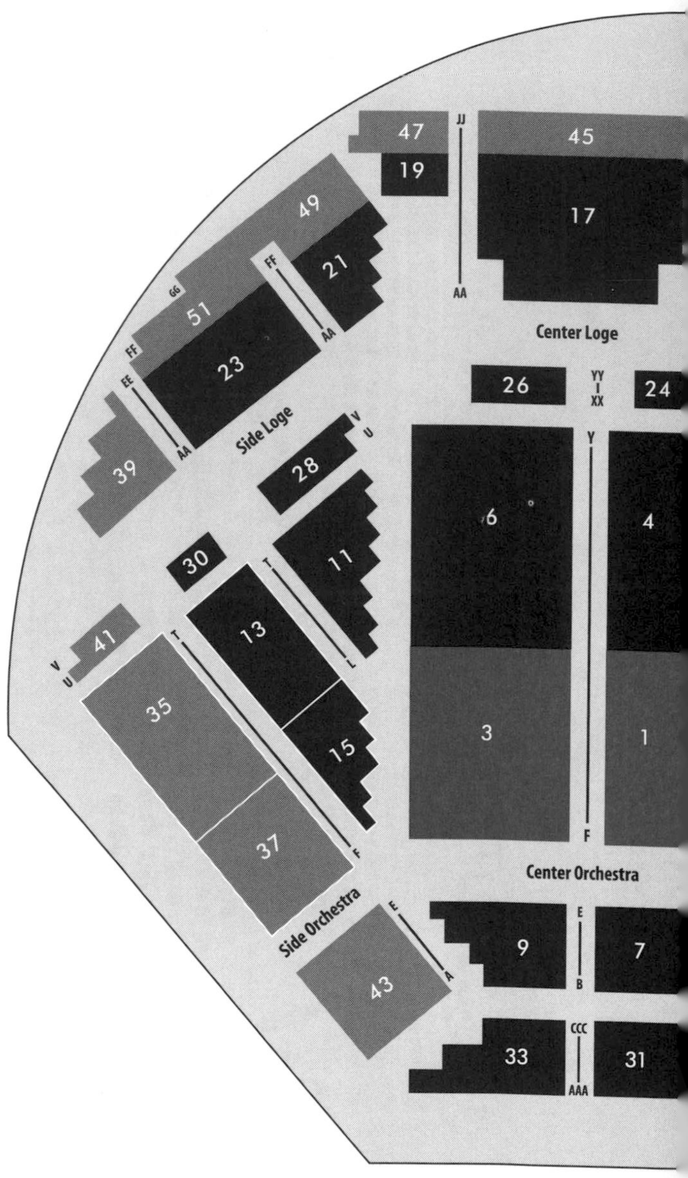

Concert/Orchestra Seating Plan

LIE [495] to Exit 39N, turn right on Rte. 25A
C.W. Post is on the right at the fifth light

Free Parking On Premises

LIRR to Hicksville, Pt. Washington, or Greenvale Station;
Bus service to C.W. Post Campus [Call [516] 822-LIRR for train schedule]

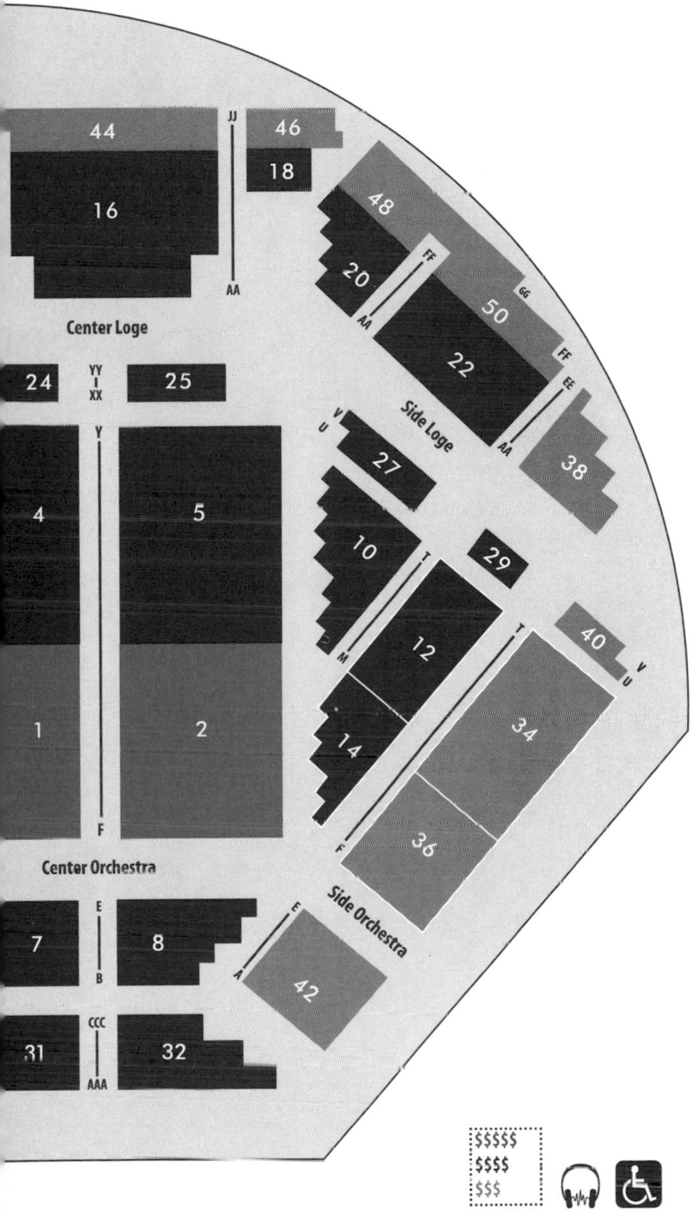

This is the seating plan for:
Concert Series, Orchestral Variations & Grand Duo Miniseries

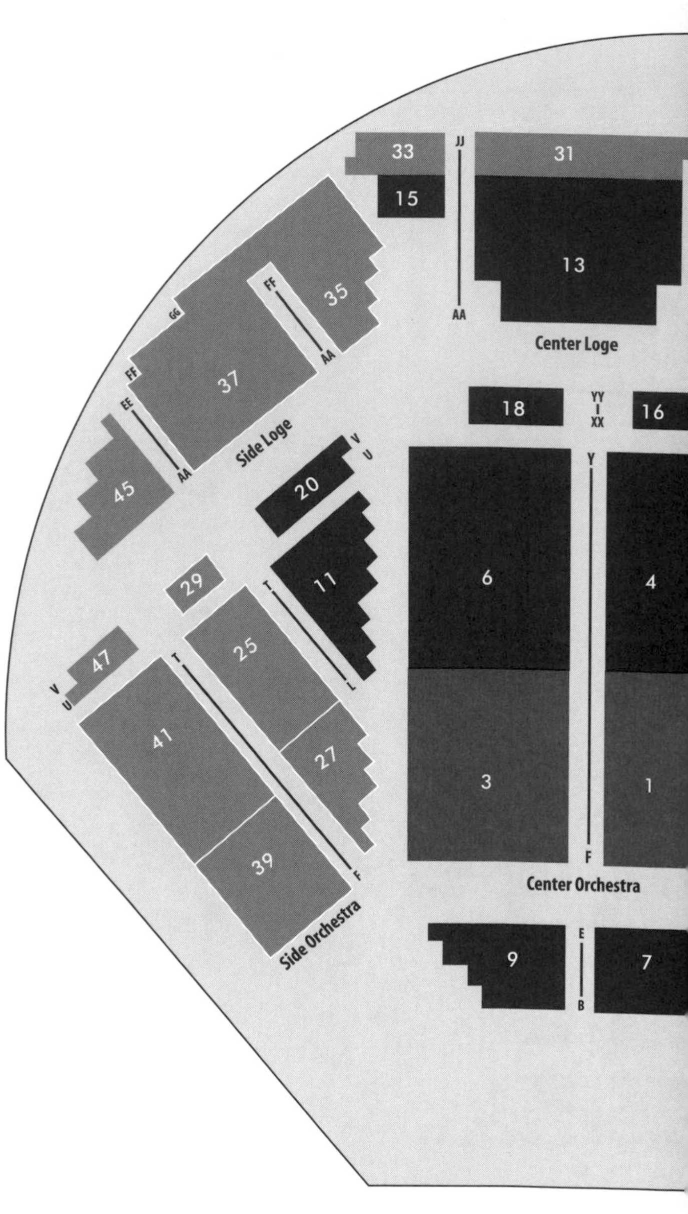

Dance/Broadway Seating Plan

30
JJ
32
14
12
AA
Center Loge
34
FF
AA
GG
36
FF
EE
AA
44
Side Loge
16
YY
XX
17
Y
V
U
19
4
5
10
T
28
24
M
T
46
V
U
1
2
26
40
F
F
38
Center Orchestra
Side Orchestra
E
7
8
B

$$$$$
$$$$
$$$

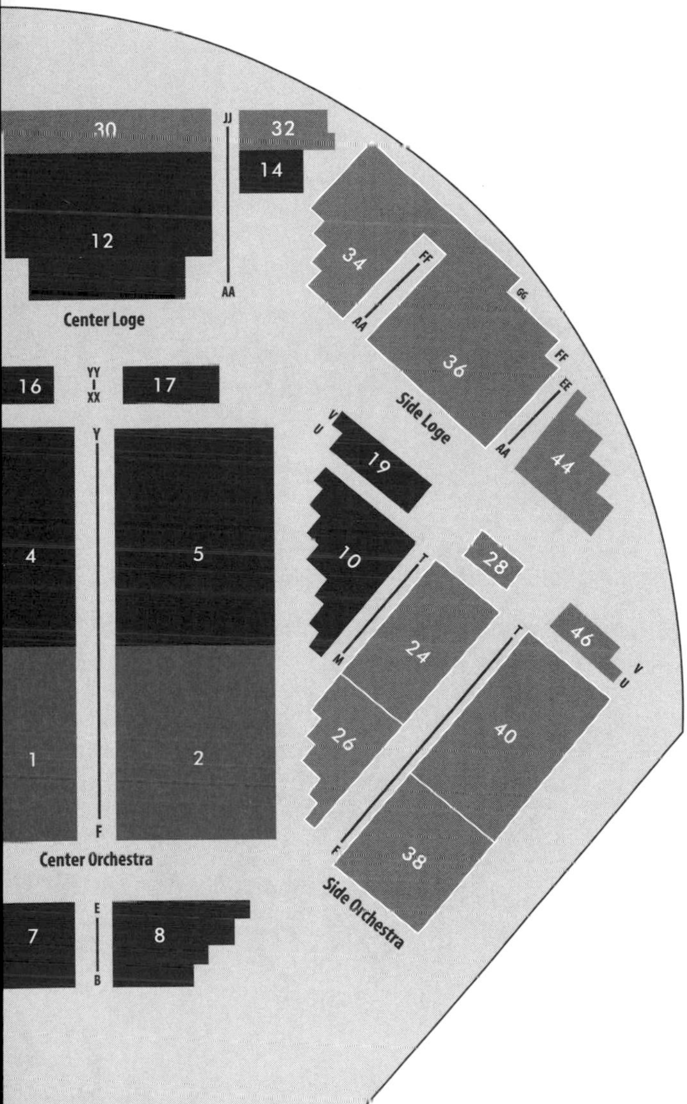

This is the seating plan for:
Showcase, Pall Dance, World Stage, A Night at the Opera, Reckson Jazz at Tilles, Broadway Classics & Specials

Tommy Hilfiger at Jones Beach Theater

Wantagh, NY

Ticketmaster: (212) 307-7171 // VIP AMEX Seating: (212) 307-GOLD

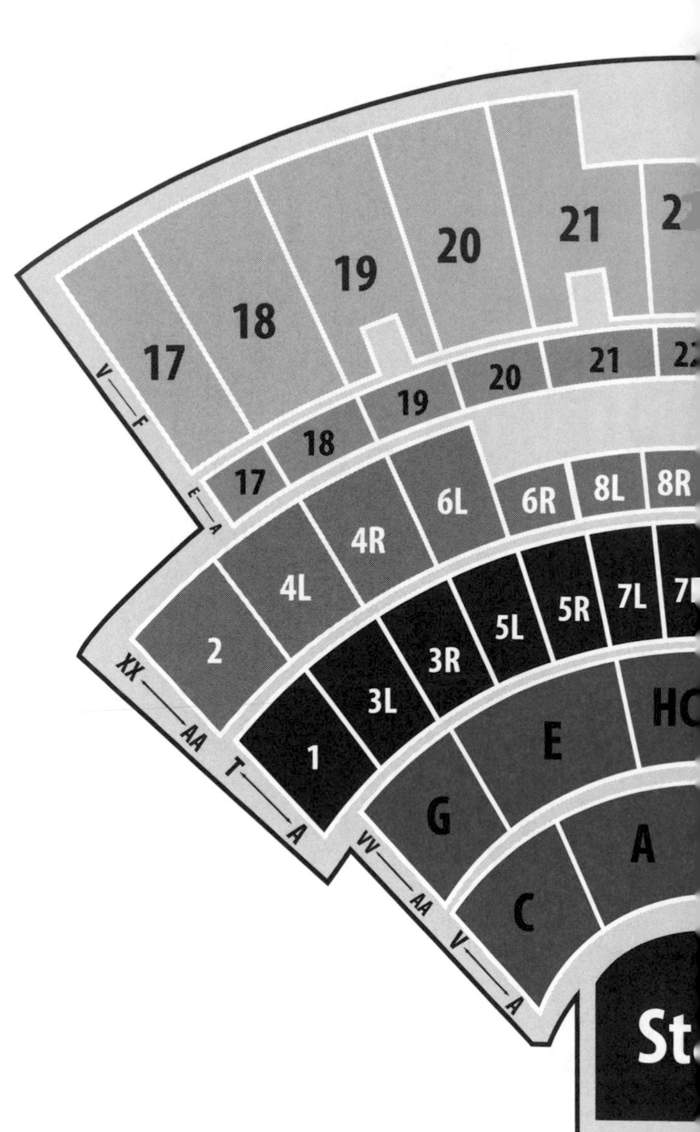

Southern State Pkwy to Wantagh Pkwy South
Follow signs to Jones Beach

Parking on Premises

22 23 24 25 26 27

22 23 24 25 26 27

F—V

A—E

10L 10R 12L 12R 14L 14R 16

9L 9R 11L 11R 13L 13R 15

AA—XX

A—T

HC F H

B D

AA—VV

E—V

ge

$$$$$
$$$$
$$$
$$
$

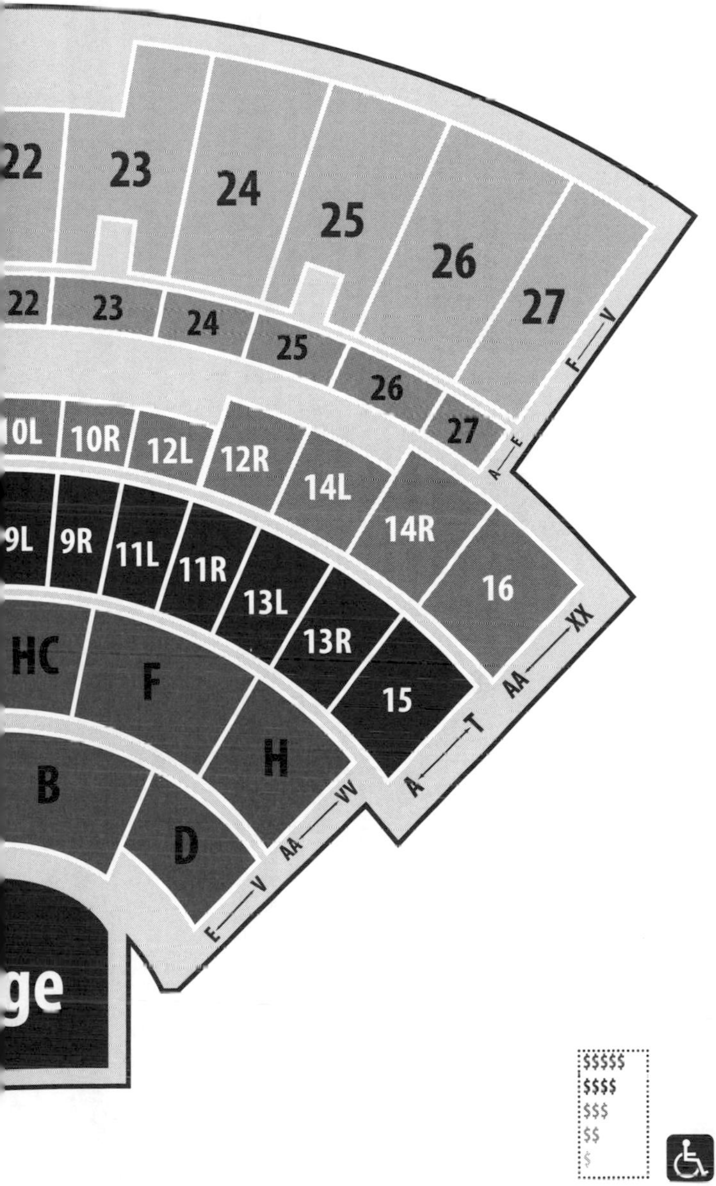

Town Hall

123 West 43rd Street // New York, NY [between Broadway & 6th Avenue]

Box Office: (212) 840-2824 [www.the-townhall-nyc.org]

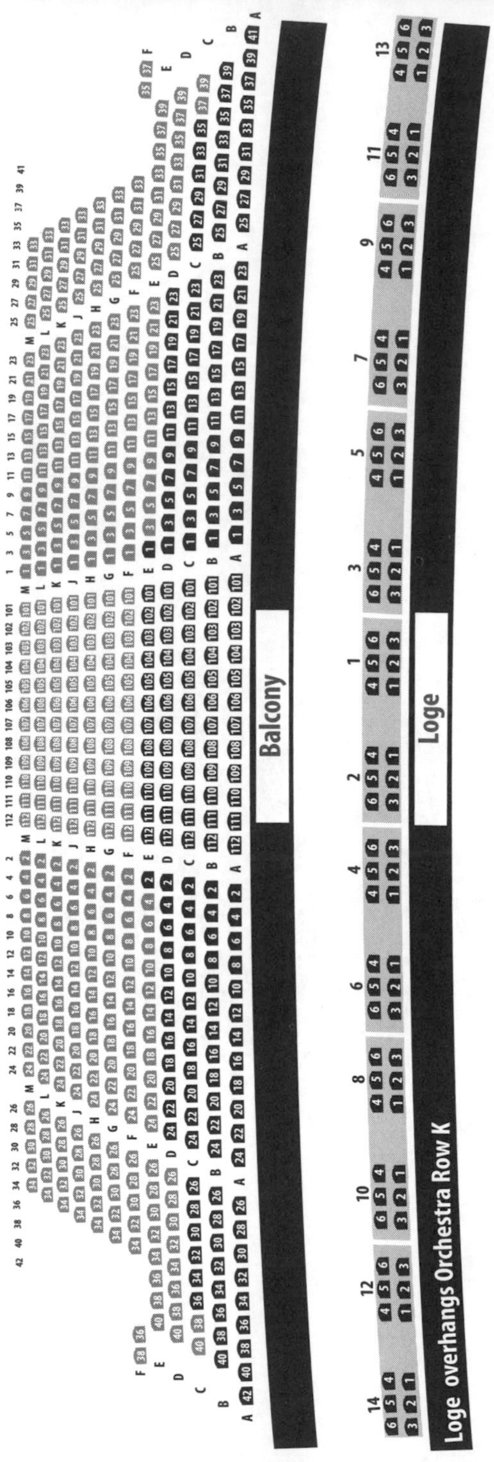

Balcony

Loge

Loge overhangs Orchestra Row K

1,2,3,N,R,Q to 42nd St. & 7th Ave.
A,C,E to 42nd Street & 8th Ave.

Adrana: 250 West 43rd St.
Icon 24hr Parking: 1114 6th Ave. [under Grace Bldg]

M1, M2, M3, M4, M5, M6, M7, M42, M104, Q32

Midtown Map #39

Orchestra

$$$$$
$$$$
$$$
$$
$

Tribeca Performing Arts Center

199 Chambers Street // New York, NY [between Greenwich & West Street]

Box Office: (212) 220-1460 **[www.tribecapac.org]**

A,1,2,3,9 to Chambers Street

Kinney: 50 North Moore St

M1, M6, M10, M22

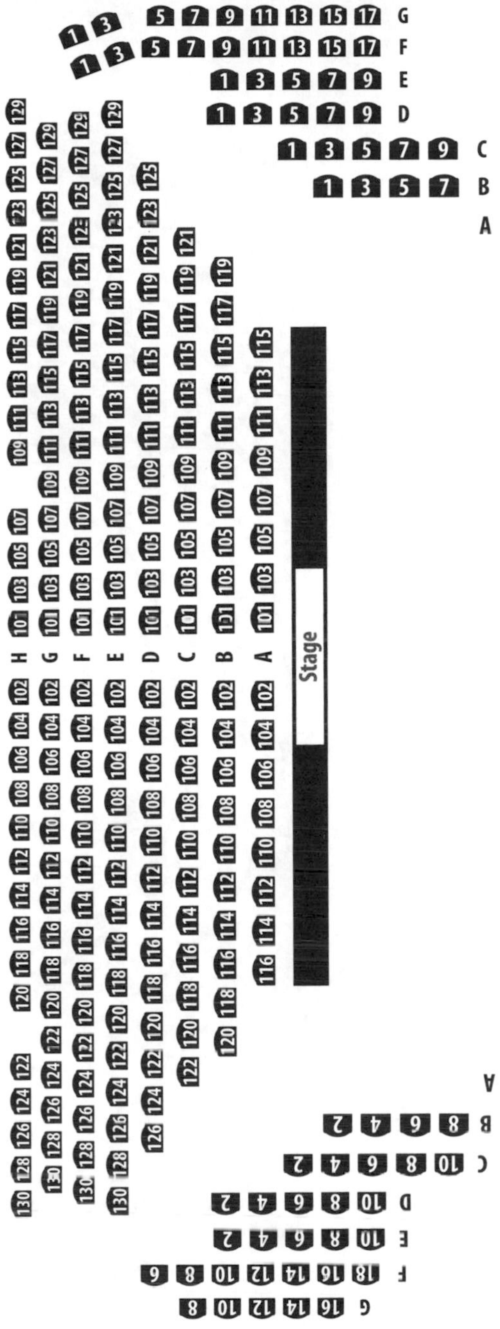

◂Theater One ▴Theater Two

960 Brush Hollow Road // Westbury, NY

Box Office: (516) 334-0800 [www.musicfair.com]

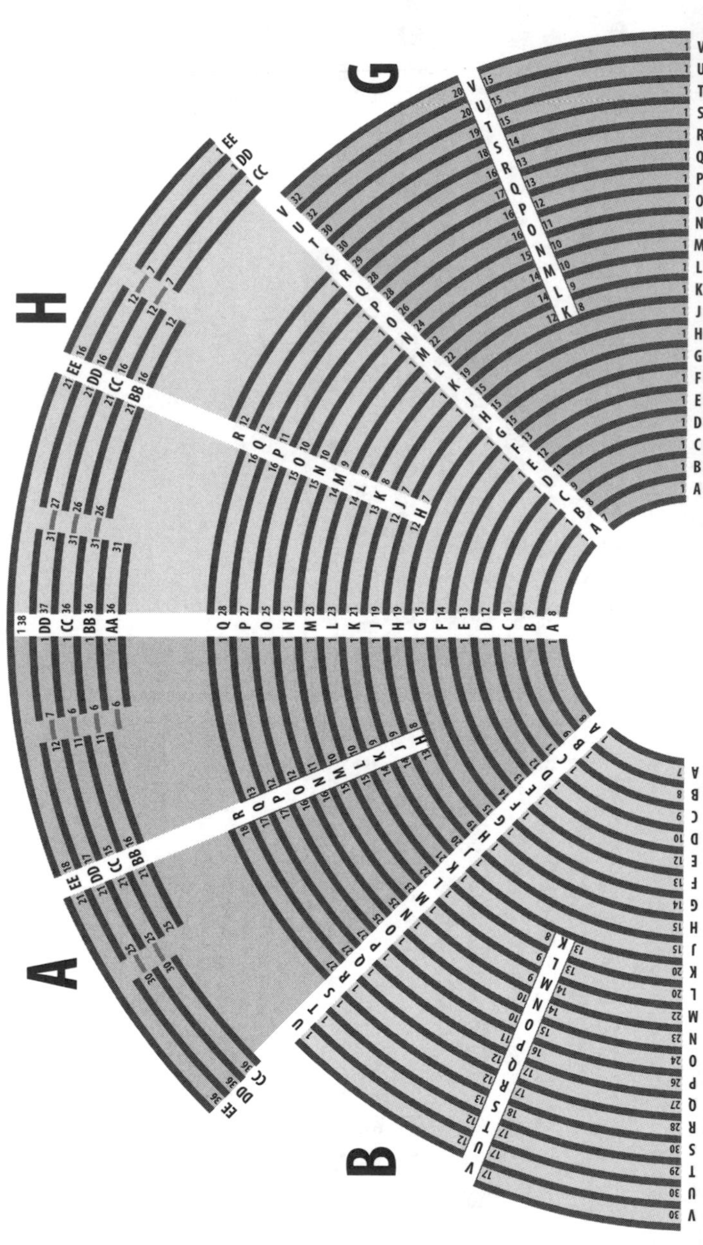

LIE [495] East to Exit 40W [Jericho/Westbury]
Turn right at light; left onto Brush Hollow Rd.

P Parking in ticket price

LIRR to Westbury Station. Cab to theater. [Call [516] 822-LIRR for train schedule]

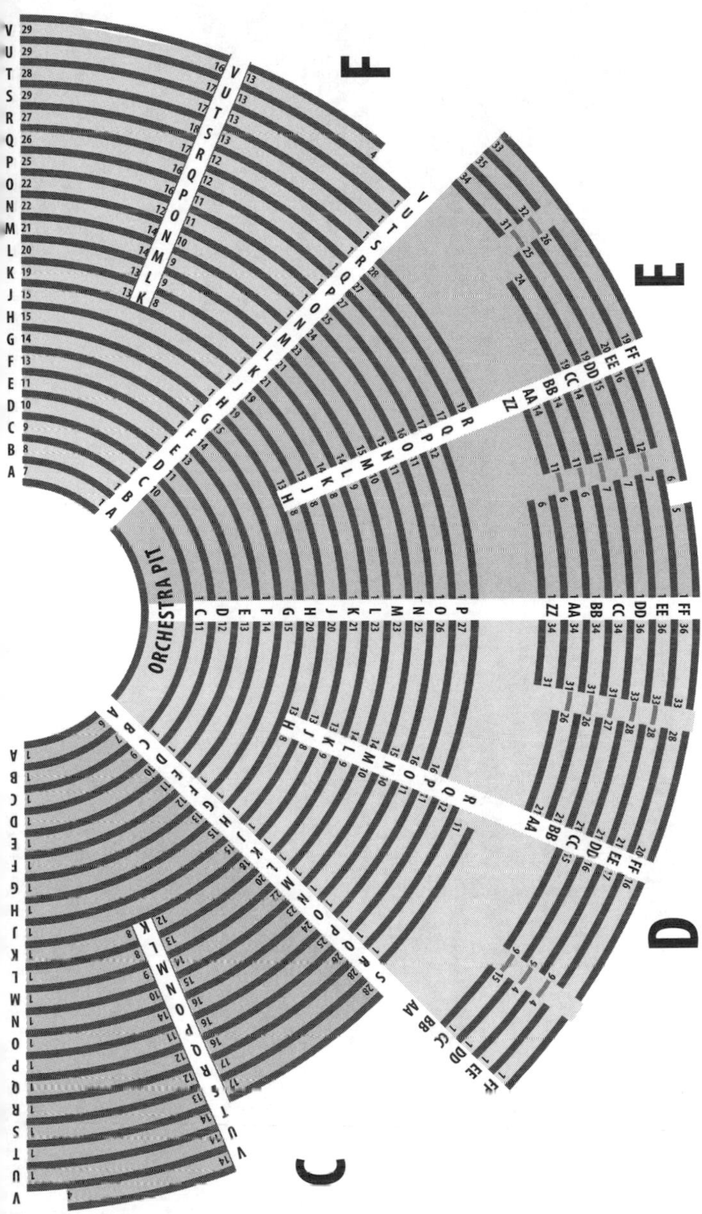

ORCHESTRA PIT

C D E F

stadiums

"There are three things you can do in a baseball game. You can win, or you can lose, or it can rain."

—Casey Stengel

Madison Square Garden
- Boxing in Stadium
- Concerts in Stadium
- Knicks/Liberty Basketball
- Rangers Hockey
- Theater at Madison Square Garden

Meadowlands Sports Complex
- Giants Stadium Concerts
- Giants/Jets Football
- Metrostars Soccer

Continental Airlines Arena
- Concerts in Arena
- New Jersey Devils Hockey
- New Jersey Nets Basketball

Nassau Veterans Memorial Coliseum
- End Stage Concert
- Islanders Hockey

Shea Stadium

USTA Tennis Center
- Arthur Ashe Stadium

Yankee Stadium

Madison Square Garden

4 Penn Plaza // New York, NY [between 31st & 33rd Street]

Information: (212) 465-MSG1 // Ticketmaster: (212) 307-7171

Group Sales: (212) 465-6080 // Disabled Access: (212) 465-6034

[www.thegarden.com]

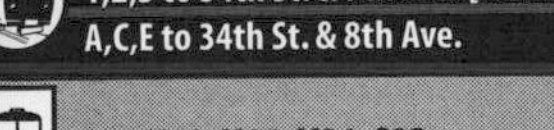

1,2,3 to 34th St. & 7th Ave. [Penn Sta.]
A,C,E to 34th St. & 8th Ave.

Meyers: 324 West 34th Street
Penn Plaza: 1 Penn Plaza [bet. 33rd & 34th St.]

M4, M10, M16, M34, Q32

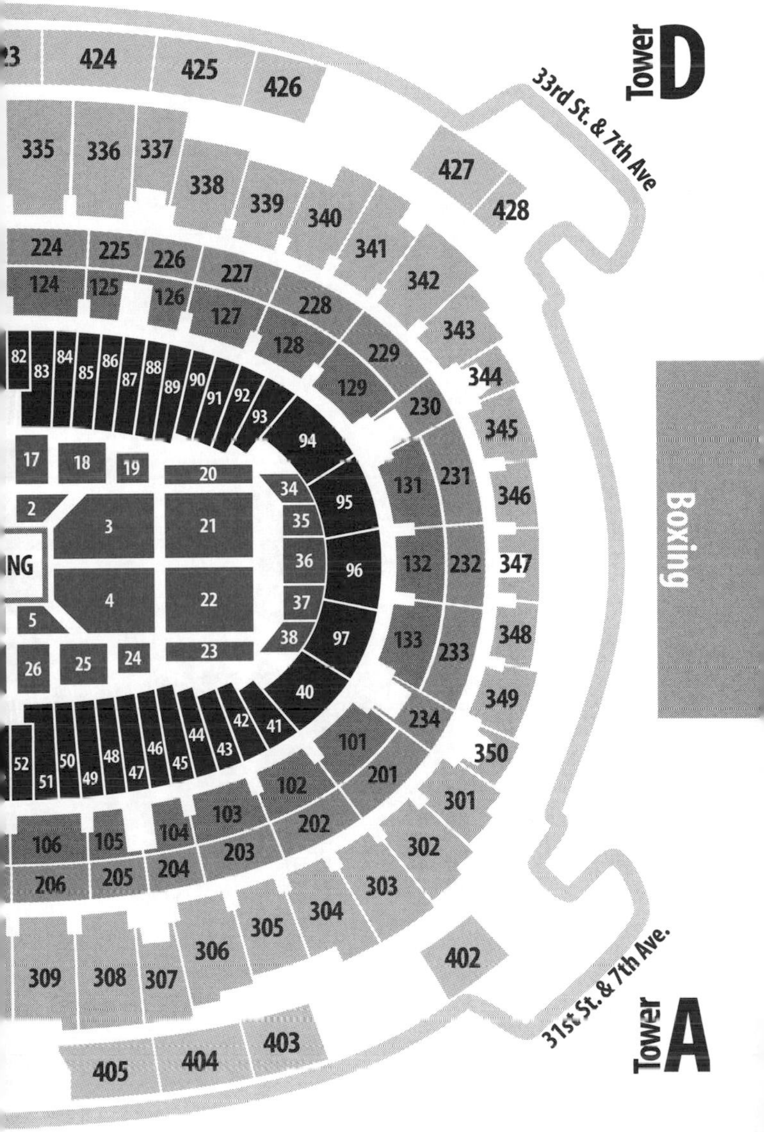

Tower D

33rd St. & 7th Ave

23 424 425 426 427 428

335 336 337 338 339 340 341 342 343 344 345 346 347 348 349 350

224 225 226 227 228 229 230 231 232 233 234

124 125 126 127 128 129 131 132 133

82 83 84 85 86 87 88 89 90 91 92 93 94 95 96 97 40 41 42 43 44 45 46 47 48 49 50 51 52

17 18 19 20 21 22 23 24 25 26 2 3 4 5 34 35 36 37 38

NG

101 102 103 104 105 106

201 202 203 204 205 206

301 302 303 304 305 306 307 308 309

402 403 404 405

Boxing

31st St. & 7th Ave.

Tower A

Madison Square Garden

4 Penn Plaza // New York, NY [between 31st & 33rd Street]

Information: (212) 465-MSG1 // Ticketmaster: (212) 307-7171

Group Sales: (212) 465-6080 // Disabled Access: (212) 465-6034
[www.thegarden.com]

Concerts

1,2,3 to 34th St. & 7th Ave. [Penn Sta.]
A,C,E to 34th St. & 8th Ave.

Meyers: 324 West 34th S[treet]
Penn Plaza: 1 Penn Plaza [bet. 33rd & 34th St.]

M4, M10, M16, M34, Q32

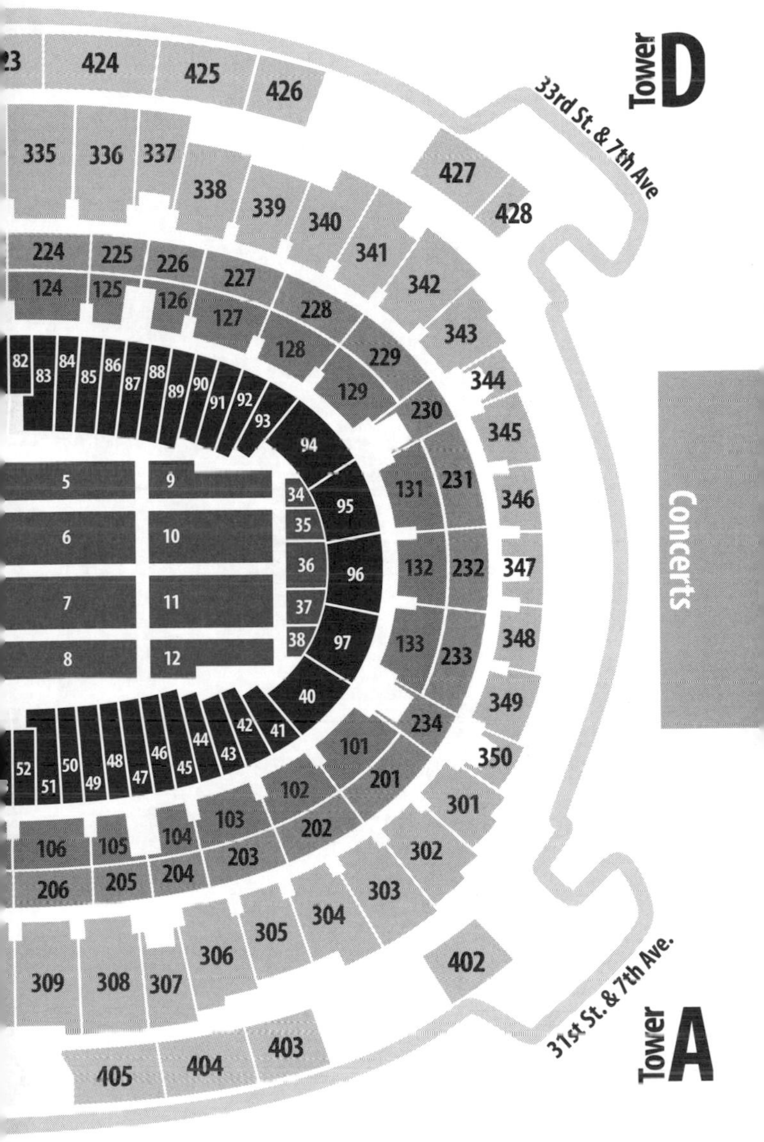

Tower D
33rd St. & 7th Ave

23 424 425 426
427 428
335 336 337 338 339 340 341 342 343 344 345 346 347 348 349 350
224 225 226 227 228 229 230 231 232 233 234
124 125 126 127 128 129 131 132 133
82 83 84 85 86 87 88 89 90 91 92 93 94 95 96 97 40 41 42 43 44 45 46 47 48 49 50 51 52
5 6 7 8 9 10 11 12
34 35 36 37 38

Concerts

101 102 103 104 105 106
201 202 203 204 205 206
301 302 303 304 305 306 307 308 309
402 403 404 405

31st St. & 7th Ave.
Tower A

Floor level configurations are subject to change

Madison Square Garden

4 Penn Plaza // New York, NY [between 31st & 33rd Street]

Knicks Info: (212) 465-JUMP // Liberty Info: (212) 564-WNBA

Ticketmaster: (212) 307-7171 // Disabled Access: (212) 465-6034

[www.nba.com/knicks] [www.wnba.com/liberty]

1,2,3 to 34th St. & 7th Ave. [Penn Sta.]
A,C,E to 34th St. & 8th Ave.

P
Meyers: 324 West 34th Street
Penn Plaza: 1 Penn Plaza [bet. 33rd & 34th St.]

M4, M10, M16, M34, Q32

Madison Square Garden

4 Penn Plaza // New York, NY [between 31st & 33rd Street]

Information: (212) 465-NYRS // Ticketmaster: (212) 307-7171

Group Sales: (212) 465-6080 // Season Tickets: (212) 465-6073

Disabled Access: (212) 465-6034 [www. newyorkrangers.com]

Rangers Hockey

1,2,3 to 34th St. & 7th Ave. [Penn Sta.]
A,C,E to 34th St. & 8th Ave.

Meyers: 324 West 34th Street
Penn Plaza: 1 Penn Plaza [bet. 33rd & 34th St.]

M4, M10, M16, M34, Q32

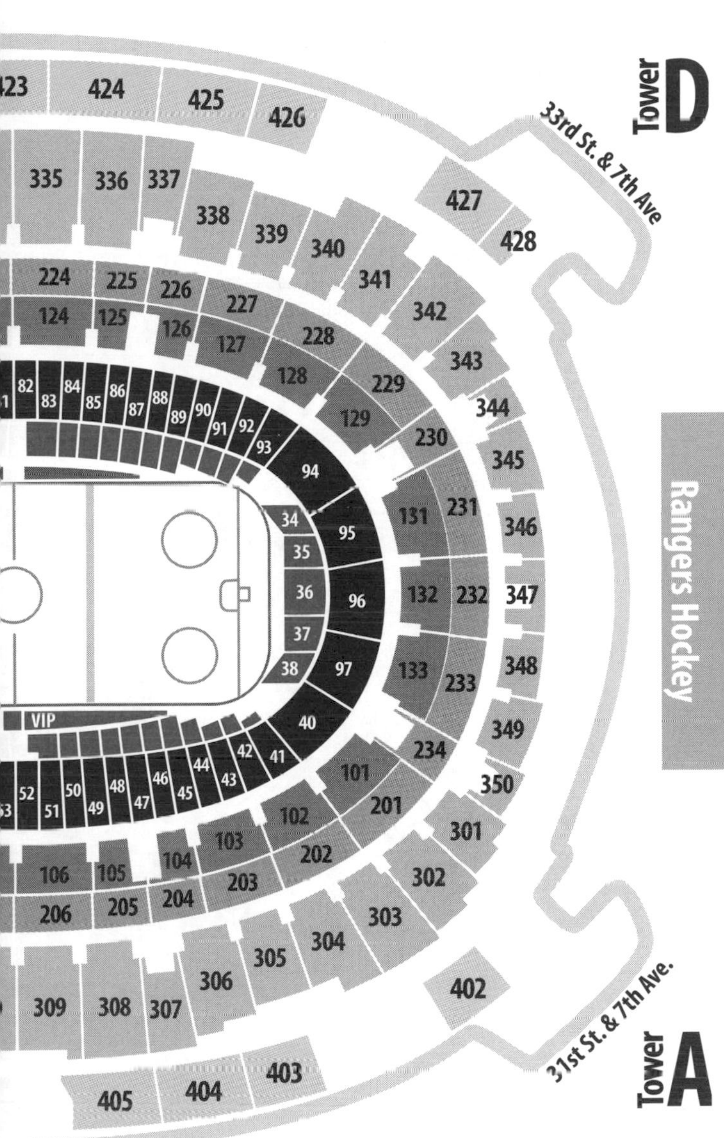

Rangers Hockey

Madison Square Garden (Theater)

4 Penn Plaza // New York, NY [between 31st & 33rd Street]

Information: (212) 465-MSG1 // Ticketmaster: (212) 307-7171

Group Sales: (212) 465-6080 // Disabled Access: (212) 465-6034
[www.radiocity.com]

AISLE A

301

303

305

201

203

205

101

50 Route 120 // East Rutherford, NJ

Information: (201) 935-3900 // Ticketmaster: (212) 307-7171

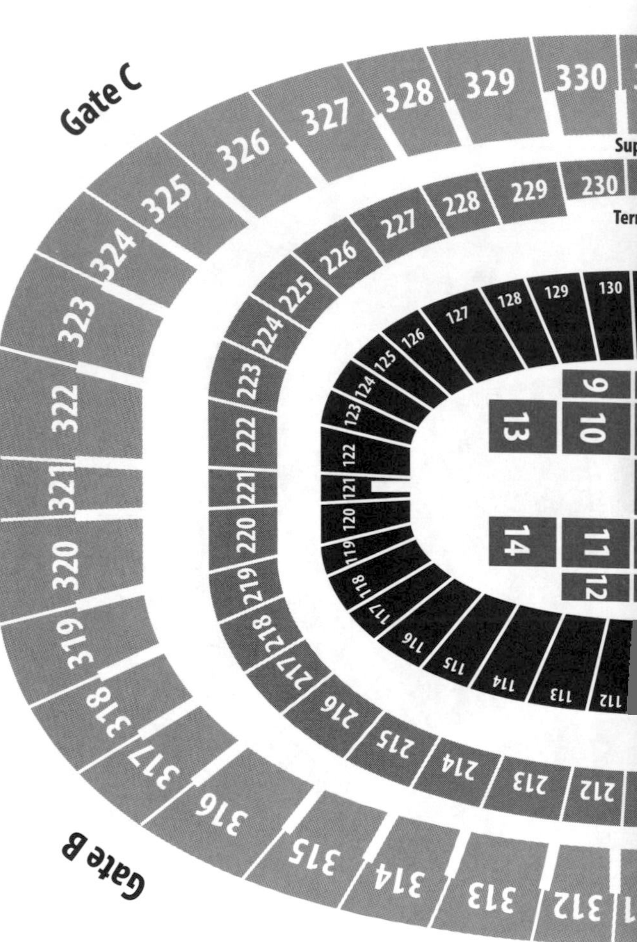

Giants Stadium

NJ Tpke to exit 16W or Lincoln Tunnel to Rte. 3W to Rte. 120N
Garden State Parkway to Rte. 153A to Rte. 3 East

Parking on Premises

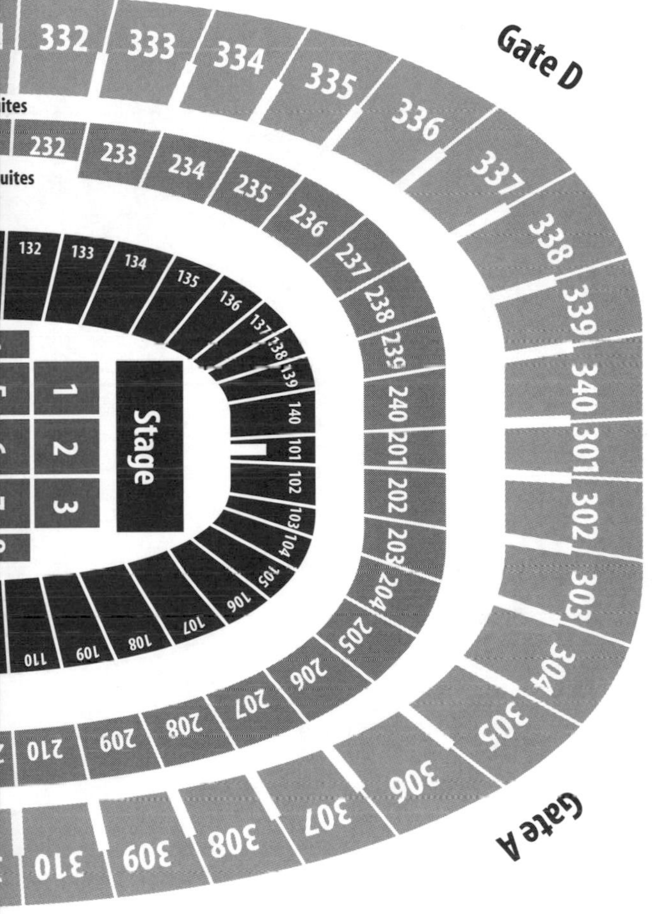

Meadowlands Sports Complex

50 Route 120 // East Rutherford, NJ

Information: (201) 935-3900 // Ticketmaster: (212) 307-7171

Giants Season Tickets: (201) 935-8222 [www.giants.com]

Jets Season Tickets: (516) 560-8200 [www.newyorkjets.com]

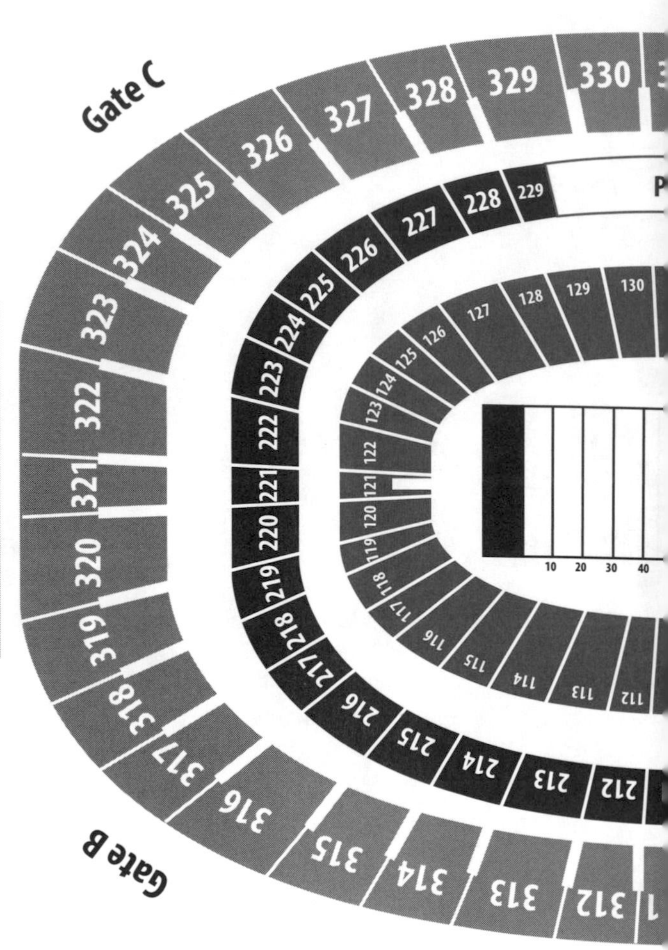

Giants & Jets Football

Giants Stadium

NJ Tpke to exit 16W or Lincoln Tunnel to Rte. 3W to Rte. 120N
Garden State Parkway to Rte. 153A to Rte. 3 East

Parking on Premises

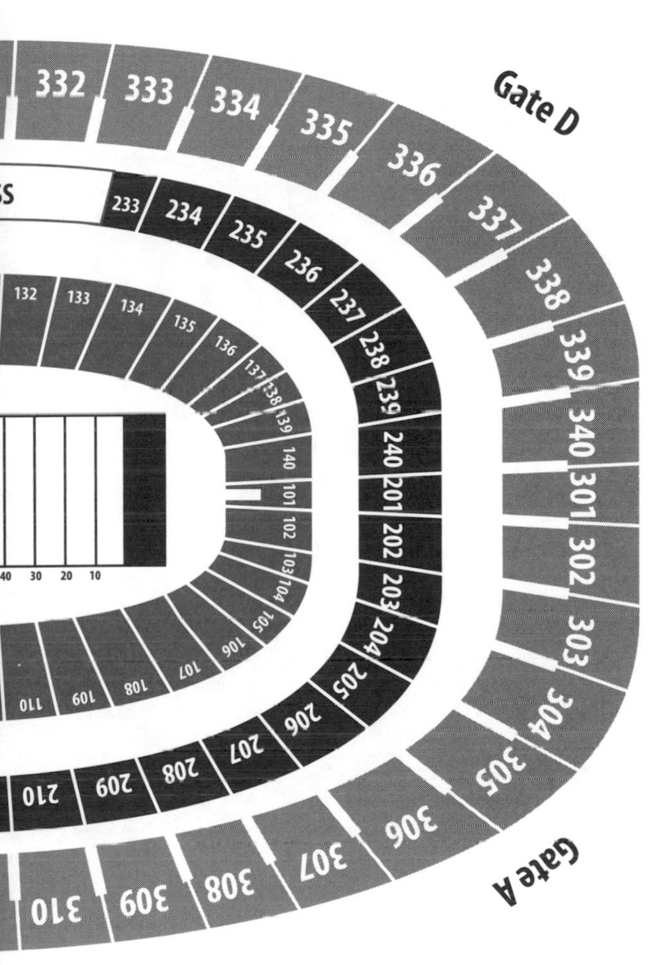

Giants & Jets Football

Meadowlands Sports Complex

50 Route 120 // East Rutherford, NJ

Information: (201) 935-3900 // Ticketmaster: (212) 307-7171

Season Tickets: (888) 4-METROTIX [www.metrostars.com]

Metrostars Soccer

NJ Tpke to exit 16W or Lincoln Tunnel to Rte. 3W to Rte. 120N
Garden State Parkway to Rte. 153A to Rte. 3 East

Parking on Premises

Metrostars Soccer

50 Route 120 // East Rutherford, NJ

Information: (201) 935-3900 // Ticketmaster: (212) 307-7171

[www.meadowlands.com]

Concerts

Continental Airlines Arena

NJ Tpke to exit 16W or Lincoln Tunnel to Rte. 3W to Rte. 120N
Garden State Parkway to Rte. 153A to Rte. 3 East

Parking on Premises

Floor level configurations are subject to change

Concerts

Meadowlands Sports Complex

50 Route 120 // East Rutherford, NJ

Information: (201) 935-3900 // Ticketmaster: (212) 307-7171

Season Tickets: (800) NJ-DEVIL [www.newjerseydevils.com]

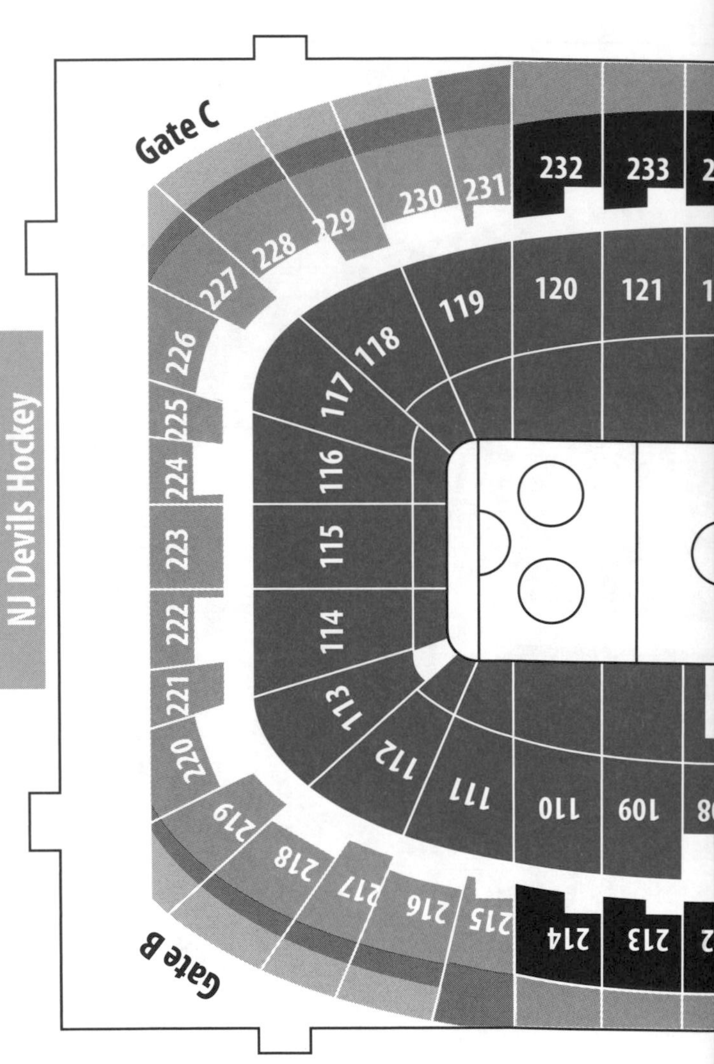

NJ Tpke to exit 16W or Lincoln Tunnel to Rte. 3W to Rte. 120N
Garden State Parkway to Rte. 153A to Rte. 3 East

Parking on Premises

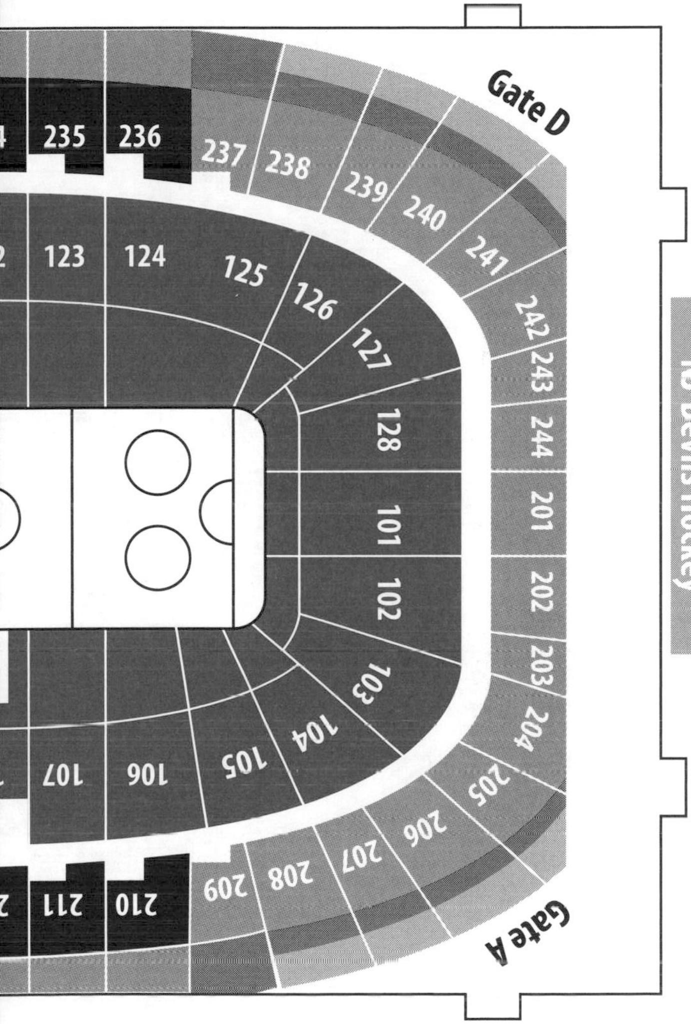

NJ Devils Hockey

50 Route 120 // East Rutherford, NJ
Information: (201) 935-3900 // Ticketmaster: (212) 307-7171
Season Tickets: (800) 7NJ-NETS [www.nba.com/nets]

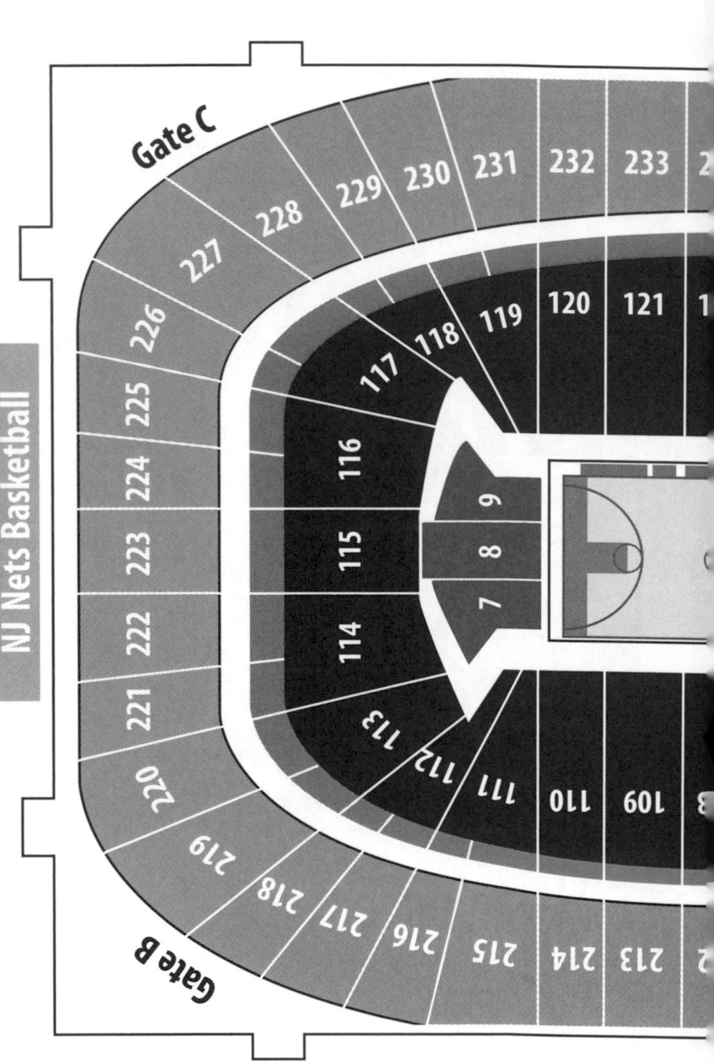

Continental Airlines Arena

 NJ Tpke to exit 16W or Lincoln Tunnel to Rte. 3W to Rte. 120N
Garden State Parkway to Rte. 153A to Rte. 3 East

Parking on Premises

Nassau Veterans Memorial Coliseum

1255 Hempstead Turnpike // Uniondale, NY

Information: (516) 794-9300 // Ticketmaster: (516) 888-9000

[www.nassaucoliseum.com]

Concerts

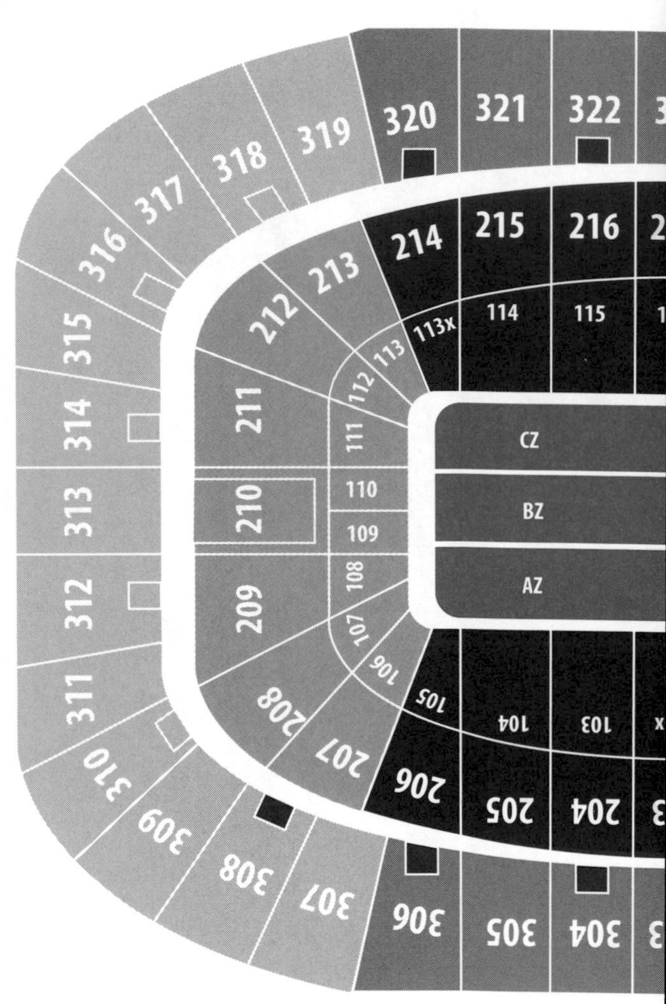

LIE [495] East to Exit 38 [Northern State Pkwy East] to Exit 31A [Meadowbrook Pkwy South] to Exit M4

Parking

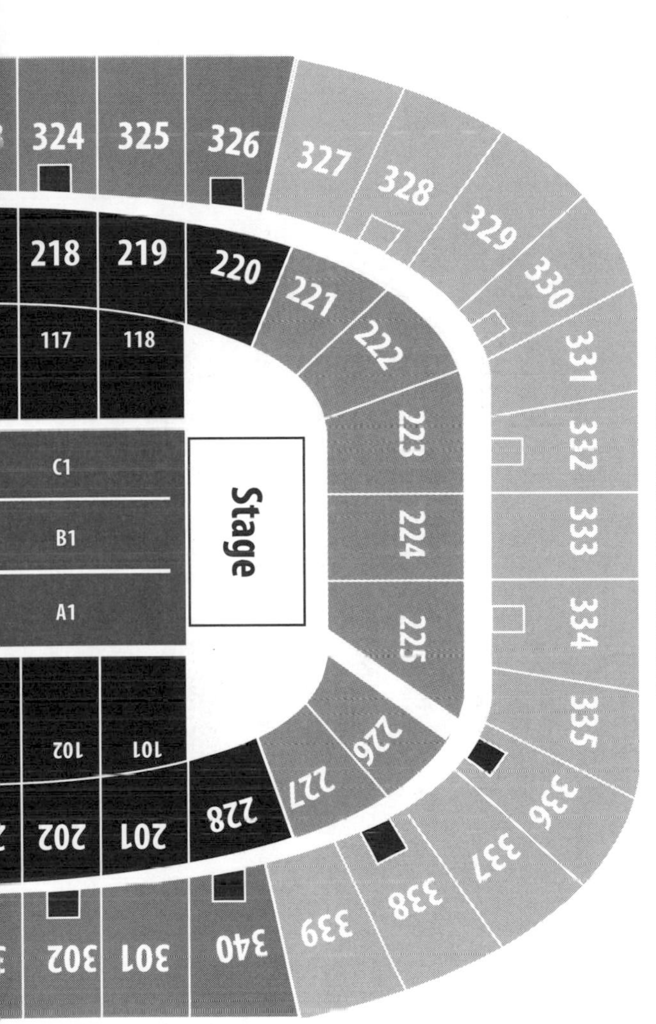

Floor level configurations are subject to change

Nassau Veterans Memorial Coliseum

1255 Hempstead Turnpike // Uniondale, NY

Information: (516) 794-9300 // Ticketmaster: (516) 888-9000

Season Tickets: (888) 822-ISLES ext. 1

[www.newyorkislanders.com] [www.nassaucoliseum.com]

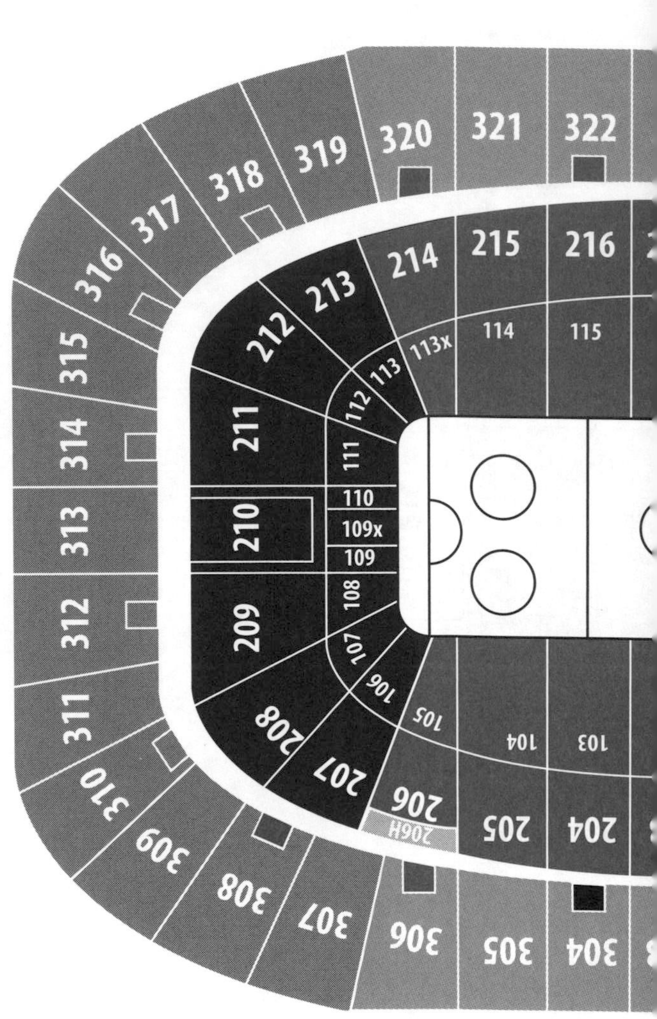

LIE [495] East to Exit 38 [Northern State Pkwy East] to Exit 31A [Meadowbrook Pkwy South] to Exit M4

Parking on Premises

Islanders Hockey

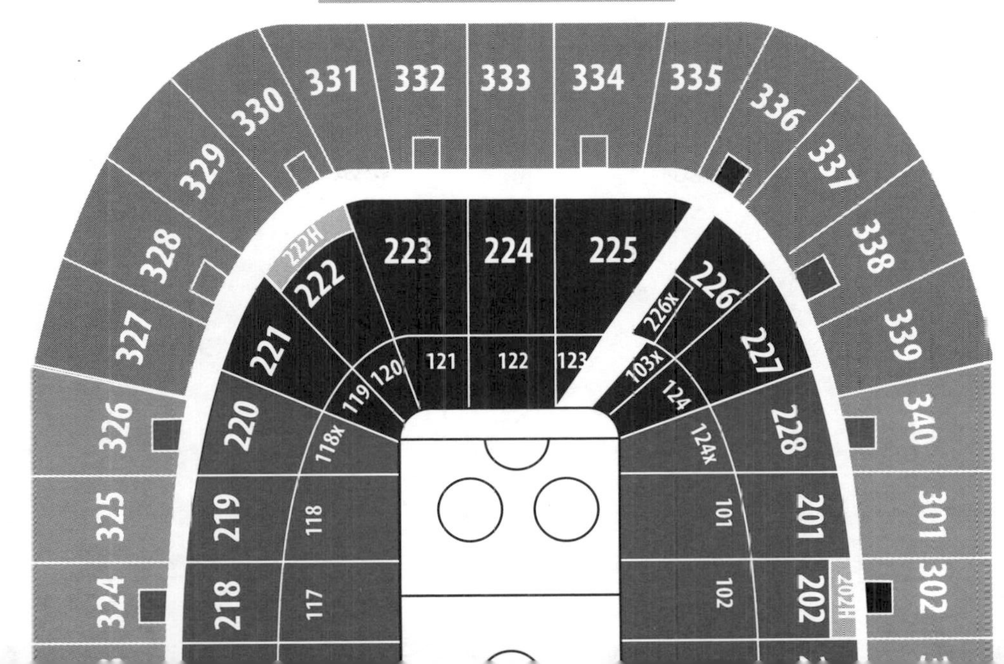

Shea Stadium

123-01 Roosevelt Avenue // Flushing, NY

Box Office: (718) 507-METS or (718) 507-TIXX

Season Tickets: (718) 565-4348 [www.newyork.mets.mlb.com]

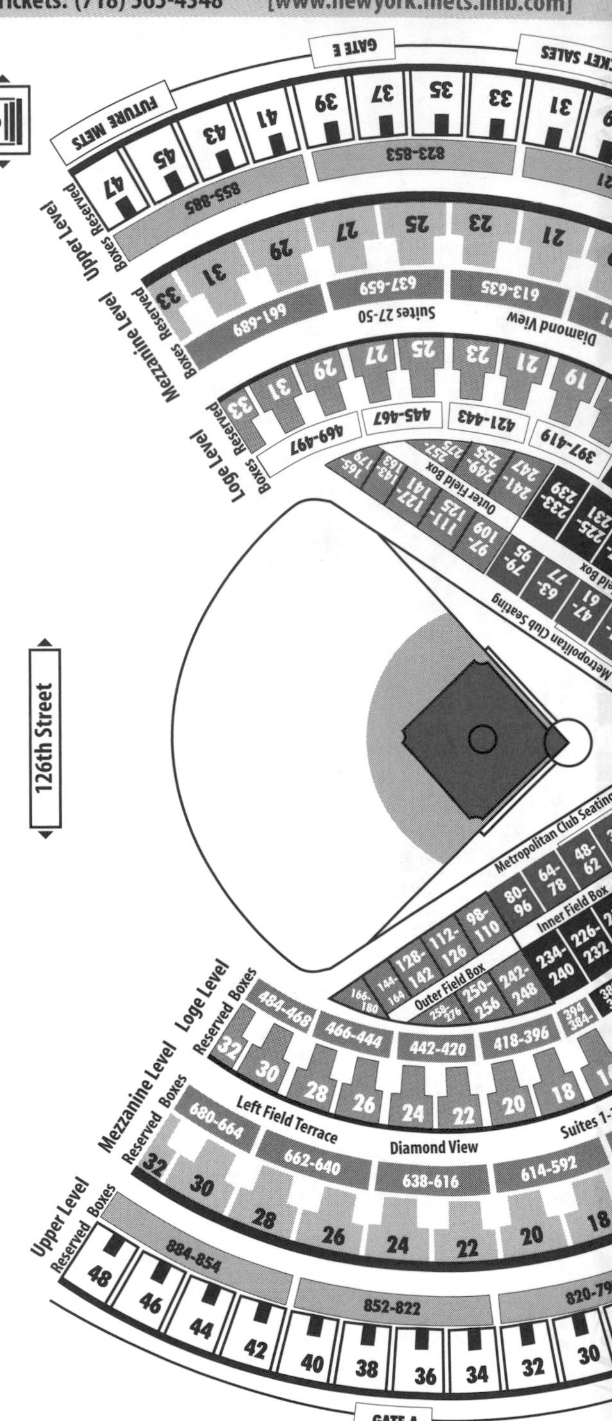

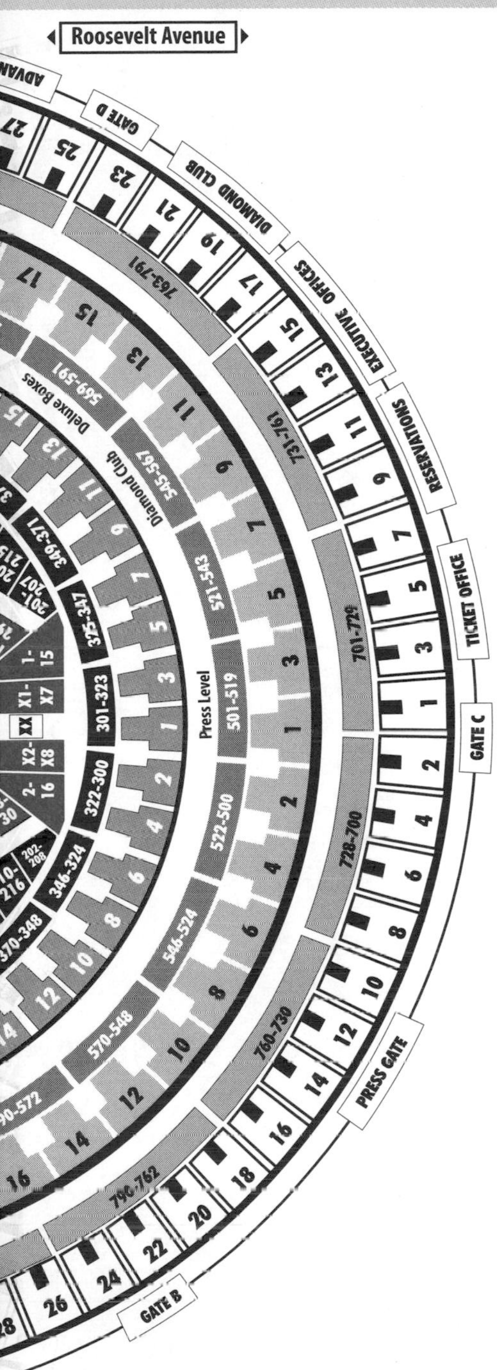

Grand Central Parkway

USTA Tennis Center (Arthur Ashe Stadium)

Flushing Meadow-Corona Park // Flushing, NY

Box Office: (866) OPEN.TIX **[www.usopen.org]**

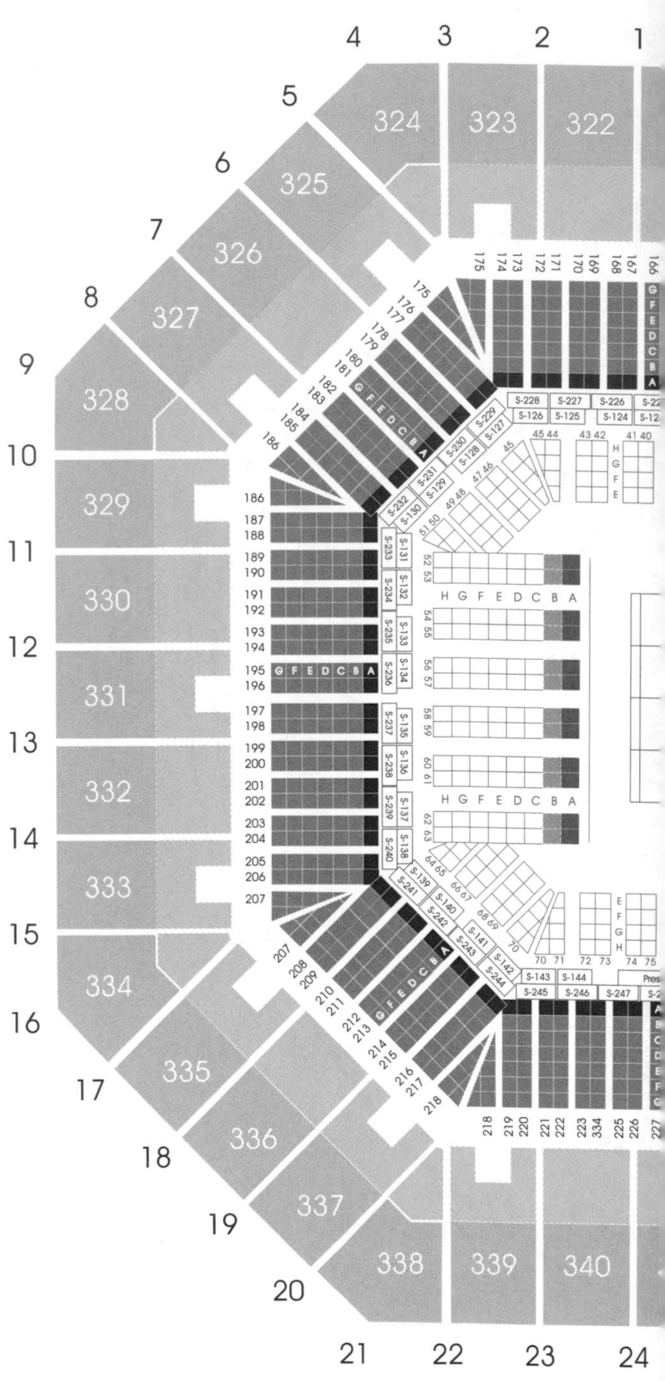

Grand Central Parkway East from New York City to Northern Blvd./Shea Stadium

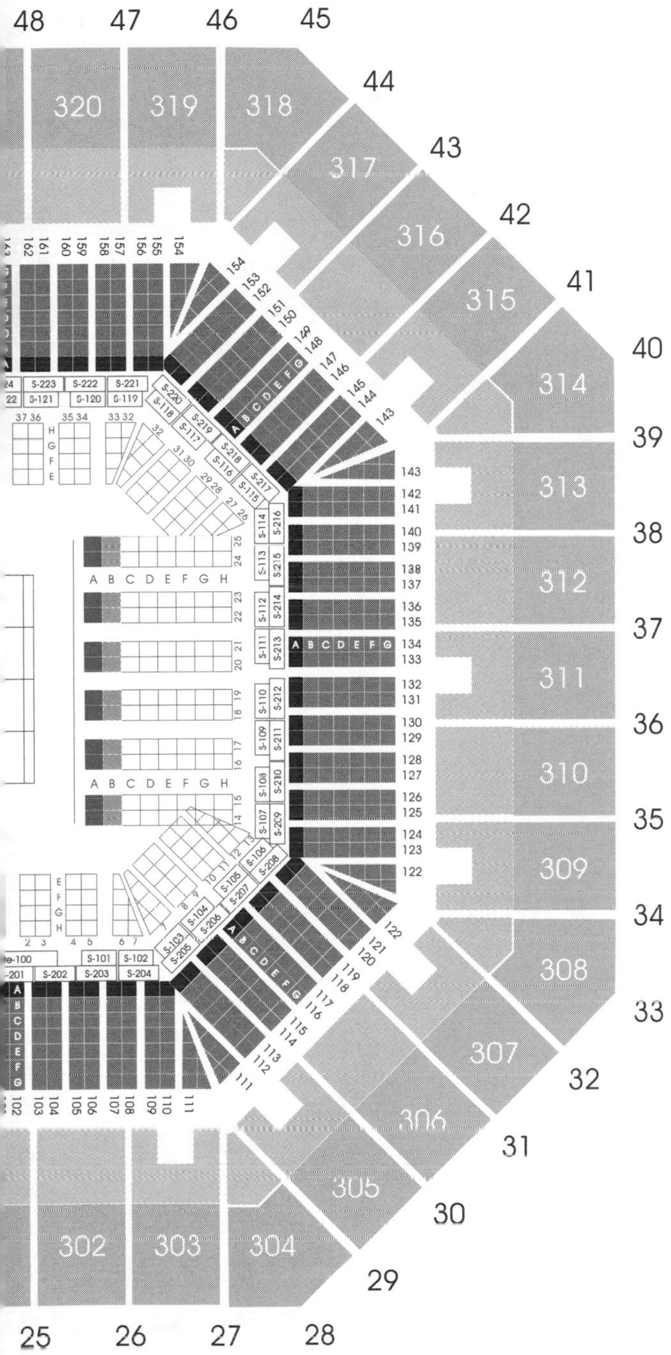

Yankee Stadium

161st Street & River Avenue // Bronx, NY

Box Office: (718) 293-6000 // Ticketmaster: (212) 307-1212

Season Tickets: (718) 293-4300 [newyork.yankees.mlb.com]

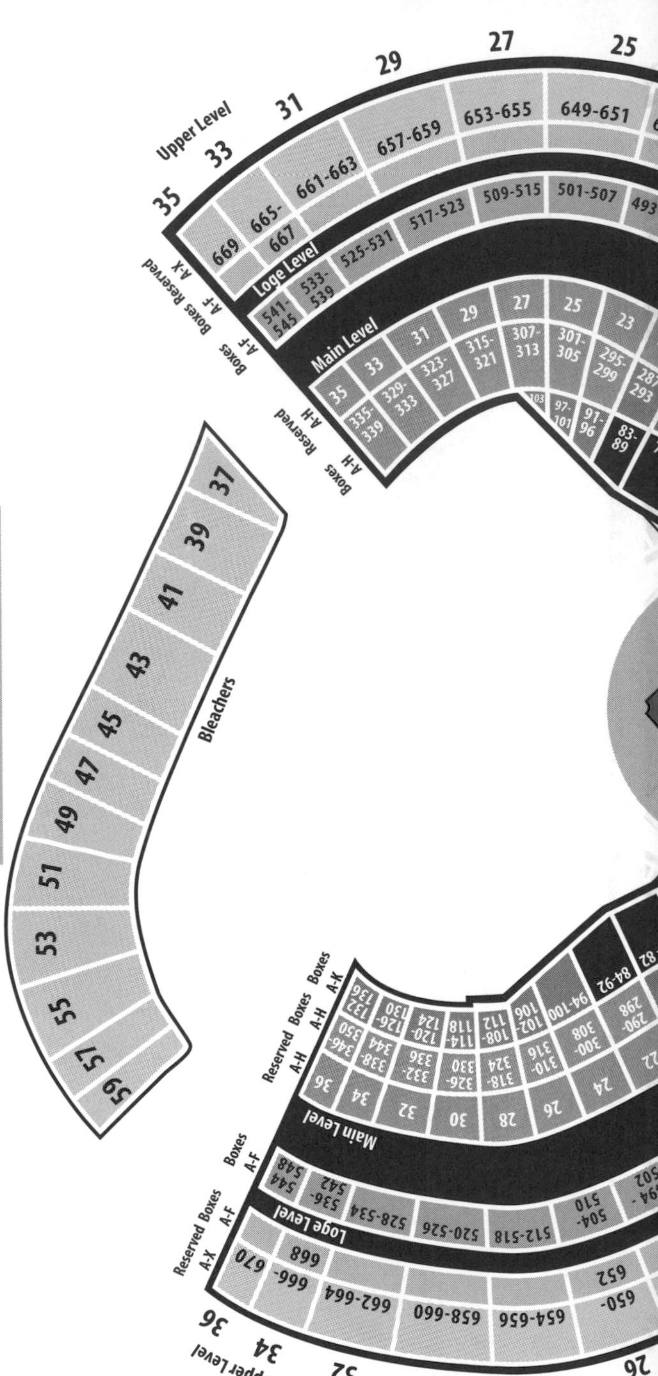

Yankees Baseball

4,B,D to 161st Street & River Avenue

East 161st Street at Jerome Ave.
East 162st Street at Jerome & River Ave.

Major Deegan Expressway/I-87 North to Exit 4 [149th St.] or Exit 5 [155th St.]

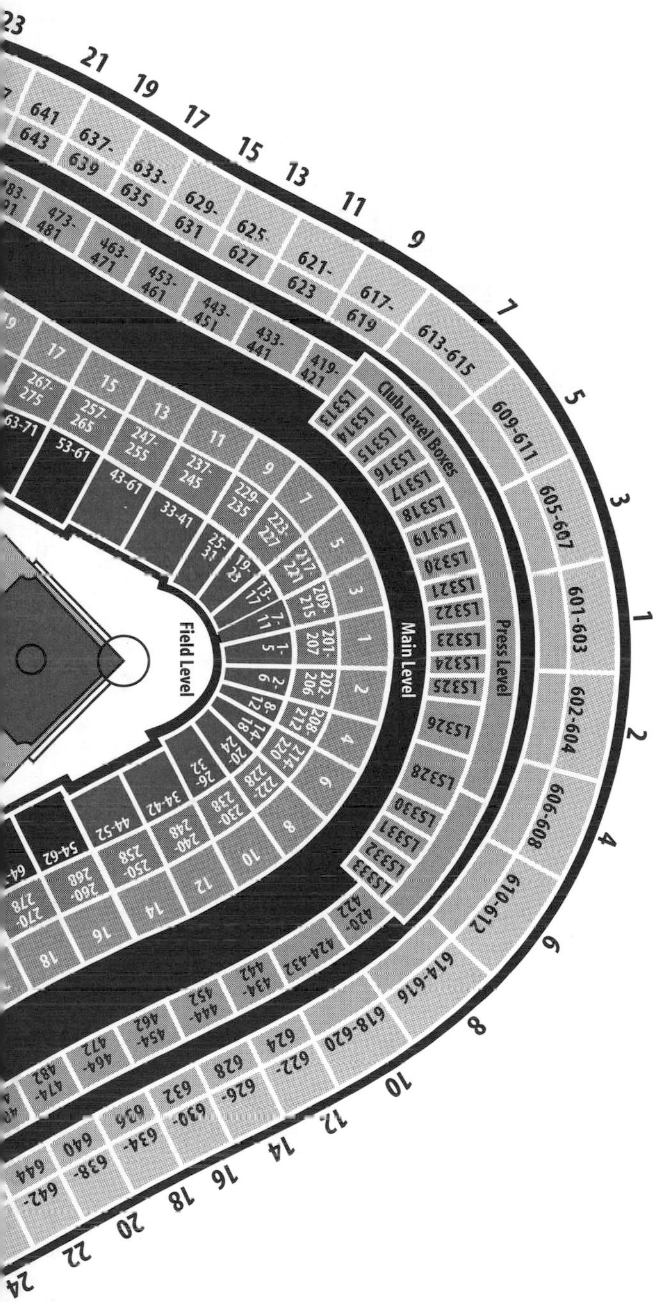

Field Level

Main Level

Club Level Boxes

Press Level

index of venues

"Give my regards to Broadway,
Remember me to Herald Square,
Tell all the gang at Forty-Second Street
That I will soon be there."

—George M. Cohan

a

b

c

d

e

f

g

h

i

j

k

l

m

n

o

p

r

s

t

u

v

w

y

midtown theatre district map

Ambassador [7]
American Airlines [37]
American Place [45]
Belasco [30]
Booth [22]
Broadhurst [26]
Broadway [1]
Broadway Ticket Center [I-1]
Brooks Atkinson [13]
Carnegie Hall [42]
Circle In The Square [Uptown] [5]
City Center [41]
Cort [12]
Duffy [48]
Ethel Barrymore [11]
Eugene O'Neill [8]
Ford Center [33]
Gershwin [4]
Helen Hayes [31]
Henry Miller's [40]
Imperial [20]
John Golden [25]
Longacre [10]
Lunt-Fontanne [15]
Lyceum [18]
Majestic [27]
Manhattan Theatre Club [47]
Marquis [17]
Martin Beck [28]
Minskoff [21]
Music Box [19]
Nederlander [36]
Neil Simon [3]
New Amsterdam [35]
New Victory [34]
NY Convention & Visitor's Bureau [I-3]
OBTIC [I-2]
Palace [14]
Plymouth [23]
Radio City Music Hall [43]
Richard Rodgers [16]
Royale [24]
Shubert [29]
St. James [32]
Studio 54 [44]
The Duke on 42nd Street [38]
Town Hall [39]
Virginia [2]
Walter Kerr [9]
Winter Garden [6]
World Underground [46]

map icons

east/west village theatre district map

Actors Playhouse [72]
Amato Opera [73]
Astor Place Theatre [74]
45 Bleecker [75]
Bouwerie Lane Theatre [76]
Cherry Lane Theatre [77]
Circle In The Square [Downtown] [94]
Joseph Papp Public Theater [84]
Lucille Lortel Theatre [78]
Manhattan Ensemble Theater [52]
Minetta Lane Theatre [79]
New York Theatre Workshop [80]
Orpheum Theatre [81]
Pearl Theatre Company [82]
Players Theatre [83]

westside theatre district map

Douglas Fairbanks Theatre [49]
John Houseman Theatre [50]
Jose Quintero Theatre [51]
Playwrights Horizon [53]
Primary Stages [54]
Second Stage Theatre [55]
Signature Theatre [56]
St. Luke's Church [58]
The Samuel Beckett [59]
The Theatre at St. Clements [57]
Westside Theater [60]
47th Street Theatre [61]

lincoln center map

Alice Tully Hall [91]
Avery Fisher Hall [90]
Damrosch Park [86]
Merkin Concert Hall [93]
Metropolitan Opera House [87]
Mitzi Newhouse Theater [89]
New York Public Library for the Arts [88]
New York State Theater [85]
The Julliard School [92]
Vivian Beaumont Theater [89]

union square theatre district map

Century Center for the Performing Arts [62]
Classic Stage Company [63]
Daryl Roth Theatre [64]
Union Square Theatre [65]
Variety Arts [66]
Vineyard Theatre [67]

chelsea theatre district map

Atlantic Theatre [68]
Chelsea Playhouse [69]
Irish Repertory theatre [70]
Joyce Theater [71]

1 Union Square

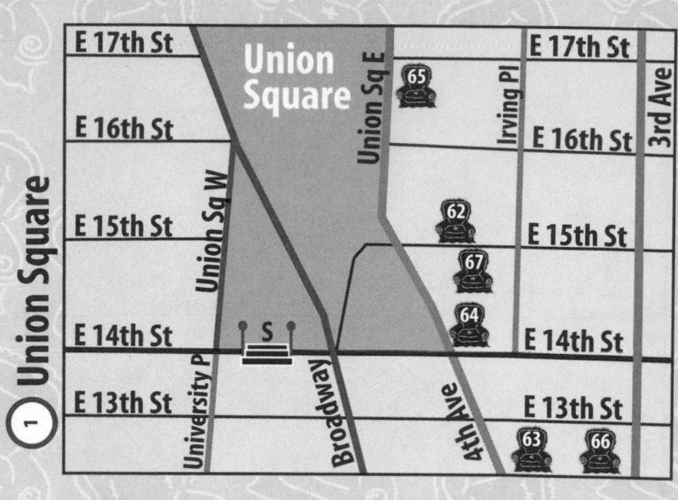

Union Square
E 17th St
E 16th St
E 15th St
E 14th St
E 13th St
Union Sq E
Union Sq W
Irving Pl
3rd Ave
University Pl
Broadway
4th Ave
S
65
62
67
64
63
66

2 Chelsea

9th Ave
8th Ave
7th Ave
W 24th St
W 23rd St
W 22st St
W 21st St
W 20th St
W 19th St
W 18th St
Avenue Of The Americas
S
69
70
68
71

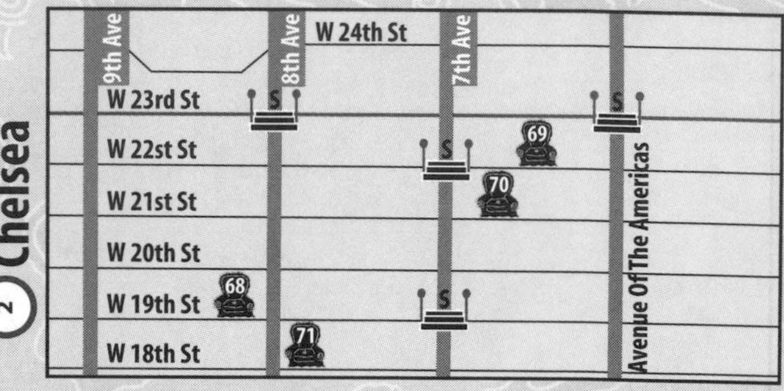

3 Lincoln Center

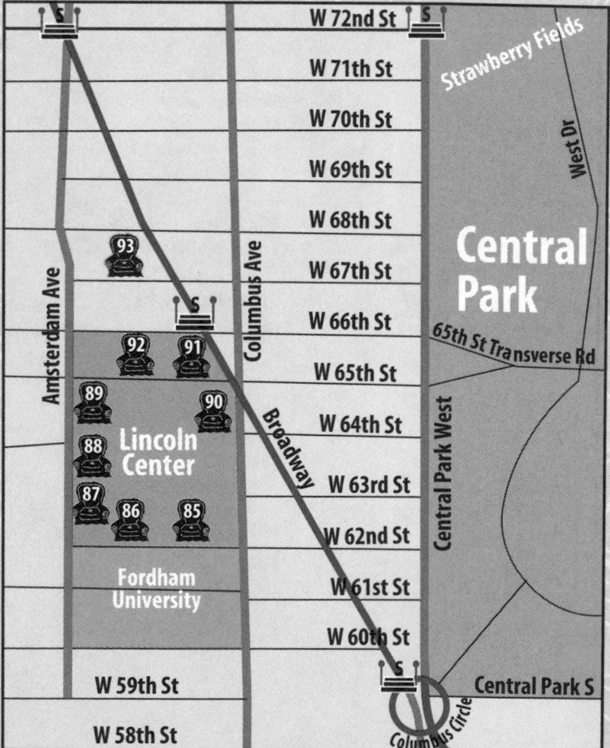

W 72nd St
W 71th St
W 70th St
W 69th St
W 68th St
W 67th St
W 66th St
W 65th St
W 64th St
W 63rd St
W 62nd St
W 61st St
W 60th St
W 59th St
W 58th St
Amsterdam Ave
Columbus Ave
Broadway
Central Park West
Central Park S
Columbus Circle
Strawberry Fields
West Dr
Central Park
65th St Transverse Rd
Lincoln Center
Fordham University
S
93
92
91
89
90
88
87
86
85

4 East/West Village

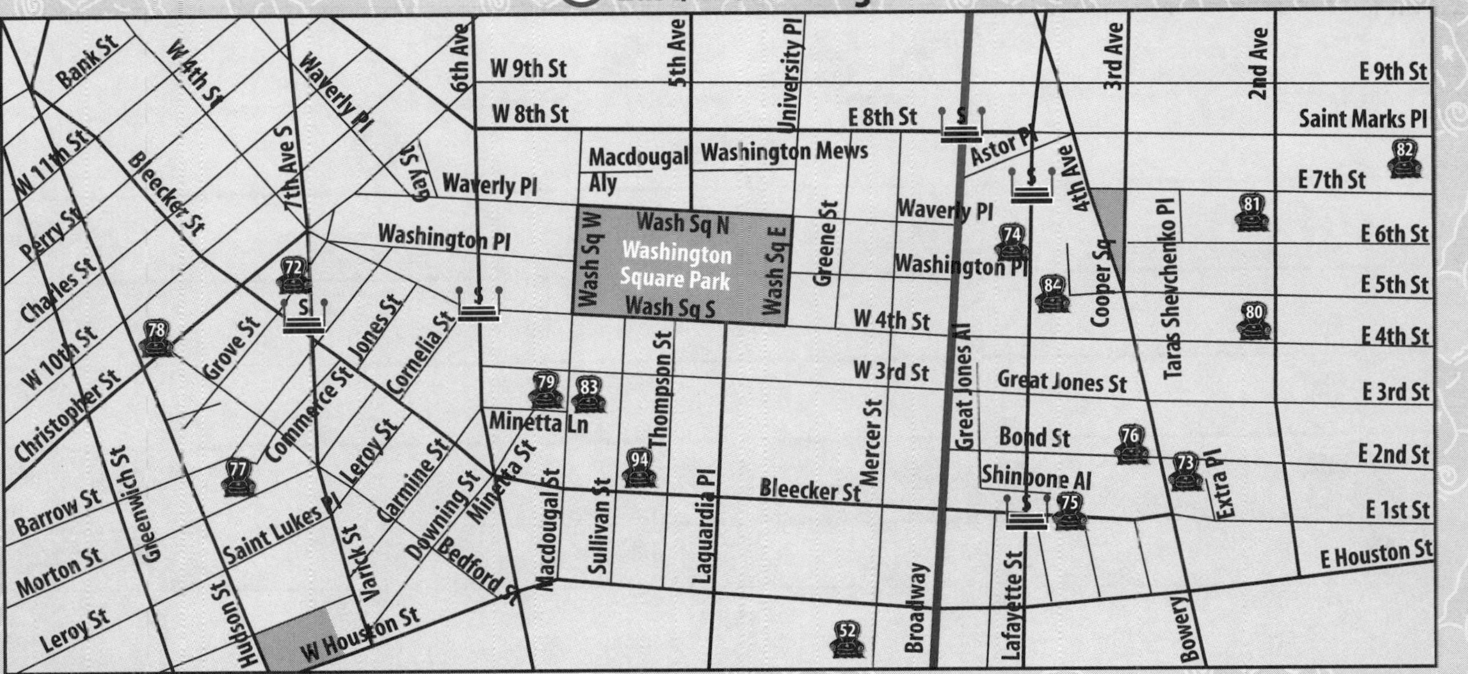

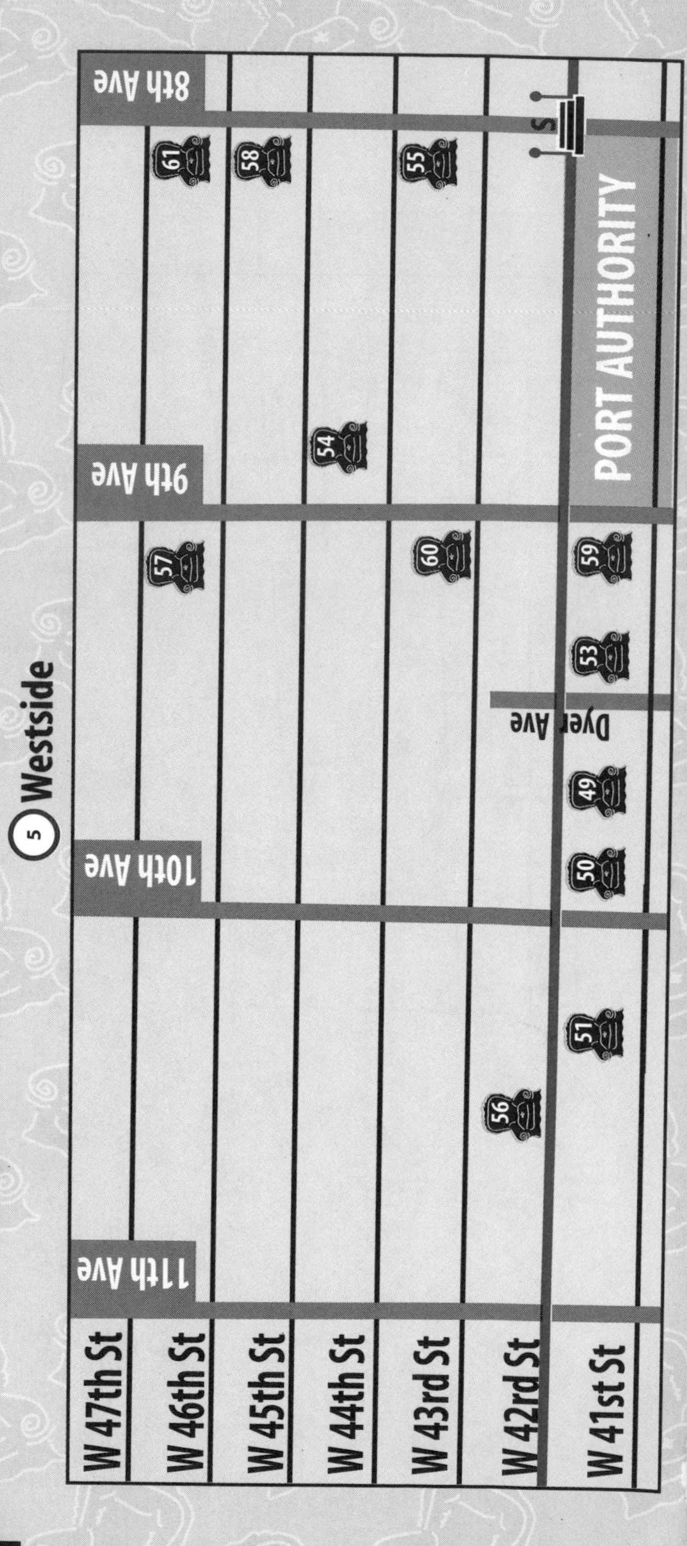

5 Westside

W 47th St
W 46th St
W 45th St
W 44th St
W 43rd St
W 42rd St
W 41st St
11th Ave
10th Ave
9th Ave
8th Ave
Dyer Ave
57
61
58
54
60
55
56
51
50
49
53
59
PORT AUTHORITY
S

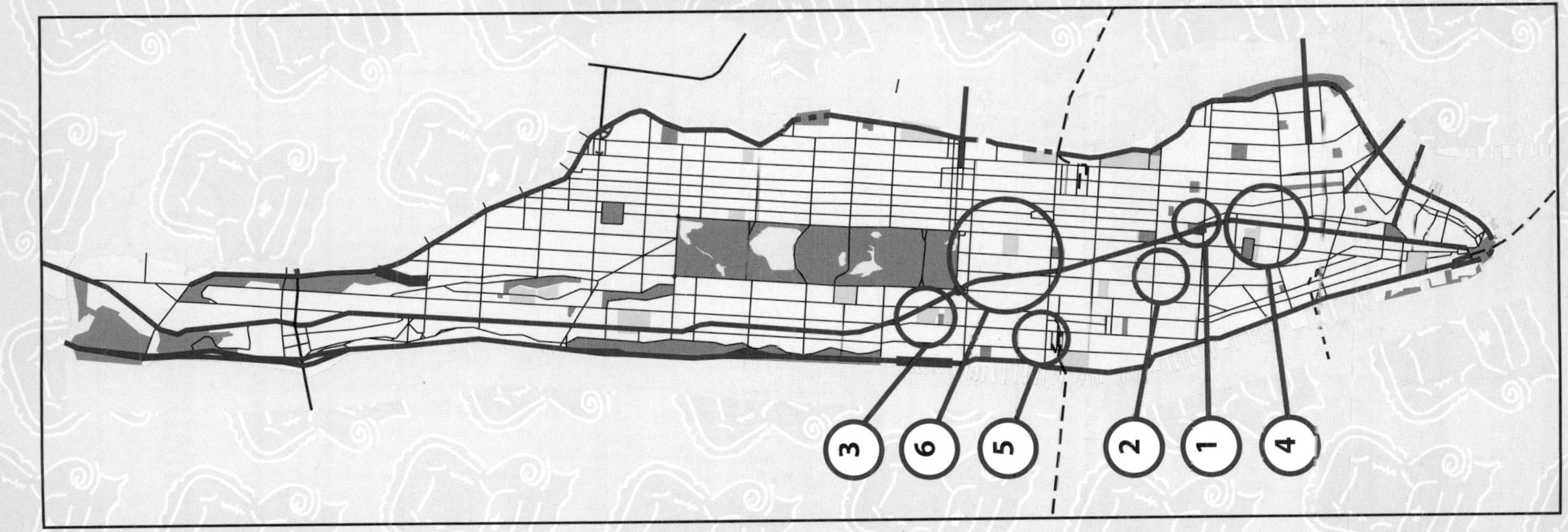
3
6
5
2
1
4